"This book is as relevant today as the stories it tells. It is more than a book on AIDS or the cross country travels of two gay men. It is a testament to George and Wil's courageous answer to a clarion call to follow in Faith and bring a message of Hope to a world of despair. Together they set out on a journey to inform and serve the communities of people who, ready or not, were about to shift their point of view about their diagnosis being a death sentence, and more importantly, open themselves up to discover the very core of who they are in Truth and Consciousness.

Rev. Matt Garrigan, Radiant Light Ministries

For everyone, at least once is their life, there is the chance for a "great adventure" that stands out from them all and opens the door to the rest. This is the story of one of those great adventures and the men who had the courage to take it. Read it, change the circumstances, change the names, and the story will be about you. If you have already taken the journey, you will identify with this book and it will deepen your own insight. If you haven't, read this one and know that your "Winnebago" awaits. You have nothing to fear and everything to discover.

Dr. William K. Larkin
The Applied Neuroscience Institute

George Melton has provided valuable insight into the experience of life, shared with his life partner Wil, as they faced the condition of hiv/aids. Those of us who have lived this experience over the past 20-25 years can surely relate to the ride as being "shot" from a slingshot. I laughed, I cried and I recalled many heartfelt memories from friends and lovers who have since transitioned into eternal life. This story is for those who wish to affirm the thrill of living life through any and all conditions and yet be able to enjoy every moment.

Rev. Michael J Kearney, D.Div. 26 years of su~~~~~~~

A Ride on the Cosmic
Slingshot

A metaphysical memoir by

George R. Melton
author of Beyond AIDS

iUniverse, Inc.
Bloomington

A Ride on the Cosmic Slingshot
A Metaphysical Memoir

iUniverse books may be ordered through booksellers or by contacting:

iUniverse
1663 Liberty Drive
Bloomington, IN 47403
www.iuniverse.com
1-800-Authors (1-800-288-4677)

ISBN: 978-1-4620-0994-7 (sc)
ISBN: 978-1-4620-0995-4 (e)
ISBN: 978-1-4620-0996-1 (dj)

Printed in the United States of America

iUniverse rev. date: 7/21/2011

For Wil

cos•mic (köz′mik) sling•shot (sling′shöt)′ *n.* The intersection of passion and intention with a date on the Mayan calendar.

Contents

Part Three Healing into Life and Death

Introduction

I N 1985, WHEN GEORGE MELTON AND Wil Garcia were diagnosed with HIV and AIDS, there was no treatment for the disease, no hope of recovery, and the Cavalry was definitely not on its way. Everywhere they turned, they were confronted with a relentless message of die, die, die, and that message was reinforced by the mounting death toll in the community in which they lived: New York's Greenwich Village.

RATHER THAN SUCCUMB TO THE OVERWHELMING climate of hysteria and going home and waiting to die, they refused to accept their diagnosis as an inevitable death sentence and set out against impossible odds to discover the means by which to live. Ultimately, the journey they would embark upon would challenge their core beliefs and force them to confront this one, very important question: Who am I, really, and what is the nature of Reality?

From a disappointing experiment with antiviral drugs obtained from Mexico, they found hope in the progressive work of Dr. Carl Simonton with cancer patients. Adopting the tools described in his ground breaking book, *Getting Well Again*, they reconstructed their diet and lifestyle to support their goal of healing. And still it was not enough.

On a trip to a local bookstore, George was drawn to the metaphysical and occult section where a book on the life of Edgar Cayce caught his attention. The Cayce readings provided a bridge from traditional religious beliefs, to an exploration of metaphysics and channeled information. There, far beyond the brick and mortar world of Newtonian physics, lay a quantum reality at the very heart of humanity's innate birthright as spiritual beings and co creators of their experience.

As a result of a profound spiritual awakening, the two men shifted their focus away from the pursuit of allopathic medicine, to an internal process of self- discovery and self-healing. In time, they reclaimed loving relationships with themselves and their families, replacing lifetimes of guilt, anger, and fear with trust, self-esteem and love. Within a year, their disease was in remission and they were both symptom free. But while they had seemingly managed to transform their own lives, the reality of the AIDS epidemic raged on around them, unchecked. They watched helplessly as friends and strangers alike perished in the growing holocaust. What could they possibly do to make a difference?

In his first book, *Beyond AIDS*, George Melton describes the inspiring story of their intense exploration of the interplay between body, mind and Spirit. In this, his latest book, he relates the incredible, never- before told story of what happened next; of the remarkable chain of events resulting from the intersection of their passion and intention with the channeled spirit of Benjamin Franklin and an auspicious date on the Mayan Calendar. The story will both entertain and enlighten you. Join these two men as they embark upon an incredible, life-changing ride on the Cosmic Slingshot!

Part One
Leaving New York City

They drew a circle to keep me out,
Heretic, a rebel, a thing to flout.
But Love and I had the wit to win.
We drew a circle that took them in.

Edwin Markham

1 Shifting Sands

AVING LIVED IN MANHATTAN FOR MOST of my adult life, I had long since come to think of it as home. In fact, my precise attitude about living there could best be described by that now classic cover of The New Yorker magazine depicting the city bound up on the west by the Hudson River, beyond which nothing but a vast wasteland can be seen--except for California on the far horizon. I simply couldn't imagine living anywhere else.

Like a shining city on a hill, New York City stood as a rare bastion of safety in a world that was basically hostile to people with the wrong skin color or background, or in my case, the wrong sexual orientation. Through the lens of my youthful idealism, I saw it as a place where misfits from all over America--indeed the world-- could find the anonymity in which to pursue their lives in peace. In New York, I was free to walk down the street without having to worry about whether people approved of me or not, or what they might do if they didn't. In the little Central Florida towns that I grew up in, that kind of freedom simply didn't exist.

Because of my deep attachment to New York, it had never occurred to me that I would ever choose to live anywhere else, at least not of my own free will. Yet somewhere in the far, deep recesses of my being, the faint stirrings of an unfamiliar dissatisfaction with my present set of circumstances had gradually begun to awaken and make itself known. For reasons I couldn't fully articulate, even to myself, the incessant crowds and ever-present noise--aspects of urban life I had once reveled in--had begun to wear on my nerves, as of late.

At the time, I and my partner of 8 years--Wil Garcia, a strong-willed Puerto Rican with piercing eyes and an overly dry wit--owned a spectacular beach house in the Pines, the fashionably gay, resort community situated on a barrier island just off the south shore of Long Island. Originally, the house had functioned mostly as a place to party and unwind from the stress of our successful careers: Wil's as a trader at Drexell Burnham Lambert, the notorious Wall Street investment firm, and mine as a successful hair colorist in a trendy Trump Tower salon. But more recently, it had found new life as a healing retreat; a place we could withdraw to, to nurture our health and rethink our lives after Wil's diagnosis with AIDS in the spring of 1985, and mine with ARC--a less advanced stage of the disease--later that same year.

When I think about it now, in retrospect, neither of us was entirely conscious of our precise reasons for wanting to sell our beloved beach house, but were simply responding to the vague stirrings of desire to be free of the commitment it represented. We wanted the option of doing something different with our summers, even if neither of us knew just exactly what that something different might actually be.

Eventually, after mulling the situation over, we decided to list the house with a realtor, trusting that if it were meant to be then someone would make an appropriate offer. Unlike Wil's nonchalant approach to the matter, I had a very definite idea about how much the house should fetch on the open market. We had purchased it in 1979 for around $160,000, and with the way real estate values had escalated in the ensuing six years, I knew it had to be worth a whole lot more. In any case, my study of metaphysics had taught me that you had to ask for what you wanted, and I figured now was certainly not the time to be shy.

"We're going to get $295,000 for the house, I just know it," I predicted one Sunday morning, as Wil and I sat at the kitchen table together, drinking endless cups of coffee and reading The New York Times.

He looked up only briefly from the movie section, to cast a skeptical eye in my direction. "You're out of your mind, George," came his deadpan response. "It'll be a cold day in hell before anyone pays that much for *this* house, no matter how inflated the market is right now. You really don't have a clue about these things, do you?"

The exchange fit an old, familiar, pattern of ours. I'd invariably come up with some overly exuberant estimation of a situation, for which Wil could always be counted on to temper with his unfailing grounding in reality. If it was my job in our relationship to jazz things up a bit, then it was his to save us both from what he feared might be the more drastic results of my spontaneous nature. We counted on this dynamic to keep our lives on an even keel.

The house had been on the market for less than a week when the agent called to inform us that she had received an offer for slightly less than the amount I had imagined and put out to the Universe for. Undaunted by this apparent rebuff of my precognitive talents, I insisted on making a counter-offer, which was soon answered with the perspective buyer's final bid.

"How much?" I asked, cradling the receiver under my chin and grabbing a pen from the kitchen drawer.

"$295,000, and not a penny more," came the reply. "I'm afraid it's their final offer."

I bit my lip and glanced up at Wil, who was outside sunning himself by the pool. He came into the kitchen and peered over my shoulder, obviously frustrated at his inability to hear both sides of the conversation, and nervous, quite frankly, about my handling such a delicate financial matter. Business, after all, was the sort of thing *he* usually took the lead on.

In a sprawling hand, I scribbled down the dollar amount and underlined it emphatically several times. Wil glanced at the number and his eyes widened. He nodded his head in the affirmative.

"We'll take it," I said, gauging from Wil's reaction that the offer met with his approval. "When do we sign the papers?"

Wil might have been skeptical about my psychic abilities when I had first predicted what the house would sell for, but he was more than pleased with the final outcome. Later in the week, we dropped by the realtor's office in the Village and signed the necessary papers, before catching an Islander's Club bus back to the island for the weekend. We had exactly one month to pack up our belongings and turn the house over to its new owners.

While both of us undoubtedly felt a twinge of remorse at the sale of the house having gone through as quickly as it had, our grief was substantially allayed by the hefty sum of cash that now filled our burgeoning bank account. And having heard all sorts of horror stories about what could sometimes be involved in such transactions, we chose to be grateful for how simple the entire process had turned out to be. Beyond our immediate sense of relief, however, was an uncomfortable churning sensation in the pit of both our stomachs, of uncertainty about why we had sold the house in the first place, and what the future had in store for us now that we had let it go.

While to the casual observer, our basic circumstances might have seemed relatively stable for two men diagnosed with HIV and AIDS, a tremendous reorientation in the way we viewed ourselves was emerging from deep inside, thanks to the accelerated spiritual journey we had been on for most of the last two years. Since then, a seemingly endless progression of psychological and spiritual shifts had opened our eyes to a world that neither of us had known existed, revealing an exquisite reality in which our circumstances were nothing more than an elaborate projection of our habitual modes of thinking.

This new reality we had embraced, undergirded by a Gnostic view of the Universe and of ourselves, transcended the usual mentality of duality and blame. We were neither the victims of a deadly virus or of a punishing God, but simply two sovereign individuals interacting with ourselves. For better or for worse, our experiences were strictly of our own making.

After months of gripping fear and hopelessness, the first rays of a new understanding had dawned into the fear-darkened recesses of our AIDS saturated minds, and in that light clarity was beginning to emerge. In less than a year's time since we had heard those awful words, "you have AIDS and you're going to die," our overwhelming fear of inevitable death at the hands of a killer virus had been replaced with a growing sense of excitement about what was possible in our lives. We had managed, somehow, to pierce the apparent horror of our diagnosis and find the reality of its larger purpose: AIDS was here to heal us, not to kill us. *That*, we had been doing to ourselves for years, with too much sex, drugs and rock and roll, and all of the other distractions the 80's popular culture had to offer two young, gay men from Manhattan with loads of disposable income.

AIDS, it had turned out, wasn't a punishment from God, after all, as the fundamentalists happily proclaimed it was, but simply a message from our inner being, spoken in the language of biology, telling us that there was more to our lives than we had ever imagined and that it was time to step out of the limiting box we had been living in for most of the last decade.

As our process of transformation continued to unfold, we experienced significant turnover in the people closest to us, as those friends, unable to deal with the changes we were making in our lives, lost interest in keeping us company and drifted off to find more suitable playmates. Needless to say, we were sad to see them go. Even so, we knew that their departure was an inevitable side effect of the healing process we had embarked upon; that it was inevitable that people who saw themselves as victims of this horrible plague would be threatened by the level of responsibility we were taking for our illness and want to distance themselves from us.

Literally turning on a dime, we had shifted our focus from the familiar pursuits of the party circuit, to a search for deeper meaning in our lives. Frequent all-nighters at the baths and our favorite disco, The Saint, suddenly lost their appeal. Our personal odyssey of self-discovery, fueled by an intense desire to live in the face of an incurable illness and the onset of its horrifying symptoms, consumed our time and dominated our every waking moments.

It was difficult for many of the people who knew us, unaccustomed as they were to our new-found spiritual interests and not sharing the urgency of our particular health challenge (not that they were aware of, anyway), to understand the radical transformation taking place in both our lives. Many of them chalked it up to fear, preferring to believe that we were acting out of desperation, just as Wil had originally perceived my actions when I had first seen the light, so to speak, and started sharing some of my new-found metaphysical beliefs with him.

Certainly, desperation might have been the catalyst that had started us down the path we were now firmly ensconced upon, but it was by no means the entire story. It was simply easier for some people to believe we were crazy than to examine the shaky foundations of their own crumbling belief systems. In some people's minds, no matter how heroic our will to live might be, our fate was irreversibly sealed by the finality of our diagnosis. We were doomed to die, no matter what. And in the end, all our brave actions and good intentions would count for nothing.

When it came to AIDS, the entire energy of social consciousness was pitted against our recovery, and the insidious drumbeat of negativity demanded we simply accept our fate and die. Yet, miraculously, Wil and

I had come to realize the insanity of buying into the mass hysteria. There *was* a cure for AIDS; we were sure of it. It might not be in the form of a pill, perhaps, but it was tangible all the same.

Our challenge, as we saw it, was not to cure ourselves by finding a drug to rid ourselves of symptoms, but to transform ourselves from the inside out using the experience of illness as a teacher and a guide. Healing lay in a transformation of consciousness, not in the suppression of unrelenting symptoms. When the lessons the disease had come to teach were learned, the experience would no longer be necessary.

It was in the midst of these tumultuous times that I had what would be the first of many opportunities to share my ideas about self-healing, and the details of my personal spiritual journey, with other people facing the same challenge. The opportunity presented itself at one of the weekly meetings of the Power Seven, the small, rag-tag band of psychic explorers I belonged to, of which several of its members were HIV positive, like myself.

Dana, the solitary girl in the group, showed up at one of our gathering with a flyer she had found on a telephone pole in the Village, advertising a potluck evening of metaphysics and channeling at a private loft on 24th St, just off Broadway. After a brief discussion of the event's merits, we all decided to attend as a group.

On the night in question, Wil accompanied me the short distance from our apartment on 12th Street, up Broadway in the direction of Madison Park. Along the way, we met up with several other members of the group who lived in the general vicinity. At 24th street, we turned and headed down an unfamiliar block, searching for the address in question.

At first glance, the grimy industrial building we stopped in front of appeared to be boarded up and abandoned. Thinking we might have gotten the address wrong, Dana rummaged through her purse in search of the illusive flyer.

"No," she insisted, pointing to the address in tiny letters at the bottom of the page. "This is it: 17 West 24th St."

We stood there for a moment, unsure of just what to do. Suddenly, the front door to the building swung open and a harmless-enough looking young man motioned for us to come inside.

"Are you here for the channeling?" he asked, sensing our confusion.

"Just take the stairs over there to the top floor. Watch your step, though. It's pretty dark in here."

We headed for the stairs at the back of the lobby and began the long, slow climb to the top. Except for the occasional votive candle placed at strategic intervals along the landing, the stairwell was mostly dark. Floor after floor was boarded up and abandoned.

"I think our host is an urban squatter," Dana giggled, attempting to break the tension with a little stab at humor. Her observation was answered by a smattering of nervous giggles, as each of us contemplated just what we might have gotten ourselves into.

Upon scaling the final flight of stairs, we found ourselves standing in the entrance to a large industrial space, filled nearly to capacity with an eclectic group of people, some of which we knew. Taking our cue from Wil, we snaked our way through the crowd to a spot, a little to the side of front and center of what appeared to be a make shift stage, and found a place where we could all sit together. No sooner had we settled into our seats than the lights dimmed and a slightly-built young man with curly, brown hair made his way to the front of the room. He cleared his throat and waited for the crowd to settle down.

"My name is Mark Veneglia" he announced. "I want to thank each of you for choosing to be here this evening. Tonight, I have the pleasure of introducing you to my good friend and spirit in residence, the honorable Benjamin Franklin." With that, a murmur of excitement rippled through the crown.

"Yeah, this I've got to see," Wil muttered, loud enough for only me to hear. "I can't believe I let you talk me into this!"

I had to stifle the urge to laugh out loud. This evening certainly wasn't the first unorthodox situation I had ever involved him in, and I had the distinct feeling it wouldn't be the last. Like so many times before, he'd just have to grin and bear it.

When the room had quieted down again, Mark took a few moments to explain a little bit about his relationship with Benjamin, and the basic format for the evening. Then, with the formalities out of the way, he quieted himself in a large, overstuffed chair and prepared to go into trance by taking a series of long, deep, connected breaths. Moments later, his small body gave a few, awkward jerks and his head lurched up from where it had fallen onto his chest; his eyes opened and fluttered a number of times, and finally the spirit of Benjamin Franklin peered out into the room.

After a spirited introduction of himself which had everyone in the room rolling on the floor in fits of laughter, the irreverent spirit of Benjamin Franklin launched into a rather lengthy explanation of why it had been so important for us to be there in the loft this particular night. He was particularly excited about the AIDS epidemic and its implications for the future of the world, his rather curious interest in the topic growing out of his previous background as a revolutionary in colonial times.

"Surely, most of you must remember that I was intimately involved in the secession of the colonies and the subsequent founding of this country," he reminded us proudly, injecting a bit of history lesson into the mix.

From there, Benjamin went on to speak at great length about the metaphysical and spiritual principles upon which the United States had been founded and to express bitter disappointment at what such a noble experiment had degenerated into in the course of only a few hundred years. He then proposed that AIDS would be part of the greatest revolution in the history of mankind--that the disease would be a catalyst for the most profound transformation in human consciousness ever to occur on Planet Earth.

"And having revolution in my blood," he declared mischievously, his voice crackling with electricity, "I just couldn't resist coming back to participate in this unprecedented, evolutionary leap!"

Over the course of the next hour or so, Benjamin proceeded to lecture and teach us, and tease and cajole us about AIDS and our obsessive fear of it. With incredible wit, he illustrated his many points with riddles, much in the way the Master Teacher Jesus used parables to teach his disciples two thousand years ago. But more powerful than his precise choice of words was the frequency upon which they rode. The mere sound of his voice created a shift in everyone in the room, whether they understood the precise details of what he was talking about or not.

When Benjamin was finally finished with his presentation and had answered as many questions as were asked of him, the crowd lay exhausted on the floor, stunned and unwilling to move. Then, after allowing a little time for us to digest the information, Mark brought the evening to a close by distributing copies of a compilation of Benjamin's previous channelings on the subject.

"Actually," he apologized, "I'm not really sure what all of it means, to be perfectly honest with you. Maybe one of you will resonate with the information and be able to provide the rest of us with some insights."

I lay on the floor in silence as the transcripts were bandied about the room, allowing Benjamin's words to wash over me in gentle waves. One thing was immediately clear: my presence in Mark's loft that evening was certainly not by accident. I had long ago accepted the notion that nothing happens in our lives by chance; that in its intelligence, the Universe puts us in the right place at the right time, with a specific purpose in mind. Yes, I was exactly where I was supposed to be.

"I'll take one," I called out, as the stack of transcripts was bandied about the room. "Here! Over here!"

I grabbed a copy from off the pile and settled back onto the floor to look it over. Scanning the first few pages of the document, an occasional word or phrase leapt up and grabbed my attention, drawing me deeper into the text. Before long, I had broken out into a cold sweat. From just the little I had managed to read so far, I was certain that I had more than just a passing understanding of what the transcript was attempting to communicate. Benjamin's words validated many of my own insights into the AIDS epidemic, and went a good deal further. According to his take on the subject, the disease was about more than just the healing of the people who had been unfortunate enough to contract it. "In simple terms," his words shouted up from the pages of the transcript, "AIDS is a catalyst for personal *and* planetary change!"

Needless to say, it was a little bit surreal to have the disembodied spirit of Benjamin Franklin validate the very things Wil and I had been experiencing for most of the last two years. Up until this point in time, we had mostly felt alone in our unorthodox spiritual journey. Yet, here, in a crowded loft in midtown Manhattan was a room full of people who were possibly experiencing some of the very same things that we were. Perhaps we weren't crazy after all, as some of our friend had politely suggested. Perhaps we weren't just grasping at straws. Maybe we had simply tapped into an alternative reality--one in which people didn't always die of AIDS but had choices that could make a difference in the outcome of their disease. *Perhaps, people could actually heal themselves of AIDS.*

In spite of himself, the cynic in Wil still managed to come through. "You don't really think that was Benjamin Franklin talking tonight, do you?" he asked, as we walked home together down a deserted Broadway. I think he was secretly hoping that I would rise to take the bait.

"You know Wil, I really don't know if it was him or not," I replied, after pausing to reflect upon the question. "It certainly seemed to be someone other than Mark--that's for sure. But to tell you the truth, I don't really care *who* it was; that's not really the point for me. I just know that when I heard the information, I knew it was valid. *I could feel it in my bones.*"

My answer seemed to satisfy him, at least for the time being. We walked the rest of the way home in silence, lost in our own separate worlds, neither of us willing to break the contemplative spell we had fallen under or interrupt each other's private train of thought.

Later in the week, after reading the entire transcript over thoroughly several times, I summoned up my courage and phoned Mark and had a long conversation with him about what had transpired for me that night in the loft. I explained the profound shifts that were occurring in my own life; my unlikely spiritual awakening and what I had come to believe about myself and my disease, and my unabashed excitement over the implications of the revolution Benjamin was describing.

It was immediately apparent to both of us that our individual experiences were parallel in several, remarkable ways. Although Mark wasn't HIV positive, like I was, we both seemed to have tapped into similar strands of information about AIDS and a concurrent planet-wide shift in human consciousness--Mark through the help of his good friend, Benjamin Franklin, and me through the countless books I had read on metaphysics, and the guidance of my Higher Self.

If Benjamin's predictions were correct, and Mark and I were both convinced they were, the world was on the brink of something far more significant than just the threat of a global pandemic. In a larger context, people with AIDS were merely canaries in the global coal mine for a much larger process. Behind the everyday appearance of business as usual, a paradigm shift of immense significance was percolating up from within the collective human psyche, and most people hadn't even noticed it was happening.

Before hanging up the phone, Mark asked if I would be willing to speak to one of his psychic development classes about my experiences in self-healing and AIDS. "It's a small group," he assured me, sensing the reluctance emanating from my end of the line. "Only about eight people--give or take a few. It's no big deal, really. I just think they'd benefit from hearing what you have to say."

There was an awkward moment of silence as I considered his request. "I...uh...I don't know," I hesitated. I was more than a little uncomfortable at the thought of disclosing my HIV status to a group of strangers, no matter how small and sympathetic they might be. While I had been open about my HIV status with my closest circle of friends, the thought of disclosure on the level Mark was proposing was an entirely different matter. I had legitimate concerns about what the consequences might be for my personal life and career, if word got out I was infected with HIV.

At the same time, in my heart of hearts, I knew that Mark's invitation represented an incredible opportunity for me to move through yet another level of fear and launch myself in an entirely new dimension of experience.

"Oh, just set a date," I relented, finally. "Just set a date and let me know when to be there."

Later that evening, as I lay in bed thinking about what I had agreed to, it dawned on me that my decision to share my story publicly was in some way related to the indefinable stirrings Wil and I had been responding to when we had put the Fire Island house up for sale. And while I couldn't grasp the entire picture just yet, it wouldn't be too long before more pieces of the puzzle would begin falling into place. Like it or not, for better or for worse, my life was about to change in ways I could never have imagined at the time.

☀

2 Welcome to the Revolution

THE LAST STEP IN THE TWELVE step program says that in order to keep what you have, you must give it away to someone else. In that respect, I guess it was inevitable that at some point in my spiritual journey I would begin to share my experience with others. Apparently, the time had arrived.

The crowd in Mark's loft, a week earlier, seemed to indicate that at least some people had begun to suspect that AIDS might have a deeper significance than the official story line would seem to suggest, and were looking for alternative ways of approaching the situation. While I was under no illusions that I had somehow found the answer for everyone, I did know that I was well on my way to embodying my own personal truth about the experience and had something of value to offer. As such, there was no way I could remain silent and keep my experience to myself.

On the agreed upon date and time, I caught a cab to 24th Street and climbed out onto the curb in front of Mark's dilapidated building. Pushing my way through the heavy, metal, front door, I headed for the stairs at the back of the lobby and made my way to the top floor. When I arrived there, the door to the loft was open. Peering inside, I could see a small group of students gathered in a circle on the floor at the far end of the room. Mark looked up from the conversation he was engrossed in and motioned for me to join them.

"Over here." he said. "Take off your shoes and make yourself comfortable."

I found an opening in the small circle of students and quickly settled into it. Mark wasted little in getting the class under way. He opened with a quick meditation and then introduced me to the intimate gathering of eight.

"This is the guy I've been telling you about," he enthused. "He has a lot of interesting things to share with you today. So, without further ado, I'm going to turn the class over to our guest today-- my new friend, George Melton."

With that, a residual vestige of my southern upbringing surfaced as a voice in my head, warning me in no uncertain terms that some things were better off left unsaid. I brushed the unsolicited advice aside and launched into my story.

"They say there are no atheists in foxholes," I began, choosing my words carefully, "and I guess you could say that's where my story begins. Since finding out that I'm HIV positive, I've been in a battle for my life, and that's how I became interested in spirituality and metaphysics. Being faced with the possibility of an untimely death, all of the unanswered questions I had suddenly needed answers: Am I a good person? What's going to happen to me when I die? Is there a heaven or a hell? Things like that. I needed to know the truth."

"Eventually, my search led me to the work of Edgar Cayce, a Christian minister and trance channel who lived in the early part of this century and left behind an enormous body of work that's archived in Virginia Beach. There was one question in particular he posed that really got me thinking: *Will this thing in your life be a millstone around your neck or a stepping stone to greater glory? The choice is up to you.*" I opted for the greater glory, naturally, but wasn't exactly sure how to go about claiming the prize."

"The idea that everything in your life can be used to move you into a greater expression of yourself--even something as terrifying as AIDS--really transformed the situation. But to claim the promise, I had to surrender the hope of a cure in favor of healing, which are two, very different things. If you look up the word cure in the dictionary, one of its many meanings is *to preserve*; it's what you do to ham or bacon. In the context of healing, if you cure a disease by simply removing its symptoms, you *preserve* the cause. Because the cause isn't entirely physical, you see; it's partly metaphysical. With a disease like AIDS, you have to deal with its psycho/spiritual roots or your symptoms will simply manifest again

15

and you'll be right back to where you started, dealing with a never-ending stream of opportunistic infections."

"Unfortunately, there isn't a cure--at least, not yet. Self-healing was the only option I had. *I* had to be the one to change, however, not the disease. AIDS was simply the physical expression of an acute inner condition. Instead of fixating on suppressing symptoms, I started to focus on transforming myself from the inside out with the idea that when I had learned the lessons the disease had come to teach me, the teacher would no longer be needed."

Some of the students looked a bit confused, so I brought my remarks to a close with a couple of clarifying thoughts.

"Just so I'm clear, here, let me state for the record that being gay is not the problem. In my case, the destructive beliefs and behaviors that grew out of being taught I was an abomination to God was the real problem. I've since learned that I'm worthy of love, exactly as I am, and I'm learning to treat myself accordingly. That has been, and continues to be, the basis for my continued good health. And I think it might be the key for a lot of other people too."

Later, when the class was over and everyone had gone their separate ways, Mark asked if I would come back the following week and do it all over again. "I have another class that meets here next Wednesday," he informed me. "They need to hear this, too."

In the after-glow of a job well done, there was nothing to do but say yes. After all, what was the point of trying to close the barn door when the horse was long since gone? I couldn't really think of a valid excuse.

Thankfully, these initial two, up-close and personal presentations turned out to be unqualified successes. It was the first time many of Mark's students had ever knowingly come face to face with a person with HIV or AIDS, at least one willing to admit it of his own volition. Expecting the worst, they had been drawn in instead by the power of this one idea: that illness, and more specifically AIDS, could be a catalyst for personal growth, and that this, in turn, could lead to a remission in physical symptoms.

Apparently, despite a general familiarity with the basic concepts of metaphysics and spirituality, most people seemed to draw the line when it came to AIDS, as though the disease were somehow the exception to every rule. The overwhelming climate of fear, whipped up in large part by a media obsessed with sensationalism, caused even the most spiritual person to throw out the baby of what they knew with the bath water of mass hysteria. Obviously, if the situation was ever going to change, someone would have to step forward and tell a different story.

The effect of all this negativity reminded me of an experience from my early childhood years growing up in Central Florida. By any standard of measure, my parents' relationship had been markedly dysfunctional. My father, an insurance salesman by trade, found refuge from his demons at the bottom of a bottle, while my mother found hers in the arms of Jesus and the old-time religion of no—no dancing, no movies and no tv. As a consequence, my social life revolved around the church, and I was there any time the door was open—twice on Sunday and once on Wednesday night, at a minimum.

I don't mean to imply that everything about my upbringing was negative, however. For all her faults, my mother was sincere in trying to raise me the very best she knew how. She made sure that I had braces when I needed them, and saw a dermatologist when my adolescent acne had raged out of control. She wasn't a hypocrite either, by any stretch of the definition; she practiced what she preached. And besides, not everything pertaining to church and religion was intrinsically unpleasant.

Besides my involvement in the music program (I was the church pianist, beginning in my early teens), I enjoyed those rare occasions when missionaries would visit from overseas, bringing informative slide shows and artifacts from the cultures they were ministering to. Typically, in an effort to drum up financial support for the work they were doing, they'd describe the many challenges involved in trying to convert the natives to Christianity—at times claiming to be up against no less than Satan, himself, in the form of the local witch doctor. Dark tales of black magic and voodoo were offered up as consummate proof of the existence of evil in the world and the horror that awaited those poor souls who refused to accept Jesus Christ as their personal savior.

As I listened, spellbound, to these incredible stories of faraway lands and the dark mystery surrounding them, I was overwhelmed with gratitude for the fact that I lived in America, far beyond the reach of such terrifying superstition. Thank God nothing like voodoo or black magic could touch me in the little town in Central Florida that I lived in.

I had always assumed that was true, until very recently. But lately, I had seen how shallow the veneer of civilization was in the United States, in the public's hateful and ignorant response to people with AIDS. And I had seen something else that had shocked and amazed me when I had first recognized it for what it was: This strange power the missionaries had talked about--this voodoo--was real, and was happening right here in America in the 1980's. It had nothing to do with Satan, however, but everything to do with the arrogant and unconscious abuse of the power of belief.

Too often I had seen the results of the official narrative on AIDS on the people I knew and loved. Convinced by their doctors and the media that death was their inevitable fate, and told by religious zealots that they were deserving of it, they had responded to their diagnosis in one of two seemingly, opposite ways: some went home and shut the blinds, and pulled the covers over their heads and waited to die--which happened with terrifying swiftness--while others, wanting to make the most of the little time they had left, went on a self-destructive binge of over-indulgence that ultimately ended the same way. It didn't seem to matter *which* course of action a person chose to take, they inevitably died, just as surely as if someone had taken a voodoo doll with their name on it and stuck it full of pins.

There was something about this awful situation that struck a raw nerve, somewhere, deep in the far reaches of my battered psyche. It was the nearly forgotten memory of what I had been taught back in that hometown church of mine. Hadn't the preacher insisted that human beings were created in the image and likeness of God, with something called free will? Yet, only recently had I even begun to scratch the surface of understanding what that term might actually imply in practice. Choice was two roads going in different directions, each ending in a different destination. Choice implied the possibility of different outcomes. No matter how obscure it might appear to be, the possibility of healing--even for something as dire as AIDS--had to exist!

With an AIDS diagnosis, there was a semblance of choice, but not *real* choice. True, you could choose how to spend your remaining time, but there was no possibility whatsoever of a last minute pardon or reprieve. You could take your vitamins and herbs or your antibiotics and AZT, but these too would buy only a precious few months of time--and only then if you were lucky. In the end, no matter what you did or how hard you tried, you were expected to die and to do it as quickly as possible.

"How can this represent choice?" I pontificated to Wil as he lounged on the bed beside me, trying to concentrate on the book on psychoneuroimmunology he was reading. "Can you call it choice when the effect of any decision you make ends in the same result?"

I knew that healing was possible from what was happening in my own life, in my spiritual quest for wholeness and the remission in symptoms I had experienced as a result. Could it be that people were dying simply because they believed they must? Caught up in a deadly vortex of hysteria and fear, were they succumbing, not because the disease was 100 percent fatal, but because the underlying call for change was being ignored?

The situation certainly wasn't being helped by the nation's so-called spiritual leaders who, blinded by their own prejudices and an irrational fear of homosexuality, and unwilling or unable to tell the difference between a lifestyle and a life, were fanning the flames even higher. According to their agenda, God himself had sent AIDS as a punishment for homosexual sex.

"This is the same setup that causes people to die when a witch doctor casts a spell on them," I ranted, interrupting Wil's reading again, to reiterate my point. "No one dies because there's any actual power in voodoo. They die because they *believe* in the witch doctor's power. He has a sophisticated understanding of the power of belief and uses it to his advantage!"

Wil waited patiently for my tirade to end. He had grown accustomed to such passionate outbursts from me and had long since decided it was best just to let me vent, without being drawn into the drama. Besides, the truth was that even though we expressed things differently and to his way of thinking some of my beliefs were undoubtedly a little over the top, he experienced many of the same frustrations I did. He too had seen too many people he knew and loved die needlessly from this disease.

"Come on, George" he said gently, trying to calm me down. "Don't get yourself so worked up about it. There's not a whole lot you can do."

But I *was* worked up, and I *had* to do something about it! Benjamin's channelings on the subject and the subsequent success of my talks at the loft had filled me with a burning desire to deliver a message of empowerment to the gay community. These people were my friends. If

19

the lid was ever going to be lifted from this epidemic and the element of real choice embraced, then the current attitude of utter hopelessness would have to be challenged. Someone would have to speak up and inject a different perception into the commonly accepted scenario of how an AIDS diagnosis played itself out. Until then, people would continue to succumb in ever-increasing numbers, would shut the door on the possibility of healing, and prepare themselves to die.

Certainly, Mark knew that this was the case. And Wil and I knew it too, as well as a number of other people who had come forward in the days following Benjamin's presentation at the loft. Yes, if people with AIDS were going to be saved, they were going to have to save themselves. The rest of the world had been hypnotized by a constant barrage of negativity and couldn't be relied on to help.

As an antidote to the frustration we both felt, Mark suggested that we use his loft for a series of potluck gatherings, giving people the opportunity to hear what Benjamin and I had to say. He felt that an expanded forum, with me included in it, would enable us to reach a much larger audience than just the few students in his psychic development classes, and that surely someone would resonate with what we had to say.

Unfortunately, Wil still had too much fear to participate in these first few events. He was in favor of them, however, and encouraged us to move forward with our plans. "I'll be there to support you every step of the way," he assured me. "I'd just rather work from behind the scenes, if you don't mind."

Not even Wil's reluctance to join our fledgling crusade could cool Mark's and my ardent fervor. All of the frustration that had been bottled up inside of us came flooding out and was channeled into the preparations, as our long-term paralysis gave way to the knowledge that indeed we could make a difference in the course of people's lives.

Energized by the subversive nature of our plans, we eagerly set about putting them into play. A series of dates was decided upon and Mark set about designing a flyer to announce the events. At each step along the way, we checked in with Benjamin who was there to offer his sage counsel and advice. We were caught up in a revolutionary spirit, driven by at least a partial recognition of how powerful an impact our ideas might ultimately provoke.

The first in the series of potluck events was a modest success in terms of the number of people who showed up, but it was a triumph in terms of its effects upon those that did. Between what Benjamin had to say and what I was able to add to it, it was as though a light had gone off in the room, shinning deep into the hearts and minds of every person there. People seemed to glimpse the power of what was being offered and took it home with them and shared it with their friends. Little by little, our revolution began to grow by word of mouth. Each successive event drew an increasingly larger crowd until eventually the loft was packed to capacity with over 300 infected and affected people, and more clamoring to get inside.

Emboldened by the success of our efforts, Wil overcame his fear of public disclosure and threw himself headlong into the fray. One evening, after I fumbled a question that had been hurled at me by a young man in the audience, he unexpectedly jumped in and answered it for me. From then on, he was right there in the middle of the action, sharing his story and offering hope and compassion in his own inimitable way. A few weeks later, we made the acquaintance of Niro Assistant, a Swedish woman who claimed to have reversed her antibody status from positive to negative, and her story was added to our budding roster of testimonials.

Even now, as I look back at these events over twenty years later, I still feel a powerful sense of nostalgia for those passionate early days of revolution in Mark's loft in New York City. To have been there and ridden the initial wave of healing energy as the first few cracks appeared in the monolithic wall of hopelessness surrounding AIDS, was to be alive in a way that many of us had never before experienced. While the rest of the world labored on under the illusion of business as usual, Wil and I, along with Mark and a growing number of other people with HIV and AIDS, had to face the fact that in our lives it was now or never. With no promise of tomorrow, we had to pursue our dreams *now*.

Surprisingly, being forced to confront my own mortality at the relatively young age of 33, came with a laundry list of unexpected blessings. Over time and with intense scrutiny, the dreaded diagnosis had morphed into a liberator, rather than the executioner I had first mistaken it for. As a result, my priorities changed dramatically. What had been important to me before my diagnosis didn't seem to matter much anymore. What had been completely overlooked was now incredibly precious. All the little grey areas that had once been so confusing to me crystallized into black and white, framed by the urgency of the situation so that I could see them as simple choices between yes or no, love or fear, life or death. In that context, even someone as dysfunctional as I was could understand what needed to be done.

Crisis was the catalyst that mobilized our growing army of revolutionaries into action on behalf of a purpose greater than ourselves, in the form of educational forums at the loft. The energy created there proved highly contagious, particularly for a group of people drowning in overwhelming hopelessness. We drank deeply of the empowerment these evenings offered and took what we learned there back into our daily lives, checking it against our own inner knowing, trying it on for size as if it were an unfamiliar piece of clothing.

Many of the people who attended these events experienced an immediate and total resonance with the hope our message proclaimed. It offered them rare validation for an inner experience not fully understood or given voice to before. Others, the leap in perception too great and too far reaching for them to make, weren't as thoroughly convinced. These individuals took away just the bits and pieces of what they had heard, that fit within their own personal picture of reality, and added it to their survival strategies in whatever way suited them best.

Finally, there were those who responded to our message with anger and fear, who could only interpret the idea of personal responsibility through the lens of self-judgment and blame. These angry souls branded us as lunatics and went off to fight their own battles. What *was* certain, however, was that no one left the loft after hearing the message being offered there without being moved in some deep, profound, life-changing way. *It was simply impossible to ignore such a compelling message of hope!*

3　The Miracle of the Foils

EVENTUALLY, WIL'S AND MY PARTICIPATION IN the events at the loft created numerous opportunities for us to speak to other interested groups in and around the tri-state area. As more of our time and energy was spent pursuing these extra-curricular activities, I found it increasingly difficult to keep my new life as a spiritual revolutionary separate from my everyday reality as an upscale hair colorist, in a fancy uptown salon.

My career, once the most important thing in my life, increasingly seemed of little actual value in light of my new-found, spiritual priorities. I wanted to quit and simply walk away from it all to do something more meaningful with my life. A talent for making a person's hair color complement their skin tones felt rather insignificant, pitted against the bigger picture of the enormous changes I could see looming on the horizon.

And to be perfectly honest, I wasn't sure how my clientele would react to knowing I had HIV, and was afraid it might cost me my career. After all, the nightly news was full of stories about the terrible things that could happen to a person when news of their infection leaked out. I certainly didn't want that happening to me.

On the other hand, I was learning to trust the Universe to support me in being true to myself, no matter how scary a proposition that might be. Here again, I could sense the opportunity in my dilemma; the reward that comes from facing your fears head on and moving through them into a deeper experience of trust. Besides, it wouldn't be the first risk I had ever taken to prove that my newfound beliefs were more than just fancy new-age theories. I had jumped off the proverbial cliff more than once in the last few years. If I wanted to continue to grow and thrive, I'd have to face my fears like an adult. I'd have to reach deep down inside myself and find the courage to walk my talk.

Ultimately, it was in the overwhelmingly positive response to our talks at the loft that I found the courage to come out about my HIV status and new-found spiritual beliefs, to my clientele and the people I worked with. At first, I took only a few, close friends into my confidence, broaching the subject of metaphysics and healing abstractly, without specifically implicating myself. Later, when this tactic proved to be successful, I upped the ante and disclosed on a slightly more personal level--testing the waters, so to speak, before finally divulging the whole enchilada.

Fortunately, most people responded to my confession with an overwhelming show of support, rather than recoiling in horror and running away like I had feared they might. As a result, the dynamics of my work life changed dramatically. Where before, my clients had always come to me for advice about superficial matters such as their hair color or fashion advice, they were now asking questions of a much more substantial nature. They wanted to know about belief systems and affirmations, and practical advice on how to integrate metaphysics into their daily lives.

Most, if not all of my clients were attracted to my new-found spiritual beliefs and optimistic new outlook on life. Even so, there were some who had little or no interest in spirituality and metaphysics, their focus being more of a material nature. Over time, they drifted away to find other hairdressers with whom they had more in common. In the past, the prospect of losing business to the competition would have upset me. Their leaving would have been seen as a threat to both my income and fragile ego. Now, however, as I let go and allowed myself to trust the flow of change that was occurring in my life, I couldn't help but be amazed and delighted when a client I had been trying to get rid of for years left of her own accord.

I had tried every trick in the book to discourage her patronage, to no avail. No matter how hard I tried, she'd invariably show up in my chair for a touchup each month like a bad penny. Now, after just a few passing references to AIDS and spirituality, she was out of my life for good. And in her place, new clients, many of them just embarking upon spiritual journeys of their own, appeared to fill the void.

Disclosing my HIV status provided me with more blessings than I could have ever imagined. Much of my work related stress simply evaporated as my most difficult clients fell by the wayside, only to be replaced by a new group of open and loving women. I didn't have to maintain a façade any longer, but was free simply to be myself. And I didn't have to waste precious energy trying to conceal my terrible secret.

How often, in the past, I had clung to relationships that no longer served me, hiding bits and pieces of myself, afraid that someone might reject me if they caught a glimpse of who I *really* was. Ultimately, it had taken a disease like AIDS to teach me that love with conditions attached wasn't really love at all. As difficult as this lesson had been to learn, embracing it created miracles in my life and opened up space for new people to enter it who loved me unconditionally.

Not only did this new-found sense of honesty prove to be a boon to my physical health and well-being, it was incredibly good for business. As clients I could never seem to please abandoned ship, the tips I received from those who remained behind increased exponentially. And I wasn't the only one to reap the benefits, either. My clients benefited, too. They would float out of the salon with their feet barely touching the ground, all the while enthusing about how great their hair looked. No doubt their hair did look great; I was an excellent hair colorist. But more importantly, they had been uplifted in ways that were not always obvious to the casual observer. Not only their hair but their spirits had been lightened too.

As my work as a hair colorist took on a deeper purpose--that of healing--I found a level of satisfaction in it that had been missing for quite some time. Interestingly enough, the change hadn't come about through finding a more spiritual line of work, as I had once thought it might, but through infusing the work I was already doing with a deeper meaning and purpose. Like every other area of my life, my job was being transformed by the healing power of love.

In the weeks and months that followed, my energy and confidence in my chosen spiritual path grew by leaps and bounds. Not only was my continued good health challenging what it meant to be infected with

HIV, my day to day experiences were stretching the very boundaries of time and space. Miracles were quickly becoming routine.

One extremely busy Saturday, I had an extraordinary experience, although extraordinary experiences were quickly becoming the norm. On arriving at work this particular Saturday, and seeing that my schedule was completely booked, I checked to see if there were sufficient supplies on hand to make it through the day. Most of my appointments were for highlights--a specialty of mine--and I didn't want to risk running out of foils in the middle of the day.

Highlighting a head of hair--at least the way I was trained to do it--involved weaving out small sections of hair by hand, applying the appropriate color and then wrapping it all up in foil to process. One head could take anywhere from forty to fifty foils, and I had at least ten clients scheduled that day. Unfortunately, I didn't have nearly enough foils to finish the job.

When my assistant, Jorge, arrived a short time later, I asked him to call the beauty supply and order more supplies, but unfortunately they were closed for the weekend. He scurried around the salon searching for any stashes I might have overlooked, before returning with some unwelcomed news.

"This is all I could find," he informed me, brandishing a thin stack of maybe a hundred foils, at most. "There aren't any more in the entire salon. I looked everywhere."

For some reason, I took the news rather calmly, considering its implications for my day. Instead, I instructed him to put the few foils we did have into my top drawer for safe keeping. Customers had a habit of taking them to wrap their eye-glass stems in to protect them from the dye, and I didn't want them wasted.

"Don't worry," I shrugged. "We'll be fine. Just put them in my drawer and keep an eye on them."

We worked the entire day without a break--not even stopping for lunch. From time to time, Jorge would take just a few foils at a time out of the drawer and put them on my tray for me to use. The possibility of running out was never mentioned again. That evening, after the shop had closed and everyone had gone home for the night, the two of us sat down together to count our tips and tally up the day's receipts.

"Did you get some more foils, by any chance, Jorge," I asked, fairly certain of the answer even before I asked. After all, he hadn't left my side the entire day.

Jorge looked up at me with a curious expression on his face. "No, I didn't," he stammered, apparently caught off guard by the question. "Did you? Where did all these foils came came from, then?"

I shrugged and shot him a patronizing glance. "Your guess is as good as mine," I said.

Just then, Jorge's partner barged into the back of the salon where the two of us were sitting. Immediately, my attention was drawn to the small, gold chain hanging around his neck, with a beautiful quartz crystal dangling from it.

"That's a beautiful crystal," I complimented him. "May I see it?"

"Go ahead," he said, leaning down so that I could get a better look. "Be my guest."

I reached up and cradled the crystal between my fingers. Immediately, the young man let out a yelp and jumped back as if he had been shocked.

"What the hell???!!" he exclaimed. "What did you do?!?"

"What?" I asked, unsure of just what had happened. "What's the matter?"

"When you picked up my crystal, the chain got really hot and burned my neck," he said, looking at me suspiciously. "What are you, some kind of a witch?"

I assured him that I wasn't. But what, then, had happened, exactly? I knew that my energy had been unusually high for the past few weeks, resulting in lights blowing out whenever I walked into a room or sudden, inexplicable static on the radio. The episode with the crystal was simply the latest installment in a whole series of strange events that were occurring with more and more frequency.

"*That's cool*," I thought to myself. "*I wonder what will happen next?*"

I returned to work the following Tuesday, after a three day weekend off, and picked up where I had left off the previous Saturday. Again, Jorge continued to take just a few foils at a time out of the drawer and place them on the tray beside me. And again, like some energizer bunny they kept coming and coming and coming.

Finally, about halfway through the afternoon, after completing at least five more heads of highlights, I looked at Jorge in disbelief.

"This can't go on forever," I announced, confused, frankly, as to why we still had any foils.

No sooner were the words out of my mouth than the drawer came up empty. A quick search of it turned up not a single, remaining foil. As soon as I had expressed doubt, the endless supply had run dry.

Jorge and I stood there for a moment, looking at each another in quiet disbelief. It seemed impossible that what had just happened had actually happened, and yet clearly it had. Neither of us had been out of each other's sight the entire day, and neither of us had gotten any additional supplies. I plopped down in a chair and let out a nervous laugh.

"It's just like the loaves and fishes," I said, "except, since I'm a hair colorist, it had to be foils, naturally. Jorge, do you realize what just happened here?"

He stared at me with his mouth open, slowly shaking his head. "This is too much," he protested. "I don't believe it."

"Believe it," I said. "I think the two of us might have just crossed over into the Twilight Zone."

All joking aside, we had inadvertently pushed up against a limiting set of concrete facts--a limited supply of foils, in this case--and reality had bent to accommodate our intention. The experience, as improbable as it was, was right in line with what I was learning about the nature of abundance and the idea of unlimited supply. For some reason --not an intellectual one, certainly--I had sensed right from the get-go that there would be enough foils to make it through the day. It wasn't a rational knowing, of course, but something deeper than that. It was cellular, perhaps; more intuitive, I suppose.

Miraculously, our limited supply of foils had lasted throughout the entire day Saturday and most of the day Tuesday, too, until the moment I had questioned its reality. Then, true to my spoken word, the endless supply had run dry.

4   An Island of the Future Amid the Seas of the Past

A S THE WINTER OF 1986 TIGHTENED its grip on the city, there was so much happening in both our lives it seemed as though every minute of the day was spoken for. We were working at our full time jobs, as usual, and still finding time to squeeze in an ever growing list of outside metaphysical activities. Activities at the loft were happening on a regular basis and drawing increasingly larger crowds.

The Power Seven psychic development group was in full swing and I rarely missed a meeting. Wil took advantage of my absence to catch up on his ever-expanding reading list, including books of a metaphysical bent and scientific journals touting the latest discoveries of psychoneuroimmunoloy.

Thursday nights meant a visit to The New York Healing Circle, facilitated by a man by the name of Samuel Kirshner who had studied self-healing with Louise Hay. While Wil was a big fan of the group, I was initially less enthusiastic about it and didn't always attend. I still had issues around intimacy and wasn't entirely comfortable with the circle's touchy-feely format. In other words, I wasn't comfortable hugging strangers. Thursday night was my opportunity to stay at home and relax, unless, of course, Marianne Williamson happened to be in town for one of her twice-monthly lectures on A Course in Miracles.

With the intense focus of time and energy, the pace of our spiritual growth was continuing to accelerate. Almost before we knew it, spring had arrived and the dog-days of summer were just around the corner.

The lifeless trees lining the dirty streets of the city emerged from their months-long hibernation, along with the city's winter-weary denizens. Throngs of happy people spilled out onto the sidewalks and into the cafes, celebrating the arrival of warm weather.

My own thoughts turned in anticipation of summer, which this year was shaping up to be quite a different affair. With no beach house of our own to escape to, for the first time in almost a decade Wil and I found ourselves without the comfort of our usual summer routine. Horrified at the thought of being stuck in the oppressive heat and humidity of the city, it took very little effort on my part to convince him that we should rent a house in the Pines.

"Well, at least we have the money to do it with," I sighed, noting the irony in the situation. Never mind that a seasonal rental cost nearly quadruple what it had cost to own.

In early April, we took an exploratory trip to the island to investigate the situation, and after looking at a dozen or so nondescript offerings found what we thought was the perfect house. Unlike the large home we had sold the year before, the small, unassuming bungalow that captivated our attention was one of the oldest structures in the Pines, having been floated across the Great South Bay on a barge and placed in its present location, years before the community had blossomed into the bustling gay mecca it had become. Despite having undergone extensive renovations, the small house still retained much of its original charm, not to mention a stellar location directly on the beach at least a mile from the hustle and bustle of the busy harbor area

"This is it, Wil" I announced, leaning against the railing of the deck surveying the broad expanse of white, sandy beach in the distance. "We don't have to look any further. This is it!."

The summer to come would prove to be unlike any that had come before, with little trace of the frenetic pace that had once passed for relaxation. Gone was the endless schedule of parties and dinners and tea dances, replaced now by ample quiet time for meditation and reflection on our new-found spiritual priorities.

I also began writing seriously for the very first time. Except for the dream journal I had been keeping, as well as a few brief notes about some of my more unusual, paranormal experiences, like the miracle of the foils, I had always been more inclined to read books than to write them. The only thing of substance I had attempted was the beginning of my life's story from what I feared at the time was my death bed of pneumonia, the winter before being diagnosed with HIV. When I had finally recovered after more than a month in bed, I had put it away and forgotten all about it.

The remote location of the house proved to be the ideal catalyst for releasing my pent-up, creative talents. Without consciously making a decision to, I began spending time each day writing in my journal, noting various events of interest and taking inventory of my evolving spiritual beliefs. I never intended for anyone else to read what I had written. It was just that after so much study of other people's ideas, it seemed important, somehow, to record *my* thoughts and feelings, particularly as they pertained to the AIDS epidemic, as a way of sorting them out and putting them all in perspective.

At the time, I never imagined that anything of substance would come from my fledgling literary endeavors. Eventually, however, the ideas in my journal morphed into the central core of my first book, *Beyond AIDS*, which I published a little more than a year later, planting the seeds of a mid-life career change as a lecturer and writer on self-healing.

Our final summer on Fire Island also brought with it drastic changes in our inner circle of friends, which up until now had actually been quite small. We had always known a lot of people, certainly, but mostly just in passing. Now, however, over the course of a single summer we managed to make more friends than in all of our other years on the island combined.

Our exposure at Mark's loft the previous winter, combined with the radical stand we had taken on AIDS, put us squarely at the center of a growing underground movement. And while some of that attention had proved to be negative, especially in the beginning, this was no longer entirely the case. Increasingly, people knew who we were and what we stood for, and were either interested or not. It was becoming commonplace for us to be approached by someone who had heard us speak, and thanked for sharing our stories. People also began sharing their stories with us.

It's not as though either of us hated the attention, mind you. In fact, we took comfort in meeting so many like-minded individuals. It offered us the validation we needed to continue on the path we had embarked on, and reinforced its importance in the larger scheme of things.

Inevitably, our bungalow at the beach became the focal point for a new and growing circle of friends pursing a spiritual approach to healing. That summer, in the midst of all the usual Fire Island festivities, a growing number of PWA's whose lives had begun to change and move in a radically different direction than the mainstream gay community, coalesced to form a community of seekers amid the life they had left behind.

To wit, Saturday nights at our cottage on the beach underwent an amazing metamorphosis. No longer were we concerned with who the DJ at the Pavilion might be, what outfit to wear or what party favor to take, and when. Saturday nights were now spent huddled in front of a roaring fire with friends, listening to the latest Marianne Williamson tape and engaging in passionate debate about the nature of healing, spirituality, earth changes and UFOs.

The irony of our situation was hardly lost on any of us. We looked upon ourselves and our unique situation with deep compassion and an unfailing sense of humor, and awe for the endless stream of miracles that were occurring in our lives. We were exactly where we were supposed to be, doing exactly what we needed to be doing, and nothing would be allowed to distract us from our purpose. There was work to do on ourselves and each other, and no promise of an awful lot of time to do it in.

In one of my favorite books at the time, *Visions*, by Ken Carey, he writes of a time during the emerging planetary shift when there would be *islands of the future amidst the seas of the past*. In my mind, that was certainly the situation we found ourselves in on Fire Island, the summer of 1987. While all around us the party continued unabated, oblivious to the disintegration of its shaky foundations, a group of mostly gay and HIV-infected, spiritual refugees came together to explore how they might be used in facilitating a new world order.

This was no global government or financial institution we were seeking to establish, but an inner reorientation of the most basic kind. We were committed to expanding our thinking beyond the level of mass consciousness to become more conscious, loving, human beings. And, we believed, everyone on the planet would be called upon to do the exact, same thing, sometime in the not too distant future. We were not special, you see. We were simply the leading edge of a growing tsunami of change.

That summer, our lives were charged with a powerful sense of purpose. Caught up on the first swells of the great wave of change engulfing the gay community and the entire planet, we were choosing to ride its crest. Despite the continuing challenges to our health, or perhaps because of them, we tasted life with an exhilarating immediacy and a new-found sense of appreciation. Live or die, and many people did die, unfortunately, there was no turning back for any of us!

Miraculously, we had somehow found the one thing we had been lacking all along; something that up until only recently most of us hadn't even noticed was missing: the knowledge that we were more than just meaningless specks of dust in an accidental universe without purpose. This alone was reason enough to celebrate, despite the growing plague of death surrounding us. Like bees to nectar, life had called to us with a vision of hope for ourselves and for the world, and we had responded to the call.

The atmosphere at the last house on the beach stood in stark contrast to the encroaching atmosphere of gloom the forced festivities of our neighbors were meant to keep at bay. Our joy, based on an understanding beyond just the cold, hard facts of the epidemic, formed a collective beacon of light, as slowly but surely other gay light workers awakened from their decades-long slumber to answer the call of Love.

As August approached, excitement began building about the impending Harmonic Convergence. Evidently, August 17th, 1987, was to be a very special date on the cosmic calendar--a rare doorway into another dimension of experience. Everyone on the planet was being asked to join together in creating a living network of light to harness the accelerating energies from the central sun and assist humanity in making a quantum leap up the evolutionary spiral. The event's success or failure would depend entirely upon whether a critical mass of support was achieved, or not.

The inspiration for the event had come from ancient Mayan prophesies, lost for hundreds of years and only recently rediscovered and deciphered by Jose Arguelles in his bestselling book, *The Mayan Factor*. Due to the considerable attention it had received in the mainstream press, the event had mushroomed onto the public's radar, catapulting it into a happening of international significance and captivating the attention of believers and non-believers alike.

Predictably, an uproar had quickly ensued from within the mainstream religious community, ever on guard against the perceived threat from anything even remotely New Age. And there had been considerable snickering in the scientific community as well, smugly entrenched as they were within their predictable, linear reality of cold, hard facts.

Though I had never personally read the book, I had learned of the Convergence through a series of articles circulating around the spiritual underground at the time. And while I was not overly familiar with Mayan prophesy, either, I did recognize the universality of what the event had to offer and felt that it was in alignment with what was happening in my own life.

As I sat sunning myself on the deck one lazy Saturday afternoon in early August, perusing the latest article on the subject, a particular paragraph leapt up from the page and grabbed hold of my attention. According to the writer, there were exactly twelve days of purification leading up to the actual date of the Convergence: twelve days to prepare one's self physically, mentally, emotionally and spiritually to take maximum advantage of the energies streaming toward Earth from the Central Sun.

I took a deep drag on the cigarette I was smoking and glanced at my watch to check the date. August 5th, the digital numbers informed me. Instantly, a light went off inside my head and I realized that now would be the perfect opportunity to kick my nasty addiction to cigarettes, once and for all. I had tried twice before and failed both times. Somehow, this third time would be the charm. This time, my efforts would have the full power of the Harmonic Convergence behind them. I smiled and reached over and snuffed out my cigarette in the ashtray on the table beside me. It would be the last one to ever touch my lips.

Not surprisingly, our entire circle of spiritual friends was in general agreement about the importance of the impending date and enthusiastically set about preparing for the celebration. We planned to have a sunrise meditation on the beach, during which we would combine and align our energies with the energy of all the other participating groups around the planet, through various rituals, yet to be determined.

I'm sure I wasn't the only person on the planet who had ambivalent feelings about all the hype surrounding this event. On the one hand, it was difficult not to be caught up in the excitement of a proposed event of this magnitude. On the other hand, it was just as hard not to think that in the absence of concrete evidence, beyond just an intuitive sense, we might just be making the whole thing up.

Yet if planetary transformation were merely a fantasy, I wasn't entirely convinced that all that group energy and intention might just be what was needed to bring it into manifestation. It was a metaphysical catch 22, like the chicken and the egg. Which had come first? The experience or the belief? I decided to lay aside my skepticism and participate as fully as I knew how. After all, in many ways the entire fabric of my present life had this same, surreal quality about it. Was my healing really happening, or was I simply making it up? Who could really say?

Wil and I invited several of our closest friends to spend Convergence weekend with us at the beach, among them, Anita Wexler, a heterosexual woman in her mid- thirties who was infected with HIV, Epstein Barr and the Herpes viruses, and just starting to manifest symptoms. I had been introduced to Anita through a client who had told her about my unorthodox approach to healing and given her my contact information. Intrigued by what her friend had told her, Anita arranged to meet me in person, hoping to pick my brain for any information I might have that could help her cope with her rapidly deteriorating health.

From all outward appearances, Anita was an extremely powerful woman: the daughter of a famous record producer; a child of wealth and privilege. She had grown up in a rarified world of fame and celebrity, and many of the major recording artists of the 60's and 70's had been her surrogate family.

Unfortunately, her family's affluence masked the deeper reality of a highly dysfunctional dynamic. Her father, an avowed atheist, was a powerful and controlling man for whose affection Anita and her mother had always been in competition. As a result, she had grown up to become excessively manipulative and had eventually turned to IV drugs as a way of handling her deep, emotional pain. What had started out as a chic little secret had quickly escalated into a nightmare of addiction and opened the door to any number of issues with her health.

Eventually, with her life and health in shambles, Anita's illusion of control had crumbled. When we met, she was completely overwhelmed and grasping desperately at anything or anyone she believed could fix her litany of problems and make them go away.

From the very start, Anita became one of our closest and dearest friends, and had dived headlong into a frantic effort to stop the slide in her condition. Naturally, she looked to Wil and me for guidance and inspiration. After a difficult period of adjustment, her condition had stabilized and she began working on a film project entitled, *AIDS Alive*, in which she hoped to document the growing underground movement of PWA's using spiritual and alternative means to heal themselves. Wil and I were first on her list to have our stories committed to film.

Mark Veneglia was our other guest for the weekend, and we were jazzed at the prospect of spending this powerful date on the cosmic calendar with him. He promised that Benjamin would be dropping in over the course of the weekend to offer his invaluable input into the process at hand. The evening before the celebration, the four of us stayed up for most of the night discussing the potential impact of the event on our lives, and on the planet at large.

True to his word, Mark channeled Benjamin on and off throughout the evening. The sessions provided us with information about various past lives we had shared together and the different ways and times we had served the human community as healers. He also described a number of lifetimes in which Wil and I had been together as a couple. In one particularly intriguing example, Wil had been killed when the small boat we were traveling in was caught up in a swiftly flowing current and swept over a raging waterfall. As we had plunged over the falls to our deaths, I had released my body and flown free. Frozen in fear, Wil had stayed in his body and crashed onto the rocks below. The story had an interesting corollary with his irrational, present-day fear of water. Perhaps my nautical skills, or lack of them, weren't the only reason I could never persuade him to go sailing with me on the Great South Bay. Perhaps it was something more deeply rooted than that.

Benjamin also described another lifetime in which I had been a Buddhist monk in flowing, orange robes--*a profound teacher of truth*, he explained. He hastened to add that I would be so, again, in this lifetime-- a teacher, not a Buddhist monk, mind you.

"The young men will sit at your feet and listen," he said, peering out at me through Mark's dark, luminous eyes. *"Aren't you lucky!?!"*

I had laughed, naturally, because to some extent his prediction had already come true at our talks at the loft the previous winter. More than once, I had found myself looking out into the beautiful, upturned faces of gay men with AIDS, sitting at my feet and listening in rapt attention as I expounded on my latest theories on healing. If this was what Benjamin had in mind, I certainly wasn't going to complain.

Finally, Benjamin warned of several dangerous, probabilities that might possibly emerge as we progressed deeper into the process of planetary transformation. Various scenarios were outlined involving physical changes in the earth and an impending crisis in the world economy.

"The financial house of cards will crumble," he predicted, prophetically, "and the entire world will feel the pain."

Before taking his leave for the night, Benjamin addressed Wil and me a final time and predicted that we would leave New York City and travel around the country, lecturing and teaching about healing AIDS.

"Because of the work you will do," he predicted, "many people will awaken to their higher purpose for being on this planet at this time. Because of you, and people like you, many people with AIDS will survive this epidemic."

Wil and I took these predictions with a grain of salt, being basically of the same mind about the information. While it was certainly entertaining to have the spirit of Benjamin Franklin tell us about our past lives together, it was not as though we had any actual memory of them. I *was* aware that I had lived before, however, owing to several spontaneous regressions I had experienced in which memories from two previous lives had come flooding back, unbidden. One had been as a soldier in 17th century England where I was involved in the kidnapping of a royal child, and the other as a young, black, female slave on a Louisiana plantation around the time of the civil war.

Whether the lives Benjamin described that night were real or not wasn't really important to either of us. We thought of them more on the order of diversionary amusements--an entertaining parlor game-- something to expand our horizons a little further than might otherwise be the case.

For my part, I was much more interested in my present life, in knowing that I wasn't the victim of karma from an unremembered past. Surely, everything I needed to heal myself was available to me here and now, in this lifetime, right where I was. Having knowledge of past lives might provide a more expansive context in which to couch my present experience, but that was all. I couldn't allow myself to be sidetracked by speculative information.

Later that night, as Wil and I prepared for bed, we discussed Benjamin's predictions and went out of our way to reassure each other that neither of us had any intention of leaving our comfortable lives in New York City to do what he predicted. We had a good laugh about it and chalked it up to Mark's overactive imagination, before settling in for a good night's sleep.

Try as I might, however, I found it impossible to fall asleep with so many questions and possibilities dancing across my synapses. I couldn't help but feel uneasy about Benjamin's predictions of earth changes and a collapsing economy. Certainly, it wasn't the first time I had heard this type of information. Some of it reminded me of Ramtha's predictions, and some of it of what I had learned as a child in church. While I no longer believed in a punishing God, these predictions did bring up long, suppressed fears that somehow we were all essentially bad at the core and would inevitably be punished no matter how we might try and redeem ourselves. Yet another layer of deeply ingrained belief in sin and guilt had been unearthed by Benjamin's words and I would now be forced to deal with it.

One of the difficulties I had in processing this type of information was that in understanding the creative power of thought and recognizing how far out of alignment mass consciousness was in relationship to Love, I could see the very real possibility of some of the disasters Benjamin predicted actually happening. I was tormented by the dilemma of how to find safety in a world that was apparently destined to disintegrate. How could anyone hope to survive if the very structures they depend upon were swept away? How could I trust and let go, in the face of events spinning out of control? And what was the point in healing yourself of AIDS, if only to die in some massive cataclysm?

This was the nature of my deepest fears rising up from the core of my being, having been stoked by Benjamin's warnings. I didn't have answers to the multitude of questions swirling around inside my head, yet I knew they would need to be addressed sooner or later, in one way or another. I had reached a point in my personal evolution and growth, beyond which I could progress no further until I had settled certain, basic questions once and for all.

For now, the best I could do was to bring myself back from the uncertainty of the future to the safety of the present moment. Here, at least for now, my world was still intact. And here, there was still plenty of everything to go around.

I turned and looked at Wil sleeping peacefully on the bed beside me, his face illuminated by the moonlight streaming in through the open window. I leaned over and kissed his forehead. With that, the vice of pressure surrounding my heart relaxed a bit and the ice in my veins began to thaw.

"At least we have each other," I thought to myself. *"I can face anything, as long as we have each other."* And with that, I rolled over and fell fast asleep.

🌤

5　*The Harmonic Convergence*

HEN I AWOKE THE MORNING OF the Harmonic Convergence, a thick layer of fog blanketed the island, obscuring my view of the beach from the bedroom window. Startled to think we might have overslept and missed the crucial moment of sunrise, I shook Wil awake and jumped out of bed, and scurried through the house to rouse the others. A quick glance at the clock confirmed that the sun would be up in less than twenty minutes. We'd have to hurry if we wanted to be on the beach by dawn.

I stepped through the sliding glass doors onto the deck and scanned the eastern horizon. Through the fog, I could just make out the faint silhouettes of people trudging silently down the beach. I turned and went inside, and called to Anita and Mark to hurry up. Wil emerged from the bedroom and announced that he was ready to go. We stepped out onto the deck and clambered down a flight of wooden stairs, and joined the silent procession. The mournful wail of a fog horn sounded in the distance.

On reaching the deserted stretch of beach that had been designated for the festivities, there were already at least fifty people there ahead of us, arranged in discreet groups of twos and threes, soaking up the predawn silence, waiting for the inevitable moment of dawn. Without a word passing between us, we selected a level spot, not far from another cluster of people, and prepared to settle in. Marc lit some incense, while the rest of us prepared for the various rituals we planned to lead. More people were arriving all the time, and someone had brought along a drum. Before long, a hypnotic beat resounded through the mist, lending a certain primeval atmosphere to the scene.

As the first rays of sunlight crested the eastern horizon, we initiated our silent prayers of surrender and slipped into meditation where we remained until the sun emerged full-blown into the sky. Then, individually and in groups, people began gathering up their belongings and heading back down the beach for home.

At this point, I was feeling a bit disappointed with the way things were turning out. As I understood it, sunrise was to be the moment when people all over the world joined together in celebration of their oneness. Though we *had* managed to come together at the designated time and place, we had remained apart in separate, distinct groups, missing the point entirely, as far as I could determine. The window of opportunity was rapidly closing and if someone didn't act soon, the crowd would disperse and this golden opportunity would be lost forever.

As I stood there, unsure of just what to do about it, Anita broke into a spontaneous grin and reached out and took Mark's hand. Immediately, Wil and I joined them, forming a small circle in the sand. Apparently, this was all that was needed to break the isolation keeping everyone apart. One by one, others joined in the circle until soon it had grown to include nearly everyone on the beach.

Seemingly out of nowhere, two men, their bodies brightly painted and sprinkled with glitter, appeared as though by magic and began dancing around the circle. A woman with sage followed close behind them, smudging each person as she passed. Around the circle, shining smiles appeared as strangers eyes met and acknowledged their kinship with one another.

This was what we had all been waiting for: the moment when each of us would step out of our individual isolation and join together as one. Out of fear of being judged or perhaps looking foolish, we had almost failed to accomplish the most important task of the day. By acting spontaneously on her feelings, Anita had salvaged the situation for everyone. At the last possible minute, a group of strangers had joined together and formed a new community of friends.

As the sun climbed higher into the sky, the day took on the atmosphere of a party. Wil and I lingered on the beach for several hours, making new friends and sharing our insights into the significance of the day. A curious group gathered around Mark, who slipped into trance bringing Benjamin through, to everyone's surprise and delight. Caught up in the festive mood, others danced to the accompaniment of an eclectic orchestra of bells, flutes and tambourines.

The celebration continued until well past noon, when finally the rest of the community woke up and wandered down to the beach to see what all the commotion was about. At this point, satisfied that we had kept faith with the day's intent, Wil and I gathered up our belongings and headed back down the beach for home where we stayed for the remainder of the day, receiving the occasional visitor who strolled up from the beach to chat and share the commitment they had made during the meditation earlier that morning.

Wil and I were delighted to discover that for all intents and purposes we had each made the same commitment: we had sworn to do whatever it took to maintain our healing and expand our efforts to share our experience with others. Anita had made a firm decision to bring AIDS ALIVE to the screen and was already busy formulating a plan to raise cash for the project by tapping into her invaluable connections in the recording industry. She hoped to begin shooting by the fall.

Both Wil and I felt strongly about the importance of Anita's project and wanted to do something to support it. Realizing that the beach house was the perfect setting for a fundraiser, we immediately offered it to her to use. The upscale crowd in the Pines was a potential gold mine of prospective donations, and would be hard pressed to resist the lure of a party.

Anita accepted our offer, but with an unexpected stipulation. "I think this would be the perfect opportunity for you to share your story with an entirely new group of people," she suggested. "Then, after you two have softened them up a bit, Judy and I could present our vision for the film and make a pitch for contributions. What do you think? Would you be willing to do it?"

For a moment, her request caught us both off guard. True, an event such as the one Anita was proposing would essentially kill two birds with one stone. It would introduce the idea that AIDS could be healed to the influential Fire Island community, while simultaneously raising funds for a film exploring the same subject. Certainly, gauging from the number of people who had participated in the morning's festivities, there was enough support in the community to make such an event a success. And, it was in perfect alignment with the commitment we had just made that morning to reach out to a larger audience. How could we refuse?.

"I don't see how we could say no, do you?" Wil said, glancing at me to make certain we were both on the same page.

"Consider it done," I concurred. "I think it's a really, good idea."

With the busy Labor Day weekend just a few short weeks away, there was barely enough time to plan and publicize the event before the summer season wound to a close and the opportunity would be lost. To take advantage of the larger than normal holiday crowds, we spent the intervening weeks hastily drawing up a plan of action. Mark designed a stunning flyer to publicize the event, and Wil and I paid to have it printed. Anita huddled at home with her co-producer, Judy, working on their pitch for contributions.

The following Saturday, the four of us spent the entire day papering the length of Fire Island Boulevard and the surrounding walks with flyers announcing the event. Then, we divided up the community between us and hand-delivered personal invitations to every house in the Pines.

We were caught up in the excitement of the moment. Yet, the further we progressed with our plans, the more I experienced cold feet about having my name plastered all over Fire Island in association with AIDS. Unlike Manhattan, where things tended to be more anonymous by nature, the Pines was a very small community. Here, people knew who I was, and the thought of disclosing my HIV status was frankly intimidating.

The more flyers Wil stapled to the telephone poles along Fire Island Boulevard, the more intense my fear and trepidation grew. Before long, I had worked myself into a real panic. I dug my heels in and tried to convince him that we had done enough.

"Let's go home," I whined. "Don't you think we've done enough, already?"

Wil, who had long since given up caring if anyone knew he had AIDS, couldn't understand why I had suddenly become so spineless. As the day progressed, he grew increasingly annoyed by my constant resistance. To his way of thinking, once a decision was made, he never questioned it again or had further reservations. For him, the matter of public disclosure had been settled earlier in the year at the loft.

Unfortunately, that wasn't the case with me. Once I had committed to speaking at the fundraiser, every hidden fear I had came bubbling up to the surface to be dealt with. There was part of me--a large part of me--that still didn't fully trust the Universe and wanted to stick with the status quo, even if the safety it offered was merely an illusion.

Despite my fears, I knew that to try and stay in a place where nothing ever changed would abort my fragile healing. Healing, first and foremost, was about growth and change, and there was no way of avoiding this fact no matter how unpleasant I might find it. I would have to bite the bullet and follow through on my commitment.

Despite my best efforts to delay it, Labor Day weekend arrived, finally, and with it the fundraiser for AIDS ALIVE. Early that Saturday morning, Anita caught the first ferry from Sayville and arrived at the house in time for breakfast, with Judy and her husband, a professional cameraman by trade, in tow. Mark arrived a short time later, along with several volunteers he had enlisted to help, carrying a flag he had designed to symbolize the self-healing movement. The flag, a black sheath brimming with colorful spirals and sacred geometric symbols, was meant to trigger the unconscious knowledge of healing in the mind of anyone who viewed it.

"That's nice, Mark," Wil commented dryly, on seeing the unusual banner. He arched an eyebrow for effect. "Very cheerful, indeed!"

Mark let Wil's remark pass without comment. By now, he was used to having to explain his art to the great, unwashed masses and wasn't the least bit apologetic about his latest creation.

"Where should I hang it," he asked, following Wil outside onto the deck.

"Over here, right next to this one," Wil said, pointing to a large, white banner hanging from the railing on the roof, with AIDS ALIVE emblazoned across it in bold black letters.

While Mark and Wil hung the banner, I polished off a few remaining details in the kitchen. The refreshments were my responsibility and I wanted everything to be perfect. Then, finally, it was time to take a break and change. As an omen of impending success, the mist parted to reveal a flawless, bright, blue sky.

Before long, the guests began to arrive, and soon the house was overflowing with people and animated conversation. The festive crowd spilled out onto the deck and around the pool in a colorful display of the latest summer fashions. After allowing plenty of time for everyone to partake of the refreshments and poke around the house, Wil signaled that it was time to begin the formal presentation.

Anita and Judy spoke first and shared their vision for AIDS ALIVE, after which Wil shared a few of his personal experience with metaphysics and self-healing. Then, when it was my turn, the fear that had held my chest in a vice-like grip for weeks evaporated as if on cue. As always, it was exhilarating to share a message of hope with people who were hungry for empowerment. As such, there was simply no room for fear.

When I had finished with my remarks, Anita and Judy returned and asked the crowd for their financial support for the film. Wil and I got things off to a running start with a $3,000 pledge. With the ice broken by our donation, several other generous pledges were made, along with quite a number of smaller ones.

The sun was low in the sky as the party wound to a close. Slowly but surely, the crowd dispersed and headed back to their separate homes. A number of stragglers hung on around the pool, engaging in small talk and finishing off the last of the refreshments. Anita and Judy set about tallying up the afternoon's take and soon announced that they had collected well over six thousand dollars.

"We can begin shooting right away," Anita crowed. "We'll start as soon as we get back to the city!"

In the afterglow of a job well done, Wil and I relaxed together on a raft in the pool. I was feeling pleased with myself for having pushed past my fear to fulfill my part in the event. With the scary part over and done with, it was easy to laugh at myself and the paralysis I had felt just a few, short hours earlier. I floated in the warm water, basking in the realization of just how supportive the Universe could be when you actually let it.

"Why do I always have to make such a big deal out of things," I asked rhetorically. "Why can't I just make a decision and stick to it, without all the drama?"

"Because you're a drama queen, that's why," Wil giggled, and pushed me off the raft into the water. Obviously, his point was well taken.

All too soon, the delicate days of Indian summer gave way to the muted grays of winter and the end to the rental season. Reluctantly, and with a twinge of sadness, Wil and I packed up our belongings and prepared to vacate the cottage, knowing full-well that this would probably be our last summer on Fire Island together. Despite the heaviness in our hearts, we were excited, nonetheless, about the many adventures that lay before us in the months ahead in the city.

In the wake of the Harmonic Convergence, the pace of our lives accelerated dramatically, as if we had suddenly been flung out of a powerful slingshot. Anita and Judy began prompt production on AIDS ALIVE, and our story was the first to be committed to film. In late November, the three of us appeared together on a local cable television show, and a few weeks later my first print interview was published in the New York Native. Opportunities for putting our message across came pouring in from every direction and we were left to adjust to being the center of so much attention, in both a positive and negative sense.

In October, I made the trip to Florida to visit my parents. While I was there, Wall Street took its steepest dive since the 1929 crash, giving up over 500 points in a single session and raising the specter of a major, financial collapse. Plugging into the fear being fomented in the press, I called Wil in New York to see how he had weathered the day and was relieved by his nonplused attitude. Taking a cue from him, I decided to forgo my usual drama and trust that events were unfolding exactly as they were meant to be. Anyway, it wasn't like there was anything I could do about it.

When I returned to New York, time continued to accelerate even faster than before. As winter tightened its grip on the city, I couldn't help but notice how much the urban environment was starting to wear on my nerves more than usual. Things that at one time would never have caught my attention seemed glaring to me now, creating an unfamiliar background of stress I couldn't seem to shake.

I was also becoming increasingly sensitive to the toxic chemicals I handled at work. Standing over bowls of bleach all day long, inhaling noxious ammonia fumes, was beginning to take its toll. My eyes burned and my sinuses became perpetually inflamed. To my dismay, the Eustachian tube in my right ear closed shut and my inner ear filled with fluid.

Repeated trips to a specialist brought about only the shortest reprieve from symptoms. To relieve the pressure, the doctor carefully inserted a hollow needle through my eardrum and suctioned out the accumulated fluid--a procedure that was both frightening and painful. I was forced to take multiple rounds of powerful antibiotics to try and prevent the infection from reoccurring. But no matter how many times my ear was drained or how many rounds of antibiotics I took, as soon as I came into contact with the offending chemicals again, my sinuses would flair up all over again and my ear would refill with fluid. As a result, I began to dread going to work.

I was also becoming increasingly irritated by the constant cacophony of background noise created through a combination of relentless traffic, the never-ending new construction, and the propensity for New York cabbies to lay on their horns at the slightest provocation. To compound my discomfort, I was being rudely awakened at least three times a week, at 3 o'clock in the morning, by an obnoxious garbage truck collecting trash from the commercial building across the street from our apartment. It seemed like the driver would deliberately pound the large, steel container up and down against the pavement just to make sure everyone in the neighborhood was awake. I thought I would lose my mind!

In truth, New York may not have been any noisier than it had ever been. I suspect I was simply more psychically open than in the past, and more sensitive to my surroundings.   Now that I had embarked upon a journey that required me to open my heart and expand my awareness, I was finding it increasingly difficult to navigate such a frenetic environment.

Unlike when I had first arrived in the city, in 1973, my outer reality no longer supported my inner growth, and the gap between the two was a growing source of stress. The solution to my problem represented a choice between shutting down or finding an environment more in alignment with my internal state of mind. I knew that shutting down would only jeopardize my healing, and that was out of the question. This left me with only one alternative: it was time to consider leaving New York City--something that I would have never imagined I would do, at least not of my own free will.

Of the two of us, I had always been the more right-brained and spontaneous, unlike Wil who was intellectually oriented and conservative in his approach to just about everything. This fundamental difference in our personalities was one of the many things that had always worked to provide us with balance in our relationship. Wil provided the stability I seemed to be lacking and I provided him with some sorely needed spontaneity.

Because our relationship contained this system of checks and balances, I had always had the luxury of acting on impulse, without having to consider the full ramifications of my actions. Wil could be counted on to veto my plans whenever they veered too far out of line.

I was counting on this dynamic when I came home from work one afternoon, shortly after my thirty-fifth birthday, in early November, and announced that I was sick of living in New York and thought we should move.

"I just can't take it anymore," I griped, barging into the apartment and throwing my coat over the back of a nearby chair. "It's just no fun, anymore. Let's get out of here and try something new."

At the same time my heart was telling me to leave New York, my mind was warning of just how insane it would be to give up a six-figure income just because I was feeling a little bit stressed out. I suppose someone more sensible than me would have simply taken a long vacation. After all, jobs like the ones Wil and I had didn't grow on trees. It had taken us years of hard work to create the success we now enjoyed.

My career had been the realization of a dream I had pursued ever since arriving in the city, fourteen years earlier. Did I really think I could just throw it away now without paying an enormous price? Money had always been important to me, and over the last ten years I had grown used to having plenty of it. It was the one thing that made me feel safe. What made me think I could get by with less of it now?

Somewhere in the back of my mind, I was counting on Wil to allow me to vent before providing a reality check. Surely, sensible old Wil would censure this insane idea of wanting to chuck it all and move. Surprisingly, however, he didn't try to talk me out of the idea or lecture me about how impractical I was being. Instead, after thinking about it for a while, he admitted to feeling the exact same way.

"I've been feeling the same kind of pressures you have," he confessed. "I'm just not exactly sure what to do about it."

A few days later, Wil arrived home from work and announced that he was leaving his job, and suggested I do the same.

"I've taken a three month leave of absence," he informed me, pausing to enjoy the look of shock that flashed across my face. "That ought to give me enough time to figure out if I *ever* want to go back or not."

To be honest, I was more than a little frightened by this uncharacteristic burst of impulsiveness on his part. At the same time, I felt an adrenaline rush just thinking about what such a radical act might actually mean. To simply drop everything the world judges as valuable and leave it behind, simply because your heart tells you to, felt incredibly reckless, yet so incredibly right.

Beneath my superficial uncertainly was a deep assuredness that we could make this work as long as we had each other. Even if we spent all our money and couldn't find comparable work elsewhere--which was highly unlikely--I still thought I could be happy. I could be happy because I possessed the one thing I valued more than anything else in the world: a loving relationship with a man who loved me unconditionally. My relationship with Wil was the one thing that made taking such a risk even remotely tenable.

The following week, I promptly initiated the necessary preparations for leaving my job. With February 1, 1988 set as our departure date and the Christmas holidays rapidly approaching, there was precious little time to waste. My co-workers took the unexpected news with varying degrees of surprise and skepticism. If any of them thought I was crazy--and some of them had decided that long ago, due to my preoccupation with metaphysics and healing--then this decision irrevocably confirmed their belief. Who but a crazy person would throw away a lucrative career, years in the making, simply because they were stressed? Certainly, such a minor annoyance didn't merit the kind of radical action Wil and I were about to take.

At the same time, I could see that on another level--one that most of them would never have admitted to--they envied me for what I was planning to do. They were just as burned out as I was but lacked the courage to break out of their comfort zones and move in a new direction. They were imprisoned by fear and by money, the same things that had kept me sweating behind a chair for most of the last ten years.

From the perspective of our spiritual growth and healing, the radical action Wil and I were about to take was exactly the leap of faith we needed in order to prove, once and for all, that the Universe would support us in following the siren call of our hearts. All of the outer signs in my life, from the problem with my ear to my growing irritation with the city, were pointing in the same direction. The bare facts were this: if we couldn't trust the Universe to support us in our desire to leave the city, there probably wasn't a spiritual basis for our healing, either. If only fear stood in the way of our dreams, it was time to put our faith to the test.

If my spiritual beliefs about a benevolent Universe were true, and my healing was based on this premise, then the move Wil and I were about to make would be just one big opportunity to go beyond belief to an actual experience of grace. If God were real, then in some way impossible for me to figure out or to explain how, support would fall into place as I stepped out in the direction my heart was leading me. Wasn't that what had happened to Luke Skywalker when he had stepped out over the abyss? Hadn't a bridge magically formed beneath his feet? Why would I expect anything less for myself?

My goal was not just the healing of my body, but a full experience of what it meant to be created in the image and likeness of God--goals that in my mind were not separate, but intertwined. The catch was this: in order to gain the experience I would have to trust enough to take at least a few tentative steps into the unknown, and trust was something I'd historically been short of. Unfortunately, this was my only option. *If I wanted to live, I would have to follow my heart.*

☀

6   *The Insidious Cloud of Fear*

IN THE BEGINNING, WIL AND I were not really sure where we would go, if and when we were to leave New York City. California loomed as a possibility, certainly, mainly because it was a known quantity. Having visited there a number of times over the years, we had made quite a number of friends, particularly in San Francisco. The fact that it was relatively gay-friendly also weighed heavily in its favor.

As we began formulating our plans for leaving New York City, numerous scenarios were considered and rejected. Our first thought was simply to take a couple of months off work to relax and see the rest of the country, after which we would return to the city and resume our respective careers, albeit at a more measured pace. I suggested that we buy a car and do a bed and breakfast tour of the entire United States. I had never driven cross-country before, and was curious about what might be out there in the vast expanse between the coasts. Besides, we would need a car if we were going to live anywhere other than New York City.

Before long, the car we had visualized evolved into a van, which seemed like a practical idea since our trip was beginning to look as though it might extend on, indefinitely. With a van, we could offset some of our lodging expenses by camping out occasionally in the various national parks we planned on visiting along the way.

Deciding that this was the way to go, we began doing the necessary research to find the perfect vehicle. Wil would arrive home each night after work, lugging a briefcase full of brochures which we would pore over until late into the night. Unfortunately, with each new brochure we looked at, our imaginations would ratchet up another notch until eventually the simple van we had intended to buy just wouldn't do. We had to have the most deluxe vehicle we could afford. Finally, we were ready to head out and do some serious shopping!

As you might imagine, it's practically impossible to buy a recreational vehicle in Manhattan. New Yorkers aren't really that big on the great outdoors, I suppose, preferring the comfort of limousines and first-class hotels to sleeping bags and tents. To find a dealership specializing in the type of vehicle we were in the market for, with a sizable inventory of stock on hand, we had to leave the safety of Manhattan for New Jersey and Pennsylvania.

Each weekend for the next two months, we followed the same routine: at the crack of dawn on Saturday, we'd roll out of bed and rent a car. Then, equipped with a map and a list of dealerships, we'd spend the entire day combing through lots and showrooms, searching for that one special vehicle. Unfortunately, the more we looked the more confused we became. Just when it seemed as though we had found the perfect vehicle, one of us would spot another model with just a few more bells and whistles we couldn't live without, and we'd have to start all over again.

Originally, I had fantasized about roughing it in the great outdoors--man alone against nature--that sort of thing. After living in the city for so long, the idea had a naive sort of romanticism about it which frankly I found appealing. Wil, on the other hand, wanted nothing to do with the idea. Roughing it was not particularly his style. He was inevitably attracted to the larger, more luxurious RV's, with fully equipped kitchens and bathrooms and comfortable beds. As he envisioned our trip, any vehicle we purchased would need to offer him the luxury of seeing the great outdoors from the comfort and safety of its mobile, living room window. To him, first class seemed like the only reasonable way to go.

Though I was not exactly opposed to such creature comforts, the sight of the price of one of these behemoths sent me into sticker shock and brought up huge levels of fear. It was one thing to buy a car, but to spend thirty to forty thousand dollars on a Winnebago when you were giving up your day job, was another matter, entirely. Money was a hot button issue for me, and the idea of letting go of such a big chunk of it made me more than a little uncomfortable.

Half joking and half in earnest, I made Wil swear that if I couldn't find a job when we got to wherever it was we were going, he'd support me in the style to which I was accustomed. At the time, he had found my request amusing and had shaken his head and assured me that he would take care of me.

"You really have nothing to worry about, you know," he had assured me. "You're one of the most resourceful people I know."

Still wrestling with uncertainty, I vacillated between being absolutely sure on the one hand that what we were doing was right and good, and panicking on the other that we were making some horrible kind of irreversible mistake. When the following weekend rolled around, I came up with every excuse in the book why we shouldn't go out looking that day. The more enthusiasm Wil exhibited for the hunt, the more I tried to throw a wet blanket over our plans.

While my erratic behavior undoubtedly annoyed him, Wil had no intention of letting me wriggle out of our agreement. He would drag me out of bed each Saturday morning and hustled me off to the car rental agency, then drive me bitching and complaining through the Lincoln Tunnel to investigate the next group of dealerships on our list. Sulking in the passenger seat beside him, I was overcome with a intense sense of dread, imaging all sorts of dire consequences for our actions and feeling completely helpless to do anything to prevent them from happening.

After a number of unpleasant excursions like this, I began to notice a curious phenomenon that occurred on each of the trips. Each time, as we were leaving the city, I would find myself smothering in the clutches of suffocating fear. Then, when we had driven another ten to fifteen miles or so and the urban landscape would give way to occasional stretches of open space, my fear would begin to ease and I would start to feel centered again, as though a huge weight had been lifted off my chest. Suddenly, I could breathe. Twenty miles outside the city and I was eagerly envisioning our departure from New York.

One Saturday in early December, after spending the entire day looking through the inventory of every dealership on our list, we began the long trip back to the city, exhausted but excited by each new piece of the puzzle that had fallen into place that day. As we approached New York from the south and west, the open countryside began to gradually give way to the shabby industrial areas flanking the city. Through the hazy polluted air, the skyscrapers of lower Manhattan appeared like ghostly sentinels on the horizon. Slowly, almost imperceptibly at first, but then growing in intensity with every passing mile, my chest started to tighten again and the fear and dread I had felt upon leaving the city returned full force.

The idea that there is no other place to live in the civilized world than New York City is an idea that is widely embraced by most people living in Manhattan. Certainly, it was by me. This living thought form of immense power hangs over the island like an invisible cloud, invisible to the naked eye. From within the cloud, it's hard to imagine living anywhere else, and any thought of ever leaving is quickly brushed aside. Yet the fear this attitude masks is seldom recognized for what it really is. It's just that it's impossible for a New Yorker to imagine living anywhere other than New York City.

Strangely enough, as soon as we would drive out from under the influence of this insidious cloud, I could see countless possibilities for our lives. There really was life outside of New York, and it had at least as many things to offer as Manhattan did. In a way I was just beginning to recognize, I had been held captive to a collective blanket of fear--one disguised as sophistication and elitism, perhaps, but fear, nevertheless. Suddenly, I could see things for what they were, and was free to take the next step in my life.

Just before the holidays, we drove to Pennsylvania to visit one of the largest R.V. dealership in the area. Exiting the New Jersey Turnpike near its southern termination point, we took a small, two-lane highway past pumpkin-studded fields and small family farms, to the small town where the dealership in question was located. To our delight, the huge lot in front of the small building housing its offices held just about every type of camper and van imaginable, including a huge array of class A vehicles.

For those that might not know the difference, a class A vehicle is different than a truck body with a camper shell mounted on the back. It's more like a bus, with the cab and body in one continuous piece. Up until this point in our search, we had been leaning toward buying a modest camper, convinced that the price of anything more luxurious would surely bust our budget. Since we were there, however, and there was such a diverse selection of vehicles to choose from, we decided to take a look at the more deluxe models just for fun. The problem was that once we had seen the nicer models, it was hard to settle for anything less.

We looked through a top of the line Winnebago with just about every feature you could imagine: a full bath and kitchen, and separate living and sleeping areas, tastefully appointed with attractive fabrics and furnishings, considering some of the tacky interiors we had seen on cheaper models. After he had opened every cabinet and door and fiddled with all the knobs, Wil looked at me and grinned.

"This is it," he said. "This is the one I want. We don't have to look any further."

Judging from his tone of voice, I quickly realized it would be pointless to argue with him. Besides, if we dared look any further, we'd undoubtedly end up with an investment even more over the top than this one. As I studied the manufacturer's sticker stuck to the passenger's side window, my stomach started to tie itself in knots: $35,500.00 and change, plus tax, the numbers stared back at me from the bottom line. This was considerably more than we had intended to spend when we had naively set out in search of a simple set of wheels. But what the hell; it was time to make a decision.

"*It's now or never*," I thought to myself. "Let's find the salesman and give him a down payment."

Before either of us had time to renege on the decision, we found the lone salesman who had greeted us upon our arrival, and ducked into his cramped and messy office to fill out the necessary paperwork. We charged the down payment on Wil's Visa card with the remainder due on delivery, the last week in January, approximately five weeks away.

When the paperwork was complete, we thanked the pleasantly surprised salesman and headed for the door. On the way back to the city, we congratulated ourselves on having finally closed the deal. We were especially pleased that money hadn't been allowed to dictate our decision. We'd bought exactly the vehicle we wanted, and money hadn't been allowed to be the deciding factor. But most of all, we were relieved that our long search was finally over. At least now, there would be no more early-morning, weekend forays out of town.

It was late in the day as we approached the outskirts of New York City, and the sun was just beginning to sink below the mountains to the west. To the east, beyond the majestic waters of the Hudson River, the skyline of Manhattan twinkled in repose. This time, as we inched our way toward the entrance to the Lincoln Tunnel, the cloud of fear that was usually there to greet us was strangely absent. Not even the frenetic energy of New York City could crush the deep sense of certainty we were feeling deep inside. All was well with the world, and everything in our lives was unfolding exactly as it should.

Back at the apartment, there was a lone message on our answering machine from a woman in Cleveland by the curious name of Bellruth Naparstek. Bellruth, a psychotherapist with a husband and three kids, had heard of Wil and I through a mutual friend and was calling to see if we would be willing to travel to Cleveland and speak. Coming as it did, on the very day we had made a down payment on the Winnebago, the request confirmed our growing suspicion that the Universe had plans for us beyond just the ones we were making for ourselves. Obviously, we would be traveling to Cleveland.

"I think that's a sign, don't you?" Wil asked, slumping onto the couch and kicking off his shoes.

"Yeah, I think your right," I nodded. "Obviously, the Universe has plans for us that we're not aware of."

The synchronicity of Bellruth's request, coming as it did from out of the blue, along with the earlier events of the day, filled us with a deep sense of connection to a much larger plan than just the ones we were making for ourselves. After dinner, Wil returned her call and accepted the invitation. At the time, neither of us had the slightest inkling of the many adventures that lay ahead of us, that Bellruth's invitation would be merely the first of many more invitations to come, and the beginning of the most outrageous adventure of our lives.

7 *Taking Care of Logistics*

H AVING JUST MADE A DOWN PAYMENT on a Winnebago, the
reality of what we were planning to do began to sink in hard. If
our departure from New York was to remain on schedule, we
couldn't afford to waste any time in getting the ball rolling. There were
decisions to make about the apartment, clients to notify of our departure,
and countless friends and acquaintances to say goodbye to. There was
also the little matter of how to handle our finances from on the road.

With Christmas just around the corner, the usual spate of holiday
parties offered the perfect opportunity to see friends and say goodbye
to them in person. At work, most of my clients were in for last-minute
touchups, and again I had the same opportunity. Though we tried our
best to explain the reasons behind our sudden departure, most people
couldn't seem to comprehend how we could be so rash as to leave two
perfectly good careers behind and strike out into the great unknown.
To be perfectly honest, neither of us was completely conscious of all our
reasons, either. Yet, despite the occasional feelings of ambivalence that
surfaced from time to time, there could be no mistaking the enthusiasm
we exuded as we tried to explain ourselves the very best we could.

There was also a strong element of sadness in our decision to leave
New York. And grief. I tried not to dwell on it too much, but the stark
truth was that I was leaving behind the best life I had ever known. I was
saying goodbye to friends and business associates, many of whom were
like members of my own family. There were the prerequisite hugs and
tears and promises to keep in touch, knowing full-well that this would
be the last time some of us would ever see each other again.

Of major importance was figuring out how to keep track of our finances from on the road. Our most pressing need was for someone to forward our mail and see to it that our rent and credit card bills were paid on time. Interstate banking didn't yet exist, and the cell phone was still an expensive novelty. We knew few people capable of handling such a job, much less someone willing to take on such a huge responsibility. After a little coaxing, Wil's best friend, Eric, agreed to act as proxy in our absence.

With much of the logistics critical to our trip handled, there was still the emotional fallout to deal with. Manhattan had been our home for most of our adult lives, and leaving felt a bit like a death in the family. The city's mean streets had taught me things that would have been impossible to learn anywhere else in the world. In the words of the popular anthem, New York, New York-- *if you can make it here, you can make it anywhere*-- the truth was that I *had* made it in New York. Yet, lurking just beneath my superficial sense of confidence was a nagging uncertainty about my ability to make it anywhere else.

Strangely enough, succeeding in New York had always come easy for me. The city's competitive atmosphere was familiar, somehow, and I instinctively understood how things worked. First of all, it wasn't a city that played by the rules, like so many other places in America I had read about. Here, anyone could make it on raw talent and sheer guts alone, and these were qualities I had plenty of. That being said, my insecurity grew mostly out of a fear that the rest of the world was much more impressed with doing things the *right* way--of playing by the rules--than a typical New Yorker was used to. I feared, and with good reason, that middle America wasn't the kind of place that looked kindly on people like me.

There was also the delicate matter of giving up our rent-stabilized apartment in the Village. Conventional wisdom had it that no one in their right mind ever gives up a New York apartment, at least not of their own free will. Wil and I had lived at the same Greenwich Village address for almost a decade, and the rent was unbeatable in terms of the amount of space we had. If we were to lose our lease, it would be next to impossible to find as advantageous a situation, given the current state of Manhattan's red- hot housing market. Predictably, my fear kept surfacing about what would happen if we left all of this behind and nothing worked out the way we planned. The apartment was my one guarantee that if all else failed I could return to New York and pick up with my life where I had left off. It was the ultimate ace up my sleeve and I was loathe to give it up.

All of these uncomfortable feelings kept bubbling up from inside me, despite my best efforts to put the bravest face possible on our plans. Unfortunately, I didn't have time to process through my tangle of conflicted emotions, given how quickly the events we had unleashed were starting to unfold. With the holidays just around the corner, work was in full swing; while at home, there was still plenty of packing left to do. I dealt with my feelings the best I knew how and pushed the rest aside, promising myself that I'd handle them as soon as all the commotion subsided.

In the days that followed, Wil and I managed to work out an arrangement to keep the apartment by subletting it to a friend with AIDS who needed a place to live. To help him out financially, we agreed to pay a portion of the rent in exchange for leaving most of our belongings in place, and the ability to stay over whenever we were passing through the city. This way, we could keep the apartment, I could have the security of an escape valve just in case things didn't work out as planned, and our friend got a much needed place to live at a price he could afford. It was a win/win situation for everyone except the landlord. The deal was technically an illegal sublet.

All too quickly, our last day on the job came and went, and with all of our goodbyes said and done with, we were ready to depart. Early in the morning, on the last Saturday in January, we rented a car for the last time and drove to Pennsylvania to pick up the Winnebago. In a shaky hand, I wrote out a check for the remaining thirty-four thousand dollars, the single, largest check I had ever written.

While there was a certain satisfaction to be had in being able to write such a hefty check, the flip side of the equation was the gnawing fear I felt at letting go of so much precious money. Unfortunately, it was too late to think about it now. We had made our decision, we had quit our jobs, and we had sublet the apartment. There was only one direction to move in.

The ink on the check was still drying when the dealer handed us the keys to our shiny, new Winnebago, and ushered us out of his office and pointed us in the direction of the lot out front. Wil unlocked the passenger-side door to our shiny, new home on wheels and scrambled up the steps, with me in hot pursuit. The Winnebago's interior was pristine with the comforting smell of a brand new car. I climbed into the driver's seat and carefully inserted the key into the ignition. Wil slipped into the Captain's chair and buckled himself in. With a turn of the key the engine roared to life.

I paused to adjust the automatic rear-view mirrors and look over the unfamiliar controls. Then, satisfied that everything was in order, I leaned on the gas and the Winnebago lurched into motion, startling the salesman who leapt deftly out of the way. I steered a course out into the street and made a right hand turn, and headed in the direction of the New Jersey turnpike. We were off for a week-long, shake-down trip, of putting the Winnebago through its paces and making sure all of its systems were go.

For such a large vehicle, the RV felt remarkably light beneath my hands. Its width, however, would take a little getting used to. It was hard to keep from straying into the adjacent lanes, and I had to really concentrate on what I was doing.

"It's nothing a little practice won't take care of," I reassured Wil, who was white-knuckling the arm rest and rolling his eyes in terror. "Have a little faith, won't you?!"

We drove slowly, taking plenty of time to get a feel for how the vehicle handled, and went as far south as South Carolina before heading east toward the Atlantic Ocean. From the coast, we took the scenic route up along splendid beaches, through rural farmland and unspoiled cypress wetlands. On a lark, we headed for Cape Hatteras and the famous light house on the beach. We fully intended to visit every place we had ever read about, and ever wanted to see.

After a couple of days on the Cape, we headed back to the mainland and rolled into Williamsburg, Virginia, just as the sun was setting for the day. Exhausted and needing to rest, I pulled into a mostly deserted campground and set up shop for the night. On awaking the following morning, I was dismayed to discover that our left, front tire had gone flat sometime during the night. It was our first test of grace under fire.

What did two guys from Manhattan know about changing a tire, especially on something as large as a Winnebago? In fact, what did two guys from Manhattan know about driving, period? While I had maintained a driver's license since I was a teen, Wil had gotten his only two months prior to our leaving town. Neither of us had even owned a car before.

The experience with the flat tire quickly taught us the value in belonging to a travel club like Triple A. Without breaking a sweat, Wil reached into the glove compartment and whipped out the official guide book, and located the nearest participating service station less than a mile away. I scurried around the tiny kitchen putting things away, before revving up the engine and limping slowly into town. In less than an hour, the tire was patched and we were as good as new. We had weathered our first crisis and were back on the road with all systems go.

As Williamsburg receded in the distance, I started to relax. "*Maybe we are up to the challenge,*" I thought. "*Maybe everything will work out, after all*".

With an entire week having come and gone since we had taken possession of the Winnebago, it was time to return to New York City and gather up our belongings, before setting back out on the road for good. Night was fast approaching as we crossed the George Washington Bridge and carefully navigated our way down the rickety West Side Highway, onto the narrow streets of Greenwich Village. Fortunately, we had timed our arrival to avoid the worst of the evening rush-hour traffic.

"Slow down and pay attention to what you're doing," Wil snapped, noticing that my attention had strayed to the majestic Palisades, silhouetted in black against the last vestiges of ambient light. "The last thing we need is for you to run off the road and get us killed!"

I was much too excited to let Wil's edginess draw me into an argument. We had a plan; we had a schedule to keep; and I intended to make sure we kept it. We hoped to secure a parking spot in front of our apartment building and spend the rest of the evening loading the Winnebago with our things. A television set, a VCR, a computer and a printer, and an assorted array of kitchen paraphernalia comprised just a partial list of what we were planning to take with us.

Easing our way down the middle of Twelfth Street, we crossed Broadway and pulled into a vacant stretch of curb just past the entrance to our building. Mark and a friend, Toni, who had volunteered to help with the move, were waiting for us in the lobby. If all went according to plan, the Winnebago would be packed and ready to go sometime around midnight, after which we planned to drive to a rest area on the New Jersey Turnpike and spend the night. That way, we could get a jump on the morning rush and avoid the hassle of having to stand guard over the Winnebago on the street.

Fortunately, the entire operation came off without a hitch. By midnight, we had finished loading our gear on board and were ready to depart. I glanced around the apartment one last time, checking to see that nothing of importance had been left behind. The rooms looked strangely vacant and unfamiliar. With all the little personal items missing, the apartment didn't feel like home anymore. It belonged to someone else-- at least for now.

The realization was setting in, and setting in hard, that neither the apartment nor New York City was really our home any longer. We now lived in the overstuffed, motor home parked outside by the curb. I stood in the doorway to the bedroom, feeling lost and empty. Unexpectedly, tears welled up in my eyes and I began to cry. From the other room, Wil called for me to hurry up.

"Come on, George. It's time to get this show on the road!"

"I'm coming," I mumbled. I wiped my eyes and glanced around the room a final time. Then, putting on the best face I could muster, I joined the others in the living room. For better or for worse, we were out of New York for good!

Part Two
The Long and
Winding Road

I shall be telling this with a sigh
Somewhere ages and ages hence.
Two roads diverged in a wood, and I-
I took the one less traveled by,
And that has made all the difference

Robert Frost

8 The Shape of Things to Come

WE WERE FREE AS BIRDS NOW, with no jobs, no home and no responsibilities. The freedom we had once only dreamed about was now the reality of our lives. As the New York skyline receded through the rear window of the Winnebago, and with it the dense cloud of mass consciousness hanging over Manhattan, we could scarcely contain our exhilaration.

"Free at last... free at last... thank God Almighty, we're free at last," Wil bellowed at the top of his lungs. I broke into a broad grin.

It didn't take us long to adjust to living in the motor home, and more than once we congratulated ourselves for not having allowed a consciousness of lack to deter us from buying the exact vehicle we had wanted. Traveling in the Winnebago proved significantly less disruptive than staying in strange hotel rooms every night, sleeping in unfamiliar beds and having to deal with the tedious job of packing and repacking every time we were ready to move on. Instead, like a gigantic suitcase on wheels, the Winnebago contained everything we could possibly need. It was completely self-contained.

We spent our first few month away from the city relaxing in my home state of Florida and getting used to the experience of being unemployed. Knowing how cold it was up north, we took advantage of our unlimited leisure time to indulge in the luxurious warmth of the subtropical Florida sun. Eventually, the tension in our bodies began to melt away and we felt rested in a deeply, unfamiliar way. As we decompressed, our skin took on a healthy glow and our eyes became brighter and more alert.

"You look at least ten years younger," I said to Wil, studying him intently from across the Winnebago's tiny kitchen table.

"And you don't look a day over forty," he shot back, sarcastically.

With more free time on our hands than either of us knew what to do with, we opted to visit my family in Central Florida where I had spent my teenage years. Our three week visit constituted the longest period of time I had spent with my family since leaving home as a pimply teenager some eighteen years before. Against both my parents' wishes, I had dropped out of college at the beginning of my junior year and moved to New York City with a couple of drag queen friends. Since then, my visits home had consisted of two or three days at the most. Now, however, having come face to face with the reality of my mortality and possible untimely death, I had begun to rethink my cavalier attitude about family. Suddenly, the idea of being involved in their lives didn't seem quite as undesirable as it had.

Initially, the disclosure of my HIV status had been stressful on both my parents. The stigma surrounding the disease was simply too much for them to handle. Yet surprisingly, my new-found spiritual beliefs met with more resistance from my mother than either my illness *or* my sexual orientation. Because of her staunch belief that Jesus was the only way to salvation, she found it difficult to accept that my spiritual life wasn't rooted in traditional Christianity. In her eyes, anything even vaguely new-age was suspect, and obviously many of my beliefs fell into the offending category.

We'd be enjoying each other's company and then suddenly we'd get on the topic of religion and end up in a big fight, trying to convince each other of the rightness of our point of view. Eventually, Wil suggested a truce, which I agreed to, at least in principle, to try and avoid any potentially controversial subjects for the remainder of our visit--particularly religion and homosexuality.

"You just have to accept that this is as far as your relationship can go right now," Wil advised me, seeing how distressed I was. "Maybe someday, you and your mother will be able to have a civilized conversation about these issues, but you might as well forget it for now. Both of you have too much of an agenda for that to happen."

Agendas aside, I actually think my mother was just a wee, bit jealous of my new found freedom and my shiny new motor home parked outside in the driveway. I couldn't blame her, really, for it had been *her* dream to retire and travel around the country, and she had articulated that dream to me only a few months earlier when I was home for one of my infrequent visits. Now, here I was living *her* dream, and it didn't seem quite fair.

She was also worried about me quitting my job and leaving New York as abruptly as I had. As a mother, she didn't want anything bad to happen to me and wasn't entirely convinced that I was acting rationally. Truth be told, I wasn't convinced of it, either.

Throughout our stay, Wil kept in constant contact with New York, particularly with our friend, Toni, who was acting as an intermediary between us and anyone wishing to contact us on the road. Toni and Wil had worked together on Wall Street and hadn't really liked each other very much in the beginning. Wil had found her aggressive demeanor offensive, while she had found his Latin attitude patently sexist. Eventually, after months of overt hostility there had been a breakthrough in the relationship, thanks to a forgiveness exercise Wil had learned at a Louise Hay workshop, and they had become fast friends.

In the months leading up to our departure from New York, we had distributed flyers at each of the events we had participated in, advertising our availability to speak and listing Toni as the person to contact if there was an interest. By the time we arrived at my parent's house in Florida, a response had begun to build and a number of inquiries had trickled in.

Through Toni, we made contact with a long-term survivor of AIDS from Charleston named Michael Mignone, who was interested in having us visit the healing circle he ran at a local Unity Church. The Church of Religious Science in Atlanta had also called and invited us to speak to their Science of Mind classes. By networking with these first two contacts, we were subsequently able to connect with interested parties in Miami, Sarasota, Orlando, Daytona Beach and Jacksonville, and preparations for our visits were underway. Finally, my younger brother, Ken, had arranged for us to speak at his local Metropolitan Community Church in Nashville, and we penciled him into our growing list of engagements. After being away from New York for less a month, the outline of what was to come was rapidly taking shape.

If either of us still harbored any doubts about why we were free of our former responsibilities and able to travel at a moment's notice, it vanished with the decisiveness of the Universe's call to action. Our growing list of invitations was confirmation enough that we were basically on the right track.

Wil and I both knew that the unrelenting hopelessness surrounding AIDS would continue unabated until someone came forward with a different point of view, preferably one of hope and the possibility of healing. We also knew that *we* could be the ones to deliver such a message or we could step back and let someone else. As far as the larger picture was concerned, it didn't really matter *who* spoke up, only that *someone* did. Eventually, with humility and more than a little trepidation, we had accepted the call to action. Now, apparently, the time had come for us to honor our commitment.

For the entire month of March, we crisscrossed the Sunshine State, camping in state parks and on beaches, speaking in churches, community centers and universities--anywhere there was an audience willing to listen to our story. As an HIV positive and healthy, out, gay man, it was gratifying to be speaking about healing and spirituality in my home state of Florida, thick as it was with virulent fundamentalism and homophobia. Obviously, I hadn't always felt this free here. But then again, I wasn't the same, insecure person I had been when I had left home fifteen years earlier. I was more centered now, and less affected by other people's opinions.

At each stop along the way, we told the story of our diagnosis and search for a way out of the seemingly impossible situation we had found ourselves in, and where that search had eventually led us. We were careful not to give the impression that our way was the only way, but simply that *there was a way.*

"If you take only one thing home with you this evening," Wil stressed in his remarks, "it's that you have options. Don't let anyone tell you that you're going to die of this disease and that there's nothing you can do about it. It simply isn't true. But healing yourself *is* a lot of work. You'll have to do more than try and fix your body. You'll need to examine your mind, your emotions and your very soul."

At first, it was a little intimidating to be speaking outside of our familiar haunts in New York City, especially since neither of us had any real feel for what was happening beyond the major cities on the coasts. Ultimately, we learned to rely on our instincts and trust that we would be guided to say the appropriate things. We were clear on one thing, however: it wasn't our responsibility to try and convince people of the validity of our message. Those who were open to our story would embrace it and respond in whatever way was appropriate to them. Those who weren't as enamored with it were free to reject it outright. Our responsibility was simply to go where there was an invitation and a welcome, and tell what had happened to us.

Don't think for a minute that any of this was particularly easy. Both of us had all of the human doubts and fears you'd expect of anyone in our shoes. Certainly, neither of us was claiming to be a perfected, spiritual being, beyond the level of human foible and fear. At best, we were simply two, sincere, gay men with a love and passion for healing, and for the community our message was intended for.

To be completely honest, more than Wil, I was terrified at the prospect of how people might react to our story, and was afraid of being hurt in some way I couldn't fully articulate--even to myself. Since its emergence onto the scene in the early 1980's, AIDS had quickly become a sacred cow in the gay community--an all powerful idol to be bowed down to and worshiped without question. As such, I had legitimate fears that people might be angry with our message and attack us for speaking out. While our intention was simply to offer hope, not add to anyone's pain, our message was not exactly politically correct, either. We were convinced that AIDS was a call for change, and that change had to begin, first and foremost, with the people most affected by the epidemic. As difficult as that might be for people to hear, it was at the very heart of our message.

To our surprise, our reputation seemed to precede us almost immediately, and the first few audiences we spoke to were larger than we had expected. There seemed to be a genuine interest in the radical stand we were taking--partly because of its novelty, I suppose, and partly because of people's terrible hunger for empowerment. At this point in the epidemic, few people had dared challenge the notion that AIDS was 100 percent fatal, and people came to our lectures just to see what two strange men from New York City might have to say that was different from what they'd been told.

To be sure, not everyone who came to hear us speak was an advocate of our beliefs or left feeling happy about what they heard. Filtered through a lifetime of internalized guilt and shame, the idea of being responsible for the conditions in your life was sometimes perceived as blame for being ill. Some people mistakenly assumed we were implying that people got AIDS because they were gay, when actually we were saying something quite different. We were, however, encouraging people to examine where they might be acting out destructively because of a deep-seated lack of self-worth. If you grew up being taught you were an abomination to God, it was only reasonable that you might sometimes act out abominably. The actual thrust of our message was that you were perfect as you are, but that there was still work to be done.

For these reasons and more, broaching the subject of spirituality with a gay audience proved to be especially tricky. Many people seemed to confuse spirituality with organized religion, and needless to say most gay people's experience in that arena--including my own--was painful, to say the least. It was fascinating to observe the many faces in the audience from our vantage point in front of the room. Certain ones would stand out above all the rest, and capture our attention. Often it would be someone who we could tell by their expression understood exactly what we were saying, and their smile would shine back at us like a beacon of support. But just as often, there were faces with deep scowls etched across them and arms folded defensively across their chests, protecting their hearts, too afraid to let hope in.

For many people with AIDS, suffering from the effects of the illness and the horrible reality of compounded grief and loss, hope seemed more like an enemy come to torture them than a friend come to set them free, and they resisted our message with all the strength left in them. Sometimes, a person's anger would be so intense that they would walk out in the middle of our talk.

At first, it was hard not to judge ourselves when something like this happened, by how many people came to hear us speak, or whether they liked what they had heard or not. Had we failed simply because someone got angry and stormed out of the room? Were we a success because the audience gazed up at us adoringly, hanging onto our every word? No matter how much we wanted people to embrace our message, we were not really there to make people like us. We were not running for Miss Congeniality. We were there to challenge people to step out of the limited boxes they had constructed around their disease, and unfortunately this sometimes made them angry.

It didn't take us long to learn that whenever we simply shared our experience honestly and from the heart, without any attachment or misplaced sense of responsibility for how it was received, our message rode on an energy far greater than just our words alone. Often, we could see that the person most deeply affected by our message was the one who stormed out of the room. Their anger was simply an indication of how profoundly they had been touched. Our job was simply to share our truth, no matter how we were received on a personal level. It was up to the Universe to nurture those seeds to fruition.

It was a relief to understand the limits of our responsibility, in terms of the effect our message had upon the people who came to hear us speak. Certainly, nothing creates stress or causes burnout faster than taking responsibility for something over which you have no real control, such as other people's perceptions of who you are. Conversely, nothing frees you up like simply letting go. We chose to let go of people's reactions and simply do the job we had been called to do.

If we had allowed people's opinions of us to hold sway over us, we would have packed it in after our first few gigs in Florida and resumed our familiar lives in New York City. Instead, we made a pact with each other that no matter how bleak things might look at any given moment, our talks were always a success, even on those rare occasions when it appeared as though we hadn't accomplished a thing. We held to this belief no matter what--especially when people got mad!

"You just have to remember that anger is sometimes the first step in the healing process," Wil reminded me. "Don't you remember how angry you were right after your diagnosis?"

He was right, of course. I did remember. I had been so mad at the fact that people assumed I was going to die and that there was nothing I could do about it, that I had vowed to heal myself to spite them. That hadn't gotten me very far, naturally, but it had gotten me off my ass and looking for a way out. Now, I would simply have to allow others the same courtesy.

9   *Taking the Good with the Bad*

W ITH SPRING IN FULL BLOOM, WE set out for Atlanta and our date with the Church of Religious Science, with a brief stop first in Gainesville, the home of my alma mater, the University of Florida. The sun was low in the sky as we exited the interstate onto the local streets of our intended destination, into a city gaily bedecked in a pink and white palette of dogwood blossoms.

Reverend Kennedy Shultz, the president of Science of Mind International and the leader of the Atlanta church we were scheduled to speak in, was from every measure a dynamic, self-made man. Somewhere in his late fifties, slightly portly with a propensity toward expensive Italian suits, the man had a charismatic personality, the sheer force of which made you think he was younger, thinner and richer than he actually was.

This clever combination of fact and illusion had obviously been a winner with the local Religious Science Community. In the decade since he had founded the Atlanta church, its membership had exploded to encompass a diverse cross-section of the community, including a considerable number of lesbians and gay men.

Besides regular Sunday services, the church offered a full complement of Science of Mind classes, as well as a support group for people with HIV and AIDS. The audience Wil and I were scheduled to speak before was our largest one to date. Suffice it to say, we both had a slight case of nerves going into the presentation.

While neither Wil nor I was a student of The Science of Mind, our message grew out of a metaphysical understanding of body, mind and spirit that was compatible with its philosophy. Predictably, then, and to our profound relief, our presentation a few nights later not only validated most of our spellbound audience's basic beliefs, but undoubtedly went beyond them.

"I'm an electrical engineer and a computer programmer by trade," Wil began, after Kennedy had given him an enthusiastic introduction. "In 1985, the year I was diagnosed with AIDS, I believed that if *anything was going to get me through this experience*--and I wasn't really sure anything was--it was going to be science and the medical profession. When George started reading Edgar Cayce and the Seth Material-- channeled information--*whatever that is*--I didn't want to have anything to do with it. If I was going to find an answer, it was going to have to be logical and scientific, and not a bunch of metaphysical mumbo jumbo." With that, a smattering of laughter erupted from the decidedly metaphysical crowd.

"Picture it, if you will," Wil continued, "our bedroom in New York City: a king size bed with night tables on either side, stacked high with all kinds of different books. On my side of the bed are medical and scientific journals, and the latest books on psychoneuroimmunology--all left-brained material. On George's side of the bed is the exact opposite: channeled books by Seth and Edgar Cayce, and every other entity you can imagine. Occasionally, when one of his books would somehow end up on my side of the bed, it immediately went flying right back to where it came from. I wasn't in the least bit interested in any of it." The audience laughed again, imagining the comical scenario.

Wil took a sip of water and cleared his throat, and then resumed with his remarks. "But after a while, I began to notice that over on George's side of the bed, he was getting better. He wasn't in as much fear as I was, and was gaining weight and seemed relatively happy. I, on the other hand, wasn't feeling very well at all. I had all these annoying little symptoms and was pretty depressed. So I said to him, *George, if I was only going to read one of your books, which one would it be?* And he said, *Oh, that's easy; read The Nature of Personal Reality*--a Seth book, if you can imagine. So I did."

"Each chapter in the book consisted of a channeling by an entity named Seth, and also some cute, little stories about Jane Roberts, the woman who channeled the books, and her husband, Robb. The part about Seth was pretty good, actually, but I hated Jane and all her stupid little stories."

"So George said, *don't bother reading that part if you don't like it. Just read Seth's part.* And so I did. And it blew me away! Here was this disembodied entity explaining all the things I had been trying so hard to understand about the mind/body connection by studying works on psychoneuroimmunology, except it was a lot more user-friendly and relevant to me as a lay person. Needless to say, in the end my exclusive scientific point of view ended up being far too narrow, and I realized that my little hairdresser lover wasn't so dumb, after all."

"The experience opened my eyes to a whole new world of information and forced me to recognize the multidimensional aspects of myself and my disease: my body, my mind, my emotions and, most importantly, my spirit. Only then, did my health begin to improve."

When Wil had finished speaking and the applause had died away, Kennedy sprinted onto the platform a second time and introduced me to the primed and waiting crowd. Instead of simply telling my story as I had mostly done so far, I decided to stretch a bit and share my own unique take on the epidemic.

"Epidemics are first and foremost epidemics of belief," I began, speaking in a calm, clear tone of voice, echoing the words of Seth. "Therefore, to be immune to a disease you must resist the beliefs that give rise to the experience in the first place."

A murmur made its way through the crowd. I waited until it had faded away, before continuing in my vein of thought.

"If you've been paying attention you'd have noticed that AIDS is a disease of the disenfranchised. It primarily affects gay men, people of color, intravenous drug abusers and women. Interestingly enough, all of these seemingly disparate groups share one important thing in common: *a deep abiding sense of their own vulnerability.* They perceive themselves as *oppressed* by the dominant powers that be, and that perception forms the central thesis of their overall world view."

I paused and took a breath, before continuing with my train of thought "At its core, I believe that AIDS is a biological reflection of our deeply ingrained perception of vulnerability. It is the most incredible example I can think of, of just how the mind/body connection actually works in real life. Our ingrained *perception* of vulnerability creates a biological environment in which a virus is able to recreate that condition *physically*. The constant drain on our energy, of having to maintain round the clock defenses, inevitably leads to exhaustion and a collapse of the very thing we are trying to protect--namely, ourselves."

"To heal our immune systems we must first dismantle our defenses so that the energy can be redirected into other areas. Yet before any of this can happen, a sense of trust in our own basic integrity must first be established. Ultimately, my quest for understanding led me into the realm of spirituality and raised a few basic questions that I had to look at very, very carefully: who am I, *really*, and what is my relationship to the whole? Nowhere, in my opinion, have the answers to those questions been more elegantly articulated than in A Course in Miracles. The healing of the immune system is best summed up in this one simple lesson from the Course: *In my defenselessness my safety lies.*"

With that, the audience rose to its feet. If going into the evening there had been any doubt in their minds about the viability of applying spiritual principle to living with HIV and AIDS, there was no trace of it now. Everyone seemed to hear our message, and hear it loud and clear.

Flushed with success, we spent the remainder of the evening answering a barrage of questions and listening to a string of personal testimonies from members of the audience. Later, as we relaxed in Kennedy's study after everyone had gone home for the night, he reiterated his unmitigated support for our work and invited us back to speak at a later date.

"Next time, we'll open it up to the entire community," he promised. "I'd like to reach as many people with this message as we can."

The next day, after a quick trip to nearby Stone Mountain to see the sights, we pulled up camp and pointed the Winnebago in the direction of my brother's house in Nashville, stopping only once along the way to check out the view from Look Out Mountain, near Chattanooga. We were on a definite high and filled with a sense of the rightness of our quest, and in our ability to see it through. With our message falling on receptive ears in Atlanta, much of the doubt that had initially plagued us was beginning to melt away. Perhaps people *were* interested in entertaining hope, after all. Maybe our efforts wouldn't be in vain.

Beyond the validation offered us by the positive reception in Atlanta, our visit there also represented a welcomed upturn in our economic fortunes. Thanks to the overwhelming generosity of Kennedy and the members of his congregation, we received our first honorarium for speaking. Up until now, our lectures had always been free with our only compensation coming through voluntary love-offerings. The effect of this arrangement had forced us into a deeper level of trust around the issue of money--particularly me, for whom money was an ongoing issue.

While intellectually, Wil and I both believed that our needs would be taken care of, in a more practical sense we had no real guarantees. We had to rely on the generosity of the Universe and the people attending our lectures, and sometimes that was incredibly stressful. Though the arrangement had sufficed to keep us in groceries and enough gas to reach our next destination, *that* was basically it. Any other expenses came directly out of our own pockets.

Having *some* money come in, no matter how little, helped me to begin letting go of the residual anxiety I still felt about giving up my regular job and the rather substantial pay check that came with it. Slowly but surely, my shaky belief in the Universe's unfailing generosity was being transformed into an actual experience of support through our day to day experiences on the road. Yet despite the numerous manifestations of grace we experienced, I still felt a knot in the pit of my stomach each time we visited a new community, never quite sure about whom we would be meeting there or what we might encounter.

If *my* confidence was growing at a snail's pace, Wil's was growing by leaps and bounds. Thankfully, his enthusiasm spilled over onto me, helping soothe my recurring fear that we would be ambushed somewhere along the line. Intellectually, I desperately wanted to believe we would be taken care of. From a practical standpoint, however, I didn't yet *know* it for a fact.

Wil had a distinct advantage over me in that he was responsible for following up on all the leads Tony relayed to us from New York. Each day, after checking in with her, he would return any and all inquiries, and if the parties were agreeable, proceed to work out the logistics for our visit. By the time we would arrive at our destination, Wil would have already established a rapport with the local sponsor and be looking forward to meeting them in person. For him, visiting a new city was like visiting an old friend; he knew what to expect. For me, however, it was to be confronted by yet another level of fear and insecurity.

Unlike Wil, I rarely had prior contact with our sponsors and had to rely on his assurances that everything was copacetic. Even so, this never seemed to be enough to assuage my fears. More than once, I wanted to run back to New York and forget the whole affair, but thanks to Wil, I didn't. His incredible patience saw me through the rough patches and helped remind me of why we were out here on the road in the first place, doing what we were doing. People we loved were dying, and we had to do something to help!

After our enthusiastic reception in Atlanta, the turnout in Nashville proved to be a bit of a disappointment, even though by now we knew better than to judge our success by the number of people that came to hear us speak. We shared our stories as usual, and afterwards opened the floor to questions from the audience. An angry young man proceeded to monopolize the mike.

"First of all, I want you to know that I think both of you are full of shit," he lashed out, angrily, stunning the audience of mostly ultra-polite Southerners. "Nobody can heal themselves of AIDS. And if you really had AIDS, then where's your blood work to prove it? *I don't think you even had it in the first place.*" Everyone in the room sat there stunned, waiting for our reaction.

"I was diagnosed with ARC, not AIDS," I responded, breaking the silence by setting our accuser straight on the facts. "Wil was diagnosed with AIDS."

Try as we might, nothing either one of us could say seemed to satisfy the man's concerns. We could see how angry he was, and beyond that, how incredibly afraid. But to be perfectly honest, while it might have been naïve on our part, it had never occurred to us to bring along copies of our lab results to prove we had actually been sick. I mean, who would make up a story about having AIDS, if it wasn't true? It wasn't like it got you invited to any of the best parties.

Wil continued to try and reason with the young man and explain where we were coming from, while I listened quietly in the background. He was having nothing to do with it, however, and continued his angry harangue. The crowd was growing increasingly restless.

Finally, my brother interrupted the man's tirade. "Excuse me," he said, forcibly injecting himself into the discussion. "I appreciate your concerns, here. Really, I do. But at this point, you're just being rude. My brother and his lover came here tonight, on their own time and at their own expense, to offer you their stories. I think I know them better than you do, and let me assure you they're telling you the truth. If you don't like what they have to say then please have the courtesy to either shut up or leave so that other people in the room can hear what they have to say. Do you think you could do that?"

Muttering to himself, the man scooped up his belongings and stormed out of the room in a huff. After several more uneventful questions, Wil brought the evening to a shaky close.

"Please feel free to accept or reject anything you heard here tonight," he reiterated, seeking to reassure the nervous crowd. "If something we said resonates with you, then take it home and do something with it. If not, leave it here and we'll take it with us when we leave. Thank you for being such a patient audience. Good night and God bless."

In the aftermath of the man's angry attack, we both felt as though we had been physically assaulted and were uncertain just what to take away from the experience.

"Maybe we *should* bring copies of our blood work with us as proof," Wil opined. "Or, perhaps, a letter from our doctor."

"Wouldn't that just be playing into people's overreliance on T-cell counts?" I objected. God knows we had seen enough people go into a tailspin after less than perfect results on a blood test. A couple of people we knew had even committed suicide.

No, we decided, *we were not going to furnish copies of our blood work to the public*. If people wanted proof of what we were saying, they could look within and discover the truth for themselves. They were adults. They were free to take our story or leave it. We were there simply to share our experience.

☀

10 Time to Face the Pain

AFTER A DAY OF SIGHTSEEING WHICH included a visit to the site of the Grand Old Opry and a full scale replica of the Parthenon, we said goodbye to my brother and set off for Charleston, the site of our next engagement. As usual, Wil had already been in contact with our sponsor there and was eagerly anticipating meeting him in person.

Michael Mignone, our host for the visit, was a long-term survivor of AIDS and a vocal proponent of a spiritual and metaphysical approach to healing much like the one Wil and I were advocating. As the facilitator of the local healing circle, he had experienced difficulty breaking through the community's entrenched resistance and was desperate for a second opinion--preferably one from out of town. After all, weren't most experts from out of town? That was where Wil and I came into the picture.

In the days leading up to our arrival, Michael had invested a great deal of time and energy preparing for our visit, publicizing it in the local press and using his personal connections with a local television anchor to arrange for us to be interviewed on the evening news. To gain maximum benefit from the exposure, the segment was scheduled to air the evening prior to our lecture. Since this was our first access to the broadcast media outside of New York City, Wil and I were understandably excited and a little nervous about how our message would be portrayed. After all, this was the South. Fortunately, our worries proved to be pointless. The woman who interviewed us was undeniably sympathetic to our message.

On the morning of the interview, I awoke with an ominous burning sensation stretching across the entire, right side of my face. A fiery pain extended from the back of my neck, across my cheek and past the corner of my eye, its path delineated by an ugly mass of angry, red blisters. The sudden onset of these unexpected symptoms threw me into a panic. I had never experienced such intense pain before and my mind immediately kicked into overdrive, imagining the worst scenario possible: I wasn't really healing myself, after all. I was probably going to die!

Here we were, miles from home and my regular doctor, and expected to give an interview later that afternoon and a talk on self-healing the following night, and suddenly I wasn't so sure I was healed, after all. A voice in my head kept screaming that my good health had nothing to do with anything I had learned or done, but was merely a stroke of luck. With my disease obviously progressing and angry, red symptoms splattered across my face as proof, I would be exposed as a fraud in front of the entire world--well, at least in front of the good citizens of Charleston.

Thankfully, Wil helped me to pull myself together so that we could give the interview as planned. With the help of a little makeup, I carefully camouflaged the blisters until the damage was mostly invisible. My pain, though still persistent, was apparent to no one but me. If my luck held, I would be able to make it through the interview and no one would be the wiser.

While it was not a particularly pleasant experience, the interview went off without a hitch. Unfortunately, I don't remember anything in particular about what I might have said, just that my heart wasn't really in it. I simply gave rote answers to whatever questions were asked of me and prayed that the whole ordeal would soon be over. Unfortunately, there was still the matter of the lecture to deal with.

In the intervening hours, the pain on my face continued to grow in intensity and the angry red swatch of blisters grew ever more pronounced. The intense pain, coupled with an overwhelming sense of failure, made the situation almost unbearable. I looked at my stricken face in the mirror and began to cry.

"Where did this come from?" I whined, overcome with an over-sized case of self- pity. "What have I done to deserve this? Why does this have to happen, *now?*"

What I really dreaded was the fact that there was no graceful way of backing out of the lecture. No matter how painful and embarrassing it might be, I would have to stand up in front of a room full of people who expected me to be well, and tell them that I wasn't.

Despite all this, I was sane enough to recognize that if I couldn't be honest enough to let people see me sick, then the sad truth was that my message was basically worthless. If I took the easy way out--if I made up an excuse and backed out of the event--I would be playing into the myth that you had done something wrong if you were sick. Cancelling might keep me on the pedestal some people had placed me on, but it would be the ultimate betrayal of myself and everyone who trusted me to be authentic.

"Am I only worthy of love if I'm well?" I wondered. *"If I'm sick, does it mean that I've done something wrong?"*

I was tormented by the questions, but I really needed to know. Running away was simply out of the question. There was nothing to do but pray for the strength to face the situation with grace.

7:00 pm the next evening came much too quickly, and finally it was time to face the music. If I was the genuine article-- if I was really healing myself, like I claimed--I couldn't afford the luxury of backing out of the talk, no matter how potentially embarrassing the experience might be. It was critical to my continued healing and spiritual growth, and to the healing of everyone who planned on attending the event, that I show up and tell the truth, the whole truth, and nothing but the truth.

As usual, Wil spoke first. Then, when he had finished, he turned the lectern over to me. Still uncertain about what I was going to say, I walked to the podium and paused a moment to compose myself.

"I have a confession to make," I began, after a long pause. "I really didn't want to be here tonight. You see, I came down with the shingles yesterday, and I was afraid of what you might think. I figured I'd better get this off my chest, first thing, so that I can get on with the job of sharing some of the ideas I came here to talk to you about this evening. So there you have it; the ugly truth. Let's see, now. Where shall I begin?"

With my confession out of the way, I proceeded to explain exactly what had happened to me during the last twenty four hours, beginning with my outbreak of the shingles, my subsequent dilemma over and showing up to speak, and my crushing sense of failure. Laying all my cards out on the table for everyone to see, I brought my remarks to a close by sharing some final thoughts about the experience.

"Like I have said many times before, symptoms are simply a message, and obviously I need to figure out what my body is trying to tell me. In spite of everything that's happened to me in the last 24 hours, I still have faith in my process and in my ability to handle whatever challenges come my way. Like one of my teacher says, *take the next step in your life and the symptoms fall away.* I guess I need to figure out what that next step is, and take it. Thank you for being so understanding. I really appreciate it."

I stepped back from the podium and a wave of relief flooded through my body, catching me off guard with its intensity. I swallowed hard and struggled to suppress a sob that was rising in the back of my throat. For a moment, the room was so quiet you could hear a pin drop. I looked out into the audience feeling utterly exposed, half expecting them to boo me off the stage. Instead, from in back of the room came the faint sound of one person clapping, followed by another and another and another, until finally everyone in the room had joined in.

Now, I was laughing and crying at the same time. The audience didn't hate me. They *loved* me! My honesty had put us all on an equal footing and dispelled the notion that I was in some way perfect or different from anyone else. I didn't have to be well for my message to be valid. No matter how flawed I might be, there was still hope for us all!

For the remainder of the eighteen months Wil and I were on the road together, this experience, more than any other, served to keep me in touch with my humility and remind me of my intimate connection to those I was attempting to minister to. It shattered any feelings of separation I might have been tempted by and smashed the inevitable pedestal people sometimes put us on. But even more importantly, it showed me that I was capable of handling the escalating attention being focused in our direction, without taking myself too seriously or allowing it to jeopardize my healing. I was worthy of love, no matter what my physical condition might be. I didn't have to pretend to be an effective role model. I simply had to be myself.

Unfortunately, the success of the previous evening, and the insights that came with it, in no way alleviated the burning sensation I felt upon awakening the following morning. To be truthful, I had half expected the blisters to be gone--vanished somehow, along with the fear and panic of the previous night. Such was not to be the case, however. The angry, red rash remained splayed across my face, as painful as ever.

With Michael's help, I managed to book an appointment with a local doctor who immediately confirmed my diagnosis of shingles and prescribed a course of Zovorax for me to take. Back in the Winnebago, away from the scrutiny of prying eyes, I took my medicine and went straight to bed. After he was certain that I was resting comfortably, Wil set off with Michael to see the sights, and then on to Columbia to speak to an HIV support group there. I was more than happy to be left alone to lick my wounds in solitude, to have the time and space I needed to pray, to meditate, and to regain my equilibrium.

Beyond the immediate drama, I knew there was an important lesson to be gleaned from the events of the last few days. Already, it was painfully obvious that part of that lesson was about learning to tell the truth, no matter how scary a proposition that might be. *That* lesson I had learned. The continuing pain on my face led me to suspect that there was even more to it than that. There was another layer of fear just waiting to be peeled away.

I prayed for guidance and let the matter go, knowing that when the time was right the answer would make itself known. It had before, and it would this time too. I didn't need to force the issue by trying to figure out every little nuance of why this had happened to me. That would simply be my ego thinking it was in charge, and only serve to complicate the situation. No, all I had to do was to rest and nurture myself until the answer showed up on its own.

I fell into a deep sleep and awoke several hours later, laying on my back looking up at the ceiling, overhead. Though it was well past midnight, Wil hadn't returned from his jaunt to Columbia with Michael. As I lay there feeling vulnerable yet surrendered, the cause of the pain on my face slowly began to crystallize in mind. The angry, red blisters were simply a manifestation of the compounded grief I had been too busy to deal with, and had repressed instead. It symbolized the pain I felt about leaving my career and New York behind, and the accumulated grief for all of my many friends who had died of AIDS and whose passing I had not found time to mourn.

As I thought about it lying there alone in bed, it had always seemed odd to me how I could be surrounded by so much death and still be relatively unaffected--or so I thought. I don't mean to say that I wasn't sorry people were dying. It's just that I had never been able to fully access my grief and it had been building up inside me ever since.

I thought that perhaps I was just a very strong person, emotionally. Yet like many people in my situation, I had been too busy and too afraid to acknowledge my grief for fear of being overwhelmed by it. With no other outlet available to it, my grief had finally released itself through my body, by way of the painful symptoms on my face.

My symptoms were merely my unacknowledged pain attempting to gain my attention in the only way it knew how. It was telling me *it was time to face the pain.* In its own inimitable way, my body had done for me what I had been unable to do myself. It had put me in touch with my grief.

As the realization of what was happening exploded into my awareness, my heart felt as though it were being ripped apart by the grief and loss that emerged from deep inside me. I rolled over and curled up in a fetal position, sobbing uncontrollably into my pillow, allowing the tears to flow freely until there was nothing left to grieve. When the storm had passed, I lay there exhausted and too tired to move, a faint ringing sensation echoing in both my ears. A deep stillness registered throughout every cell in my body. I had passed through the void and emerged safely onto the other side. The healing crisis was over. The physical results were simply a matter of time.

I awoke the next day feeling immeasurably better. With nothing more to do in Charleston, we hugged Michael goodbye and broke camp and headed for the nearest interstate out of town. After living in a fish bowl for most of the last two months, no one was more grateful than I was for the precious anonymity of the road. Finally, I could focus on my own needs, instead of worrying about everyone else.

This was particularly important now, especially where I was concerned. In our first few months on the road, Wil and I had experienced the full gamete of emotions, from the thrill of victory to the agony of defeat. We had been lauded as saviors and slandered as quacks. But more than anything, my recent bout with the shingles had shaken my confidence and brought a plethora of buried fears to the surface. If I wanted to stay on course, I would need to make myself my first priority. This was easier to accomplish on the road, far from the demands of our sponsor's expectations. With every passing mile, it was easier to hear even the slightest promptings of your heart. My inner self didn't need to shout to get my attention, and it didn't need to make me sick. I could simply take the next step in my life and my symptoms would remain at bay.

11 Shuffle off to Buffalo

WITH SEVERAL WEEKS OF FREE TIME on our hands, Wil and I were headed for Buffalo, across the lower great lakes through Cleveland and on into Chicago, with a stopover in New York City first. After so many months away from home, we were looking forward to visiting with friends and bringing them up to speed on our latest adventures.

I was especially anxious to see my regular doctor, Dr. Ronald Grossman. After my recent outbreak with the shingles, I wouldn't be able to relax until he had checked me over thoroughly and given me a clean bill of health. Thankfully, by the time my appointment rolled around a week later, no trace of the angry, red blisters remained. In less than two weeks time, my body had healed itself of any visible signs of the outbreak.

Dr. Grossman was pleased, if not a little surprised, by my rapid recovery, and congratulated me on a job well done. "I don't know what you're doing," he said, shaking his head in amazement, "but whatever it is, keep up the good work."

Taking advantage of the opening, I explained how I had handled my recent healing crisis. Besides just taking Zovorax, I wanted him to know that there were other effective ways of approaching illness beyond just the traditional allopathic fixation on suppressing symptom. Surely, it was as important for me to share my spiritual approach with him, as it was for him to empower me with his scientific expertise. After all, we both wanted the same thing. We both wanted to find a way to outsmart this insidious virus.

"I believe that symptoms are just the tip of the iceberg,' I began, testing the waters to see if he was receptive to my point of view. "Besides just alleviating symptoms, I'm always interested in discovering the psycho/ spiritual dynamics behind them. That way I can work on releasing the cause on an energetic level."

Dr. Grossman looked up from my chart with a glance in my direction. Interpreting that as interest, I pressed on with my train of thought.

"If you're only focused on suppressing symptoms without addressing their subjective roots, it's like putting makeup on a zit. It might look good for a while, but in the long run it doesn't really accomplish much. At some point, the infection is going to erupt again and probably get even worse. You've got to get the core out if you want it to go away."

I pantomimed popping a zit, to great effect. Dr. Grossman winced at my colorful analogy, but seemed to get the point.

"That's the mental/emotional part of the process, and that's the part that I have to take responsibility for. You can't just take a pill and expect AIDS to go away, you know. You've got to do some work on yourself."

To his credit, Dr. Grossman didn't negate my opinion or throw me out of his office. Instead, he leaned forward and invited me into his confidence.

"I'd have to agree with you," he said. "The patients of mine who do best--like you and Wil, for example--are the ones that have a positive attitude. There's no doubt it can make a tremendous difference in the progression of this disease."

With that, he closed my file and gave me a paternalistic pat on the shoulder. "Keep up the good work, George. And make sure you get in to see me occasionally, whenever you're in the city. And tell Wil I'd like to see him, too. We need to monitor his progress so I can keep abreast of how he's doing."

Later, as I stood on the curb in front of the office, waiting for a cab, I thought back over our exchange. "A positive attitude wasn't exactly what I had in mind, but at least I did manage to get in a couple of good points," I thought, wryly. "I guess I'll just have to be patient with the man. After all, he's only a doctor." For a moment, the arrogance of my last thought caught me by surprise. I blushed to myself and hopped into a waiting cab.

On a more superficial note, beyond any immediate concerns with my health, I was looking forward to getting a haircut from my regular hairdresser, Irene. So far, the one's I had gotten on the road had been unmitigated disasters, and as a hairdresser this was a particularly sensitive issue with me. I had a belief system that said nobody knew how to cut hair like a New York hairdresser, and unfortunately, as beliefs will do, my opinion had been reinforced by the awful experiences I'd been subjected to on the road.

There was an upside to all this, however. It gave me a belated appreciation for the loyalty my former clients had always shown me, particularly the ones that had flown in from other parts of the country just to have me do their hair. At the time, I had secretly thought they were exaggerating when they had insisted no one could do their hair like me. Now, after only a few months away from New York, I had a better appreciation for where they were coming from.

Haircuts aside, the biggest problem Wil and I faced being back in the city was logistics--what to do with the Winnebago for the duration of our stay. For lack of a better alternative, we parked on the street, as close to the apartment as possible. The Winnebago's hefty size presented a bit of a challenge in this regard. At over twenty seven feet in length, we needed two consecutive spaces to park in. On the crowded streets of Greenwich Village, it was almost impossible to find even a single parking space--much less two, together.

After cruising the neighborhood for the better part of an hour, we happened upon an over-sized opening several blocks from the apartment, and promptly pulled in and parked. Unfortunately, the small matter of New York City's alternate side of the street parking regulations complicated the situation. No sooner had we settled into our hard won spot than we were forced to pick up and move to the other side of the street. It was just one more unwanted element of stress that we could have just as well done without.

"Now do you remember why we wanted to leave New York?" I joked to Wil. "No matter what you want to do here, it's always a big production."

Adding to our general discomfort was how strange it felt being back in our old apartment, now that someone else was living there. Ken had been sick for most of the last month, and the apartment had been sorely neglected. A thick layer of dust lay over every visible surface.

Decidedly uncomfortable with the situation, Wil and I decided to sleep in the Winnebago and use the apartment only for its phone and bathroom facilities. Besides, an empty Winnebago made an inviting target for thieves, and our presence in it at night would provide a certain measure of security.

That Thursday night, we paid a well-deserved visit to our friends at the New York Healing Circle. Even though our appearance there was unexpected, Samuel graciously turned part of the evening over to us so that we could update the group on what we had been up to during our absence. Wil described some of the work being done in the other healing circles we had visited, and I filled in some additional details. After the closing ritual, we hung around and chatted with friends, and bask in all the love and attention.

"This evening was a real surprise," I confessed later, when we were back in the Winnebago. "I was afraid people might feel we had abandoned them, and be mad at us because of it. That certainly wasn't the case, though. All I felt was love."

"Some people might feel that way, but the majority of the people I talked to were supportive of what we are doing. Anyway, you can't really worry too much about what other people think. You just have to do what's right for you."

"Yeah, I suppose" I grunted. Certainly, we had done what we had needed to do. No one could fault us for that.

Early the following day, we surrendered our precious parking spot and made a last- minute trip upstate to speak to an interested group of college students in Woodstock, NY. Anita and Niro rendezvoused with us at the venue, and afterwards caught a ride with us back to the city in the Winnebago. The exertion of the trip had left Anita completely exhausted, and she slept most of the way home. Wil took advantage of his time with Niro to bring her up to speed on our recent exploits. He also agreed to place our trip under the auspices of her organization, SHARE, an acronym standing for Self Healing AIDS Related Experiment. For now on, our trip around the country would officially be known as SHARE on the Road.

Before leaving for Buffalo, Wil and I gave the apartment a thorough cleaning and stocked the refrigerator with a number of Ken's favorite foods. "There's nothing worse than not having any food in the house when you're sick," Wil commented, putting away the last of the groceries. "I hope someone would do as much for me if I were in the same situation."

Later, as we steered the Winnebago onto the West Side Highway and over the George Washington Bridge, the Hudson River shimmered beneath us like a mile-wide ribbon of liquid silver. A half hour later, we had cleared the last of the urban sprawl and were well on our way upstate. As New York City faded into the distance, we breathed a collective sigh of relief.

It had dawned on me during our visit that Wil and I had the best of both worlds now. We could visit the city anytime we wanted to, without the liability of being full-time residents. Perhaps all we really needed was an occasional visit like the one we had just completed.

As we skirted the Adirondack Mountains, spring followed our every move. Along the southern edge of Lake Ontario, the trees were just beginning to put forth shoots of green. All around us were seasonal reminders of renewal and rebirth.

"I think spring is my favorite season," Wil commented, as we passed a particularly beautiful stretch of woods. "Too bad we never seemed to get one in the city anymore."

He was right, of course. In recent years, spring had failed to make its usual appearance, unless the spectacular flower show at Macy's Department Store counted as the real thing. Instead, the bitter winds of winter had abruptly transitioned into the sodden, oppressive heat of the summer, with little buffer in between.

"I think it must have something to do with global warming," I hypothesized, blithely. "The weather seems to be really screwed up this year, don't you think? Doesn't it seem like it's been spring, forever?"

"Maybe it's because we've been going north for the last three months," Wil replied, shooting me an exasperated look. "*Your inner fundamentalist is showing.*"

I grimaced on hearing him say that. It was a little joke between us, something Wil liked to say to remind me whenever the apocalyptical part of my personality was beginning to rear its ugly head.

"Yeah, maybe you're right," I reconsidered my position. "Something out of the ordinary doesn't necessarily have to be a sign that the world's coming to an end. I suppose there are other, less sinister explanations."

Whichever one of us was right, we were experiencing the longest spring of our lives and loving every minute of it. It had begun in March while we were still in Florida, and was with us still, even though June was just around the corner. I forgot about global warming and chose to see spring's lingering presence as an omen of good fortune, as though the grace of God were following our every move.

After a brief detour through the finger-lakes district in upstate New York, we arrived at out intended destination: the city of Buffalo, situated on the eastern edge of Lake Erie. Prior to our talk the following evening at a stately old Presbyterian Church, we met for dinner with our sponsors from the Western New York AIDS Network and had a heartfelt discussion about the spiritual aspects of the AIDS epidemic, a subject the Buffalo community was just beginning to recognize the importance of, and one that the organization was hoping to include more prominently in their future, educational, outreach programs.

Over dinner, Ed Darstein, the friendly head of the agency, shared some of the many difficulties he encountered as a result of Buffalo's average citizen's homophobic attitudes. Eight years into the epidemic and as hard as it was for us to believe, there was only one doctor in the entire city who would treat people with HIV and AIDS. Everyone else was either afraid of being infected or of having their practice ruined by a mere association with the disease. As a result, most people went underground after receiving their diagnosis, making it nearly impossible for the agency to reach them with help--much less two, gay strangers from out of town with a radical message of hope.

During our lecture the following night, members of the press were barred from the auditorium out of respect for the privacy of those in attendance. Confidentiality, whether pertaining to sexual orientation or sero-status, was a huge issue for the Buffalo community and the agency didn't want to run the risk of outing anyone inadvertently. As usual, Wil was the first to speak and basically repeated the talk he had given at the Church of Religious Science in Atlanta, a month earlier. Then it was my turn. I was in a definite A Course of Miracles frame of mind

"If any of us hope to survive this epidemic where there's apparently no cure, it's important for each of us to answer this one, basic question, once and for all: Who am I, really?" I began by saying. "It's been said that we are spirits having a human experience--not the other way around-- and that's what I've come to believe in the course of my exploration of metaphysics. If we're not our bodies, then, what is our true relationship with our physical selves? A Course in Miracles suggests that a good question to ask ourselves is *what's the body for?* The answer depends on whom and what we believe we are."

"When our primary sense of identity is rooted in our everyday experience as imperfect, human beings, in individual, physical bodies, it's only natural to feel isolated and alone, and separate from the things we need. It's understandable, then, that we would see our bodies as a means of getting the love and validation we think we're missing in order to feel good about ourselves. This kind of external seeking can take the form of money or food or sex; it doesn't really matter. They're all basically different forms of the same thing.

Identification with Spirit, on the other hand, gives us an entirely different perspective because Spirit, you see, is whole, perfect and complete--and knows it. It doesn't need anything. It sees the body as simply a means of sharing its wholeness with others-- *of giving rather than getting.* That's what you do when you know you're whole, perfect and complete-- you share. You don't need to *get* anything from anybody."

"Simply put, it's the energy of *getting* rather than *giving* that causes the body to become sick, because we're using it inappropriately. We're running our life-force energy backwards and burning up our circuits in the process. This doesn't make us bad people, however, as some would like to think. It simply means that we're ignorant of who we are, and how things actually work."

"At its heart, I believe that the AIDS crisis is first and foremost a crisis of identity. Therefore, the first step in resolving this crisis is to correctly identify whom and what we are. From there, everything else falls naturally into place. For most of us, including myself, AIDS came into our lives by way of our sexuality, and most of the world has responded by pointing their fingers and saying this is proof that we are wrong and bad for being who we are. But they are dead wrong, and their analysis of this epidemic is superficial and distorted by their own prejudices. That being said, AIDS does have much to teach us about ourselves and our sexuality. When sex becomes strictly a means of getting the love and validation we think we're missing, the very energy of our orgasm--which is highly creative--empowers our experience of lack--our dis-ease, as

Louise Hay likes to say. That gives a nasty virus like HIV a pretty big energetic opening in which to do its dirty work."

"Before I close, tonight, I'd like to leave you with this one final thought: If AIDS can indeed be a stepping stone to greater glory as the readings of Edgar Cayce seem to suggest, then the opportunity for transformation has to be commiserate with its downside, which I think you'll agree with me is huge. Ultimately, I believe that AIDS is here to heal us, not to kill us, but the choice is ours to make. I look forward to the day when we as gay people take our rightful places as equal members of the human family, as the healers I believe we are in truth. To me, that's what AIDS is here for: to remind us of who we really are. And ultimately, that's what healing ourselves individually, and as a community, is all about."

Despite the ban on the press from inside the auditorium, each of the three local television stations covered the event from outside the church. Standing on the steps as the orderly crowd filed past, Wil and I took time to speak briefly with each reporter.

It was intimidating to be dealing with the press again--especially for me. Our last encounter had been in Charleston when I was sick with the shingles and seized with dread. While the reporter there had been sympathetic to our cause, I was still a little gun-shy from the experience. I still had an underlying fear of being ambushed that I couldn't seem to shake.

Now, here in Buffalo, a month after our last encounter with the press, Wil and I both found it hard to keep the reporters from putting *their* words into *our* mouths. Apparently, they were used to condensing a story down into a few, sensational sound bites, even at the expense of accuracy. After a bit of compromise, Wil and I managed to say our piece and the reporters raced off to file their stories in time for their deadline. In the end, everyone got what they had come for.

Later, in our hotel room, we watched the late edition of the local news to see what kind of coverage the event had gotten. Happily, every station in town carried an item about our visit. On first appraisal, we were a bit annoyed that some of what we had said had been taken out of context and its meaning slightly skewed. One station, in the interest of balance, presented their own medical expert to reassure the public that no one could possibly heal themselves of AIDS.

Even though the coverage wasn't entirely what we would have liked, we were pleased, nonetheless, that some semblance of a positive message had broken through to the public via the mass media. No doubt this scenario would need to be repeated many more times before the perception of AIDS as an inevitable death sentence would begin to change. The mere fact we had been interviewed at all, in a city as conservative as Buffalo, was a miracle in and of itself, and for that we were extremely grateful. At the very least, the experience provided us with a much- needed opportunity to refine our media skills, and that would serve us well in the weeks and months ahead. Like everything else about the trip we were on, we were learning as we went along.

Before leaving town the next day, Wil and I made a brief appearance on *A.M. Buffalo*. Arriving at the studio just before dawn, we were greeted by a burly security guard who checked our ID's and politely escorted us onto the set.

"Where is everyone?" Wil asked the stiff-mannered host who was slated to conduct the interview. "I thought the show was taped before a live audience?"

"I....uh....*we* decided it would be best to do this without an audience due to the sensitive nature of the subject matter," the man stammered, obviously caught off guard by the question. "We felt it would be in the best interest of *everyone involved* to do it this way."

"I wonder what he meant by *in everyone's best interest*," Wil whispered later, while the reporter was busy consulting with his producer.

I shrugged my shoulders and screwed up my face in disdain. "What do you think it means?" I hissed. "It means they think the public is too stupid to make up their own minds."

After an otherwise pleasant but unremarkable interview, we returned to the hotel to collect our things and moved back into the Winnebago. On the way out of town, we stopped by Ed's house to pick up a copy of the interview he had promised to record.

"Come on in and take a look," he mumbled sleepily, answering the door in his pajamas with a cup of coffee in his hands. "I think the interview went pretty well from what I could see."

We followed him into the living room where he motioned toward the couch. "Make your selves comfortable," he said. "Can I get you anything to drink?"

"No, we've both had enough coffee for one day, thanks," Wil laughed. "We must have drunk at least a gallon apiece at the studio."

Ed switched on the television and fiddled with the ancient VCR. After several failed attempts to make it work, a fuzzy image sputtered to life and our smiling, albeit slightly, puffy faces appeared on screen. Despite a bad camera angle that made it appear as though I had fallen asleep while Wil was talking, the interview was pretty much standard fare-- except for one small thing: the peculiar manner in which the editor had spliced in shots of the non-existent audience between close-ups of Wil and I. Their reactions were strangely out of sync with what was being said.

For example, when Wil said he had been diagnosed with AIDS in 1985, and had assumed he had only a few months to live, a shot of a woman, laughing, flashed across the screen. Had this been an unfortunate accident? A random example of sloppy editing? The work of a homophobe who thought that gay men getting AIDS was funny? We couldn't really decide.

12 We're Hot in Cleveland

LEAVING THE CITY OF BUFFALO BEHIND, we followed the Niagara River as it meandered its way north to the Canadian border and spent the afternoon contemplating the magnificent falls and gorge. Then, retracing our steps to Buffalo, we headed west along the southern edge of Lake Erie and arrived on the outskirts of Cleveland, tired but jazzed at the prospect of meeting the mysterious lady who in many ways had helped initiate our trip. Bellruth Naperstek's invitation to come to Cleveland and speak, coming as it had on the very day we had put a down-payment on the Winnebago, had been an important source of validation for our plans and our first invitation to speak outside of New York City.

Crossing over the city limits just as the evening commute was revving into gear, we exited the busy interstate and drove directly to Bellruth home in Cleveland Heights. Before long, we were sitting around the kitchen table of her rambling, two-story, Tudor home, sipping tea and chatting with her and her business partner, Janet Crate, as if we had known them our entire lives. The late afternoon sun streamed in through the kitchen window, casting a warm, cheery spell over the room. For a moment, it felt as though we had been transported into a classic Norman Rockwell painting.

Bellruth, a therapist and the creator of a distinct line of visualization tapes, and Janet, a housewife and mother of two, were the co-founders of *Bridges to Discovery*, an organization created for the expressed purpose of presenting self-help programs to Cleveland's rapidly growing, alternative community. Our visit was an important part of their fledgling efforts and their first attempt to address the issue of AIDS.

Almost immediately, Wil and I fell madly in love with these two endearing women, as much for their enormous sense of compassion and commitment to others as for their incredible sense of humor. For the next several days, we watched as they put the finishing touches on their plans for our visit, playing off each other like two, long-time veterans of a well-oiled, vaudeville comedy team. In private, we began referring to them as Lucy and Ethyl, something we didn't share with them until much later in the friendship. When it came to preparing for our event, however, they were not inclined to fool around. In the end, every detail had been meticulously attended to.

On the publicity end of things, Janet had arranged for us to appear on the popular, local, television show, *Morning Exchange*. Shortly before sunrise on the day in question, she picked us up at Bellruth's house and deposited us at the studio a good half-hour before we were scheduled to go on. After meeting the show's two, main co-anchors, Lee Jordan and Fred Griffith, we warmed ourselves over coffee and donuts and killed time poking around the set.

"When we come back: Two men from New York with AIDS, with a story of hope and healing." The words resounded over the studio monitors, startling Wil and I back into the present moment and triggering butterflies in both our stomachs. During the commercial break, an able-bodied production assistant led us onto the set and prepared our mikes, and a make-up artist gave our faces a quick dab of powder. *Five... four... three... two... one...*, the numbers flashed across the teleprompter. "You're on!" the director pantomimed.

Our hosts' empathy for our message was immediately apparent, particularly in how thought-provoking and carefully considered their questions were. We were thrilled at the amount of information we were able to convey in only the few, short minutes allotted us, especially since Janet had warned us earlier that one of the show's regular contributors--a balding, middle-aged man with a slight build and thin lips--was decidedly homophobic and unhappy that we were even in the studio, much less appearing as guests on the show. As the interview began, he sulked quietly in the background with his arms folded across his chest, a scowl etched upon his face.

"So," Fred Griffith began, "You young men seem to have beaten the odds somehow, at least for now. What made you think you could beat this disease in the first place?"

Wil jumped in and fielded the question. "Originally, I didn't," he said. "I accepted the fact that I was going to die and resigned myself to my fate. But after listening to George and observing the results he was achieving with his own health, I started to reconsider. Being more left brained and scientific, I studied Drs. Stephanie and Carl Simonton's work with cancer patients using dream recall, visualization and meditation to create a model of what the profile of a cancer survivor looks like. From there, it was only a short step to recognizing that AIDS could be approached in a similar manner. I would need to treat my body, my mind, *and* my spirit."

"I see," the anchorman nodded, turning his attention to me. "Tell me, George," he asked. "What would happen if you were to get sick now, after all the work you've done on yourself? Would you consider yourself a failure or say that a holistic approach doesn't work? What would *you* do?"

I had to admit it was a good question and went straight to the heart of the matter over whether telling people they were responsible for the conditions in their lives was doing them a disservice--another reason to feel guilty and wrong--or a way of empowering them to take control of the situation.

"I think it's important for people to know right up front that being holistic doesn't imply any guarantees--particularly when it comes to AIDS," I began, measuring my words carefully. "Even vegetarians die, though most of them don't really think they will." The audience let out a hearty laugh.

"But," I continued, "I think it's a disservice to victimize people twice by first telling them they're at fault for their disease, and then turning right back around and telling them that there's nothing they can do about it. That doesn't make sense to me."

"I think you must embark on a journey like the one Wil and I are prescribing with your eyes open. You can't bargain with the Universe and say *I'll do this if you'll do that in exchange.* It might be a first step, but in the long run healing doesn't really work that way. You must be motivated out of truly loving yourself enough to do what you need to do, rather than the fear that you're going to die. Ultimately, my goal is to be able to look myself in the eye, *whenever I die*, and know that I've lived a life I can be proud of--that I'm in integrity with myself. Then, it won't matter so much what happens. Either way, I'll be at peace."

After several more quick exchanges, as quickly as it had begun the interview was over, logistical details of our lecture were flashed across the screen, and the director cut to a commercial. We removed our lapel mikes and climbed down from the stage.

"Please let us know whenever you're in the area again," Lee Jordan, the female member of the team said warmly, clasping my hand in hers. "We'd like to keep the public abreast of your story and let them know how you're doing from time to time."

"They must really like what you had to say if they invited you back," Janet commented when I told her what Lee had said. "They're pretty picky about who they have on as guests."

Later, as the three of us hashed over the interview over a breakfast of hot-cakes and coffee, it was unanimously agreed that our interview had been an unqualified success. Given the brief time allotted to us, we had managed to convey our message clearly and succinctly. And we had had an extremely positive interaction with the press-- something that had mostly eluded us until now. Apparently, the adversarial nature of that all important relationship was finally beginning to shift.

The city of Cleveland turned out to be a pleasant surprise, especially in light of the many demeaning jokes we had heard made at its expense over the years. Neither Wil nor I was prepared for what we found there: a city rich in history and graced with an abundance of classical architecture. Certainly, there were the obvious signs of decay of the mighty industrial center it had once been, but there was also a considerable stock of grand old buildings and dignified monuments as telling reminders of its former glory.

In the days following our talk at a gay-friendly, Presbyterian Church in Bellruth's neighborhood, there was ample time to take in the local sights. Anxious to show off their city in the best light possible, Bellruth chauffeured us around Shaker Heights, past hundreds of graceful mansions on curving tree-lined streets. Most of the houses harkened back to the early part of the century, to the decades immediately preceding the stock market crash of 1929. At the time, Cleveland had rivaled New

York as the center of American finance and commerce, and these grand old houses were a legacy of that bygone, golden era.

After finalizing plans for a return visit in the fall, Wil and I said goodbye to our new best friends and set off in the direction of Chicago. Our schedule called for us to drop in on Test Positive Awareness, a local, HIV support group, and afterwards speak at a local MCC. On the way, we made a quick, overnight stop in South Bend, Indiana and spoke to a small support group only recently organized by an expatriate friend of ours from the healing circle in New York.

By now, word of our travels had begun to spread like wild-fire, and invitations to speak came flooding in from cities large and small. Wil and I fully intended to accept every invitation we received since the Winnebago provided us with easy access to even the most obscure, little towns. The only thing needed to make it happen was a sponsor with enough energy and enthusiasm to produce an event, and the gift of a love offering to reimburse us for our costs.

With the increasing demands on our time, keeping track of all the requests and figuring out the various logistics quickly became a full-time job. Overwhelmed by how much work our surge in popularity had created, Wil and I sat down together, one evening after dinner, and formulated a plan for handling the backlog. Placing a large map of the United States on the kitchen table, Wil took a black magic marker and proceeded to circle every city and national park he thought we might even remotely be interested in visiting, and connect them by way of the most scenic route we could find. When he had finished, a thick, black line looped lazily around the circumference of the map in a large irregular circle, intersecting with itself again in New York, where our journey had begun.

Estimating the amount of time we might want to spend in each location, we created some loose parameters for our trip. Now, whenever a request came in from Toni, we could look at the map and determine the approximate dates we would be in the area and lock it in.

Faced with the growing magnitude of the responsibility we had undertaken, it was time to do a little fine-tuning in the all important area of organization. Our simple desire to leave New York City and see the country was turning into something much bigger than either of us had envisioned when we had first set out on the road. Our trip had morphed into a full-fledged, traveling AIDS ministry, and we, in effect, had become full-time, spiritual counselors.

When Wil and I had first left New York, neither of us had stopped to consider that there would be so much interest in hearing what we had to say. True, we *had* planned to drop in on the various healing circles we encountered, but that was pretty much it. Now, simply through word of mouth, the trickle of inquiries had escalated into a raging torrent, propelling speaking into the defining element of our trip. Benjamin's words to us during the Harmonic Convergence were proving to be prophetic. Young men *were* starting to sit at our feet and listen!

We had also come to appreciate just how much power there was in simply following your heart. Yet, at times, the road this led us down seemed completely irrelevant to our original intentions. Then somehow, without our actually knowing how or why, an unforeseen set of circumstances would land us exactly in the right place at the right time, in a way we could never have planned. More than ever, we were living in a state of grace and could only sit back and marvel at the many unexpected ways the Universe moved on our behalf.

☀

13 Tiptoeing thru Texas

OUR STAY IN CHICAGO LASTED ONLY long enough to fulfill the agreements we had made, in large part due to our inability to find a satisfactory place to park the Winnebago, and partly because of an energetic discomfort we both picked up on almost immediately upon arriving in the city. The consciousness of the community seemed to have a discomforting density to it, mirroring the Midwestern bedrock on which the City of Broad Shoulders stood. As soon as we had finished our talk at the MCC, we pulled up stakes and headed out of town, bound for the state of Texas.

With at least a week before we were expected in Houston, there was ample time to explore the countryside enroute. We took our time, ambling through the flat, boring expanse of farmland south of Chicago, and crossed the southern tip of Missouri into Tennessee. Here, the highway meandered alongside the mighty Mississippi River which both of us were seeing for the very first time.

At Memphis, we crossed over the river and headed west into Arkansas through the capital of Little Rock. Taking a break from the arduous drive, we stopped overnight in the small, resort town of Hot Springs. Since neither of us had ever been in the Ozark Mountains before, we set up camp in a nearby National Park so that Wil, who had spent most his life on the mean streets of New York City, could have a firsthand experience of what America's heartland was actually like.

Since neither of us was really sure of just what kind of reception two gay men from New York City, traveling with their cats, with no discernible interest in hunting and fishing, might expect from the locals thereabout, we wisely exercised caution. The last thing either of us wanted was a confrontation with a hostile mob of rednecks. I had had enough experience growing up in Florida to know how important it was to draw as little attention to yourself as possible--especially in a place like this. Given who we were, we did the best we could and no one seemed the wiser.

Surprisingly, our presence in the park didn't seem to arouse any undue suspicion, at least not from the pair of middle-aged hunters from nearby Arkadelphia Wil mustered the courage to borrow a heavy-duty extension cord from, on finding ours missing when we went to set up camp. I had gone looking for him after he had failed to return in a reasonable amount of time, and found him squatting on an overturned bait bucket, chewing the fat with a couple of middle-aged men in plaid shirts. Amazingly, they were friendly and helpful, and offered us volumes of unsolicited information about the weather and the best fishing spots in the area. After that, we felt safe enough to drop some of our defenses and be a little more open to our surroundings. Our acute sense of being different began to soften and fade away.

The next morning, after returning the extension cord to its rightful owners, we broke camp and headed south in the direction of Texas. We had our work cut out for us in the coming weeks with major presentations planned in Houston, San Antonio, Austin and Dallas. I have to confess, I wasn't exactly thrilled at the prospect of visiting Texas, and an uncomfortable knot began to form in the pit of my stomach. Despite my reservations, promises had been made and plans for our visit were already under way. At this late date, there was no choice but to follow through on our agreements.

Our host in Houston was a man by the name of Michael Wilson, the director of a rather large, gay health-club located in an oversized warehouse, downtown. In response to the epidemic and a strong disdain for allopathic medicine, Michael had committed his considerable expertise in the field of nutrition and metaphysics to counseling HIV positive members of the gym in the art of staying well. This had turned out to be no easy task, given the pervasive atmosphere of fear permeating this very southern city.

To complicate his mission, the owner of the health club he worked for was a doctor who owned considerable stock in Burrows-Welcome, the manufacturer of AZT, the sole wonder drug of the moment. Rightly or wrongly, Michael felt that his boss had a vested interest in prescribing the drug to his patients, irrespective of its effectiveness, and was caught up in an irretractable conflict with him over the issue.

Despite landing directly in the middle of this sticky situation, our event at the gym, the night after we arrived, was a major success-- even though shortly before taking the stage, a gangly Houstonian in cowboy gear had remarked threateningly in my ear: "The last couple of holistic healers that came through here got run out of town. I'd be careful if I was you."

"I'm not a holistic healer," I replied defensively, caught off guard by the unexpected rush of fear his words sent surging up my spine. "I'm just here to share my experience. You can take it or leave it. I really don't care."

Later, as I stood at the front of the cavernous aerobics room where the event was being held and centered myself to speak, I remembered the man's remarks and made a concerted effort to address them in my talk.

"Our message is not anti-medicine," I informed the attentive audience, borrowing from the words of our friend, the AIDS activist, Sally Fisher. "That would be *exclusive* of something and our message is really more one of *inclusion*. Rather than using the word *alternative*, I like to use the word *complimentary* when it comes to describing our approach. Allopathic and naturopathic medicine must both work together if we're going to win the fight against AIDS. This, to me, is what a holistic approach would actually look like. You'd use the very best of everything available--including spirituality."

Sadly, in the wake of our controversial visit, Michael was forced to resign his job at the gym. His unemployment didn't last for long, however. Within days, a local, health- food store offered him a position where he continued to dispense nutritional advice, free of interference from his former boss.

"Getting fired actually turned out to a blessing," he related in a letter we received from him several months later. "I got so caught up in making the doctor wrong, I got distracted from what my real work was. It took me a while to get refocused, but eventually I did. Live and learn, I guess you could say."

From Houston, we headed to San Antonio, a community still in the earliest stages of organizing to deal with the raging epidemic--this in the face of a public overtly hostile to anyone or anything even remotely connected to the disease. On checking in with our sponsor, we were informed that some snags had arisen in preparing for our visit and that we'd need to check in with Papa Bear, the overweight head of the struggling, local, AIDS service organization, to straighten things out. On meeting him, Wil and I had a clearer sense of just what the problem might actually be.

Perhaps out of a misplaced sense of responsibility, or perhaps for some other reason we couldn't fully discern, Papa Bear apparently felt that it was his job to censor whatever information the local AIDS community was allowed to hear and he was definitely suspicious of what Wil and I were selling. After considerable negotiation, we convinced him, albeit begrudgingly, that our intentions were honorable and obtained his cooperation, if not his blessing, for the event to go forward. The following night, we spoke at the local MCC, to a polite crowd of around 50 people.

Despite the relative warmth of the reception, I felt uncomfortable in San Antonio and was anxious to get back on the road. "No wonder the local community is so oppressed," I complained to Wil, back in the safety of the Winnebago. "Even their so-called leaders don't trust them to think for themselves. And I thought it was just the press that was the problem."

After the gloom of San Antonio, Austin was like a breath of fresh air. In comparison to the other cities in Texas we had visited, this bright and modern city felt as though it were part of another country entirely. Even the geography was noticeably different.

"I never thought I'd say this about a city in Texas," I confessed, after we had been there for several days, "but I actually think I could live here. Too bad it happens to be in Texas."

In keeping with our positive first impression of the city, Austin's gay community was active and rather well-organized for a city of its size. As such, our event at the local Unity church, the night after we arrived, drew a large and receptive crowd, as well as considerable coverage in the local press. To our delight, there was a small story on the evening news and an article in the paper the following day.

"Things are looking up," Wil chirped over coffee, handing me the local paper. "At least nobody's throwing rocks."

I scanned the article and handed the paper back to him. "Yeah, but we've still got Dallas ahead of us," I said, frowning. "From what I've heard, it's not the most enlightened city in the world."

Wil turned and gave me a disapproving look. He didn't seem to appreciate my bad-mouthing Texas. "You need to try and be less judgmental," he scolded me. "Try and be more open minded, would you?"

I hung my head and said I'd try.

After breakfast, we made a few short phone calls before pulling up stakes and setting out on the relatively short trip to Dallas. Crossing over the city limits just as the morning rush hour was winding to a close, I eased the Winnebago into the first convenient filling station we came to and jumped out to fill it up. Wil set off in search of a pay phone to try and make contact with our sponsor, Dennis Darcy, the head of the Dallas PWA Coalition.

"We're going to meet him for dinner," he informed me upon his return. "He said we should come directly to his office and he'll show us where to park. He said to be careful, though, because the neighborhood's a little rough."

"*Remain calm,*" I muttered under my breath. "*It's only for a couple of days. We can leave as soon as we're finished with our talk.*"

Our lecture at the local MCC the following night was very well attended and received. Afterwards, we connected with a friendly young man by the name of David Amidon, who was on a spiritual journey similar to our own.

"I've got some friends in Denver I'd like you to meet," he insisted. "You've got a lot in common. I could give them a call and let them know you're coming, if you want. I'm pretty sure they'll want to meet you."

"Alright," Wil said. "If they can't make it to the lecture, perhaps we can meet them for lunch or something."

Often in our travels, people insisted on setting us up like this, and frankly the results had not always been to our liking. At times, we had found ourselves in some pretty awkward situations.

"You're not really going to call them, are you?" I asked later, betraying my reluctance to further our connection to anyone even remotely related to Texas.

Wil shot me a disapproving look. "You're better than that," he scolded me, trying to shame me into a more positive frame of mind. "I'll bet they're really wonderful people. Don't be so quick to judge."

The attitude was so typical of Wil. He seemed to see only the best in people, while often I could not. I was still wrestling with the fear that people might try and hurt me somehow, and our overall experience in Texas hadn't helped to change that perception. I felt bruised by the entire experience and wanted to get out of the state as fast as possible.

"Don't worry," Wil admonished, after I broke down and confessed my considerable misgivings. "Texas was simply a test. The Universe just wants to see if you can handle it when the chips are down. Things are bound to get better, soon. You just have to be patience, that's all."

"I'll keep it in mind," I mumbled. But secretly, I wasn't entirely convinced he was right.

☀

14 Denver and the AIDS, Medicine and Miracles Conference

TRAVELING THROUGH THE HINTERLANDS IN A Winnebago, planting seeds of hope in the consciousness of anyone who would listen, Wil and I were beginning to feel a distinct kinship with Johnny Appleseed, despite the fact that the seeds we were planting were ideas and not actual seeds. Though the soil we had encountered was uneven in places, we were convinced that our efforts would eventually bear fruit, and this belief kept us from losing faith even when we were discouraged and wanted to quit and go back home. As long as one person wanted to hear our story, we were both committed to sharing it.

The first rays of sunlight were just beginning to breach the horizon as we broke camp and headed west via the nearest interstate highway out of Dallas. As the city's distinctive skyline faded in the rear-view mirror, I sighed in relief and turned to Wil and smiled. It was good to be on the road again, with just him and the two cats for company. For a while at least, the only problems we'd have to deal with would be our own. Everyone else would just have to take care of themselves.

The time spent in Texas had been stressful on both of us--particularly me. Nothing horrible had happened, mind you, just that the constant resistance we had encountered had been a drained on both our energies. As usual, I had found it unnerving to be arriving in a different city every few days, having to deal with the various local personalities and politics. I didn't mind it when things were going smoothly, but it was another story when they weren't. As a result, I was getting an opportunity to see just how deep my commitment actually was--if I could take the heat or would turn tail and run at the first signs of difficulty. Clearly, my metal was being tested.

The longer Wil and I were on the road, the more we noticed the inordinate amount of petty, political infighting among the so-called leaders of the AIDS community, and how often their personal power struggles came at the expense of the people they were meant to serve--namely people with HIV and AIDS. More than once, we had found ourselves caught up in the drama as a sponsor attempted to use our visit to further a personal agenda. Even worse, many of the caregivers we had met, while sincerely wanting to be of service, were blatantly dysfunctional and acting out of their own unhealed issues, which didn't bode well for actual empowerment.

It was also interesting to note the different responses to the epidemic in the various parts of the country we had visited so far. In some places, an open and accepting climate had coalesced around people with AIDS, while in others the level of fear was so thick you could literally taste it in your mouth. These marked differences weren't always the result of an unsupportive attitude on the part of the larger community, either. Frequently, the biggest challenge people with AIDS faced came from within their own ranks. They were often their own worst enemies.

Often, Wil and I found that it was necessary to bypass the official AIDS organizations in order to find a sponsor for our talk. At this point in the epidemic, there was still little support for the idea that people could live with the disease, much less recover from it, and most people clung tenaciously to the belief that an AIDS diagnosis was tantamount to certain death.

Because of how deeply entrenched this belief was, more often than not Wil and I were viewed simply as two annoying voices from the lunatic fringe, best ignored or dismissed outright. It was as though the gay community was suffering from a really bad case of Stockholm syndrome and was more comfortable with fear than hope.

Though Wil and I knew that it was impossible for us to single-handedly change the course of the epidemic, we were meeting up with people who had similar ideas, but were too intimidated by the politically correct version of events to risk dissenting from the majority opinion. A visit from us seemed to provide the validation they needed in order to stand up for what they believed. Once Wil and I gave voice to their innermost thoughts and feelings, they frequently found the courage to voice it themselves.

As outsiders, Wil and I had license to say things that a person living in a particular community didn't always feel comfortable giving voice to. As our ability to catalyze spiritual activism began to expand, we could look behind us and see the profound changes taking place in the wake of our extensive travels. Emboldened by our stand, individuals in many of the communities we had visited were bravely stepping forward to ground and expand the work we had begun, and a powerful ripple effect was beginning to taking shape. Small as it was, a crack was starting to appear in the current paradigm of hopelessness.

Leaving the dry flatlands of West Texas behind, we entered the northeast corner of New Mexico and passed through Grasslands National Park into southern Colorado. Through the Winnebago's dusty windows, grassy plains stretched out on either side of us as far as the eye could see. Once, the area had rung with the sound of countless buffalo as they ranged across the plains. Now, little more than a hundred years later, there was nothing left to remind us of their existence, just the eerie whistle of the ever-present wind.

Denver was the next stop on our tour and we were looking forward to visiting the city. Our contact there, like so many others that had helped make this trip possible, was a recent transplant from the healing circle in New York City. Lisa Esposita had been living in Denver for less than a week when she had made the acquaintance of Anne Shields, the educational director of the Colorado AIDS Project, and discovered their shared interest in metaphysics and healing. In their subsequent discussions together about how best to introduce a spiritual perspective to the local gay community, Lisa had mentioned Wil and me and the work we were doing, and encouraged Anne to approach the board of directors with a proposal for a visit. While several of the board members had initially expressed reservations, Anne had ultimately prevailed and the proposal had been accepted. Our upcoming talk was to be the first presentation of a spiritual nature the agency had ever sponsored.

The evening of our talk, the auditorium of the old, inner-city, Methodist church we were scheduled to speak in was packed to capacity and humming with electricity, as people filed in and noisily found their seats. It was obvious from the energy of the crowd that news of our message had traveled ahead of us, and curiosity was running extremely high. The audience seemed to sense the importance of what they were about to hear and their enthusiasm overflowed onto us, reviving our flagging spirits.

As usual, Wil spoke first and related the story of his initial skepticism and subsequent conversion to metaphysics and spirituality. Then, when he had finished, he took a seat down front and turned the lectern over to me. Taking advantage of the audience's obvious, new-age bent, I decided to venture farther out on a limb than ever.

"I'm not a proponent of the idea that HIV is the sole cause of AIDS," I began by saying, startling the audience to attention with my unorthodox declaration. "But then again, neither do I believe it has nothing to do with it, like the followers of Dr. Peter Duesburg. I think there has to be a marriage of the behavioral and viral theories if we're ever going to understand this disease in its entirety."

"It's important to realize that viruses don't exist in a vacuum," I continued. "Their behaviors are not a given, but are determined by the energetic quality of the environment in which they exist. *Energetically, then, viruses*-- and I mean *all* viruses, not just HIV--are by nature resonance structures. They have no distinct energy pattern of their own, but resonate to the energy of their host. The same virus can exhibit different behaviors in different hosts because ultimately they respond to their host's unique, individual *vibration*. In this respect, you have an effect on how HIV behaves in your body, because you're responsible for your vibration. You create this frequency through your mental/emotional body, through your thoughts, feelings, beliefs and intentions."

I stopped and gave my words time to sink in, before starting back up again. "When you're full of fear--and you know there's plenty of that going around-- you're feeding the virus the very energy that activates it into a level of activity which enables it to destroy your immune system. When you go against your own inner knowing that you're not a victim of this or any other disease, or default to the opinions of the so-called experts, you are essentially giving your power away."

"The AIDS virus thrives on fear and conflict. Healing yourself, as opposed to curing your disease, means healing your mental/emotional bodies, as well as giving your physical body everything it needs to repair itself. Healing happens through seeing your disease from a spiritual perspective *as an issue involving consciousness*. If we fail to address the conditions that fester beneath the biology of AIDS, then for every opportunistic infection we do manage to suppress, we're simply setting ourselves up for another, more serious one. This disease must be addresses physically, mentally, emotionally *and* spiritually if we're going to gain the upper hand."

When I had finished speaking, Wil joined me on the platform for a lengthy question and answer period, after which several members of the audience came forward to share their own recovery stories achieved through holistic and spiritual means. These testimonies offered the strongest validation yet for the stand we had taken, and their timing was impeccable. After our difficult trip through Texas, we had begun to feel as though we were fighting a losing battle and to question whether or not to continue, or quit and go back home. Now, here in Denver, after six months of whistling into the wind, we had finally met up with a group of like-minded people who were using metaphysics to defy the odds. If we were crazy, then apparently a lot of other people were too.

David Amidon's friends were in the audience that night, having come in late after Wil had started his presentation. Afterwards, because of the crush of well-wishers and the lateness of the hour, we spoke with them only briefly before agreeing to meet them for lunch the following day.

Almost immediately, Wil and I felt a deep kinship with the three strangers, especially the two women, who were students of *A Course in Miracles* and spoke pretty much the same language as we did. Sandy, Angel and Ascension lived together on a ranch, high up in the Rocky Mountains outside of Denver, called Heaven on Earth, which they hoped to develop into a retreat center for people with HIV and AIDS. Because Wil and I had often dreamed of doing something similar, we naturally wanted to see the ranch and learn more about their plans. Unfortunately, due to our crowded schedule we took a pass. We asked for a rain check and promised to visit them the next time we were in the area.

On our way out of town, we stopped by the offices of the Colorado AIDS Project to say good bye to Anne. Before letting us go, she extracted a promise from us to return in the spring to participate in the city's first annual AIDS Walk.

"You could be honorary grand marshals and lead the parade" she argued, standing in the door to her office, dangling the offer in front of us like a carrot on a stick. "It would be quite an honor to lead the very first one, don't you think?"

Wil glanced over at me for confirmation, before giving her our answer. "We'd love to," he said, his face breaking into a broad grin. "Just let me check our calendar and make sure there isn't a scheduling conflict."

He opened his leather-bound binder and thumbed through it to the month in question. "No," he said, pointing to the empty page. "There's nothing here. Next year it is then!"

From Ann's office, it was only a short drive to the Clarion Hotel in Boulder, where the second annual AIDS, Medicine and Miracles conference was being held. The conference, which had taken its name from the title of Dr. Bernie Siegel's best-selling book, *Love, Medicine, and Miracles*, was unusual as far as AIDS Conferences go in that it wasn't strictly a scientific affair. Its real focus was on community building and alternative approaches to healing. This year's keynote speaker was Louise Hay, and Wil and I were looking forward to furthering the fledgling friendship we had begun with her when we had attended her workshop in New York City, in 1986.

The conference opened on Friday evening with Louise's keynote address and resumed the following morning in the main Ballroom of the Clarion Hotel. Promptly at 9 am, Don Holloway, the executive director of AM&M, mounted the stage and welcomed everyone to Boulder. Then, after a flurry of announcements clarifying a number of last minute changes to the program, the first plenary speaker of the morning, the lesbian humorist, Fran Peavey, warmed up the crowd with a humorous monologue on the challenges of living with AIDS.

Wil and I were the next on the bill. Our presentation, which lasted for exactly an hour, began with the story of our diagnosis and subsequent trips to Mexico for drugs, and ended with our forays into metaphysics, spirituality and the mind/body connection. Wil wrapped things up with some final thought on the subject.

"The end result of everything we've told you here this morning is that despite everything you may have heard, an AIDS diagnosis doesn't necessarily equal death. It's really important for you to know that. But even more important, it's essential that you consider this disease in a multi-dimensional context. You need to understand yourself as a body, a mind and a spirit." The audience burst into applause.

With a fifteen minute break before the next speaker, we took a quick bathroom break and slipped back into the auditorium and found two seats next to Louise. Dr. Candace Pert, the current wunderkind of immunological research and the discoverer of peptide T, took the stage and immediately filled it with her electrifying presence. The fact that she couldn't seem to stand still readily betrayed the considerable excitement she was feeling. In the presentation that followed, she wiggled and swayed and paced back and forth across the stage like a woman possessed, mesmerizing the spellbound audience with her genius and enthusiasm.

"She's certainly not your typical scientist, I'll grant you that," Wil whispered in my ear.

"Neuro-peptides are literally the molecules through which our emotions communicate with our immune systems," Dr. Pert was saying, using laymen's term so that the audience could better understand the complicated subject matter. "Now, we not only know that the mind and immune system talk to each, we know *how they do it*. This opens up a whole new area of research for us to learn to manipulate the conversation. It will allow us to develop powerful new drugs that literally program the immune system to attack the virus that causes AIDS!"

"That's the first time I've heard about a treatment that sounds like it might actually work," Wil remarked on the sly, obviously taking a dig at the controversial new drug, AZT. "And have you noticed all her references to metaphysics and spirituality? Here's a doctor that really understands their importance in the healing process!"

I nodded in agreement, before turning my attention back to the platform where Dr. Pert was just finishing her remarks. If she was any indication of the caliber of people on the front lines of AIDS research, then there really wasn't very much to worry about. The virus would succumb to the sheer enthusiasm of the researchers. *Thank God for doctors like her,* I thought.

That afternoon, Wil and I took part in a panel of long-term survivors, which at this point in the epidemic was anyone who had survived their diagnosis for more than two or three years. "This question is for either Wil or George," the young man who was first in line at the microphone indicated. "I was wondering what you thought about AZT, and if either one of you were on it?"

Never one to shy away from controversy, Wil jumped in and fielded the tricky question. "I'm not taking any medication, at this time," he said. "I'm not really sure that in the case of AZT the benefits outweigh the risks, if you know what I mean. If you look at the label on the bottle the drug originally came in, you'd see a skull and crossbones and a strong warning to not even let it to touch your skin. That being the case, you can imagine what it must do to you when you take it internally. Personally, I think it's making a lot of people sick and I would never want to take it, myself."

"I have something I'd like to add to that," I chimed in, taking the microphone from Wil. "I agree with a lot of what Wil just said, but not all of it. I think every person and situation is unique and requires an individual response. I've seen people do well on AZT, and I've seen it make others really, really sick."

"Being a metaphysician and a student of *A Course in Miracles*, I try to look at every decision I'm faced with from a spiritual perspective. The Course says that *healing is the release from fear*. So in regards to your question, I think the first thing you need to consider is what your greater fear is: taking AZT-- which is all the medical profession has to offer, right now--or not taking it and dealing with the fear of having a potentially lethal virus running loose inside your body."

"If you think AZT is poison, then don't take it; if you do, you'll be out of integrity with yourself and you'll be violating your own belief system. Viruses feed on this kind of internal conflict. If you think it might help, then take it and bless it, just like you would your food, and see if it works for you. You can always change your mind."

I felt strongly that this was a point that needed to be made, given a very vocal segment of the community that was running around the country scaring the wits out of people on AZT, screaming that it was poison and going to kill them. If, indeed, fear was the basis for most disease as *The Course in Miracles* suggested, then trying to help people by telling them what they should and shouldn't do might actually be causing them harm. If, on the other hand, a person were taking AZT simply because their doctor pressured them into it, then that needed to be addressed, too. It was just plain wrong to make absolute pronouncements about what was essentially a personal decision. One man's poison might very well be another man's cure. It was dysfunctional, black and white thinking to think otherwise.

15 Visiting Christine in Sedona

O N THE MONDAY AFTER THE CONFERENCE disbanded, we checked out of the hotel and moved back into the Winnebago, and headed south through the Rocky Mountains by way of the most scenic route we could find. With time on our hands, we ambled south though the high deserts valleys of Southern Colorado and into New Mexico, and passed through Taos enroute to Santa Fe. Centuries of Indian and Spanish occupation and the sensuous lines of the indigenous adobe architecture gave this part of the country a rather unique ambience and distinctive, old-world charm, unlike so much of the rest of the country we had been in with its hodge-podge of tacky strip malls, fast-food joints and the like. New Mexico felt like an entirely different country.

"I could see myself living in an adobe, writing books and wearing lots of turquoise jewelry," I remarked, as Wil and I sauntered around Santa Fe town square, poking our heads into the cornucopia of shops and galleries. "And you could run a small educational outreach to the Spanish speaking community. What do you think?"

"It's always the same with you," Wil laughed, mocking me in his gentle way. "Everywhere we go, you say the exact same thing. First, you wanted to live on Miami Beach, then a huge house in Shaker Heights, and now a little adobe in Santa Fe. How will you ever decide?"

I laughed. With so many wonderful places in the world, it was hard to imagine having to choose just one. "I guess I could be happy anywhere, as long as I'm with you," I sighed, dreamily. Certainly, he couldn't argue with that.

The following evening, we spoke to a small but attentive audience of PWAs and their caregivers, organized by a petite, red-haired Englishwoman named Debra Bryant who had moved to Santa Fe from London a number of years earlier. Wil and I had made her acquaintance when she had visited the healing circle on a trip to New York, and an invitation to Santa Fe had quickly ensued.

At her insistence, we checked out of the small RV park we were staying in on the outskirts of town, and moved into the narrow alley behind her small casita off Old Santa Fe Trail. With our talk out of the way, there was ample time to play and see the sights. We explored the Indian pueblo at Taos and stopped at the chapel in Chimayo to collect some healing mud. Then, with our schedule beckoning us westward, we said goodbye and hit the road at a clip.

On our way to California, we planned to make an important stop in Arizona to visit a close friend who had recently settled in the small town of Cornville, just outside Sedona. We had met Christine Hartman one Sunday morning at Unity services in Lincoln Center, when she had come in late and been forced to take one of the few remaining seats, which just happened to be next to me. Though I had noticed her before on several occasions--she bore an uncanny resemblance to Lauren Hutton--the slight gap between her two, front teeth, I suppose--this particular Sunday was the first time we had ever had the pleasure of meeting face to face. When the service was over, we invited her back to the apartment for brunch, along with a small group of friends.

As fate would have it, Christine was a devout follower of Ramtha, the 35,000 year- old, spirit guide channeled through J. Z. Knight, and much of our first afternoon together was spent sharing our metaphysical philosophies and listening to Christine expound upon Ramtha's latest teachings. Having recently read *The Ramtha White Book*, I found the conversation rather intriguing and was eager to find out more.

Over the next few months, we continued to see each other at Sunday services, and our friendship steadily deepened. Many subsequent Sunday afternoons were spent together watching Ramtha videos, among which were a number predicting catastrophic earth changes and economic and political upheaval.

Obviously, prophesies such as these were not entirely alien to me. I had been exposed to them any number of times in my own metaphysical studies, and in my fundamentalist upbringing as a child. While Christine was firmly convinced that we were on the edge of an apocalypse, I vacillated between denial and the recognition that unless things changed, and changed soon, many of the Ramtha's predictions had a distinct possibility of coming true. The future wasn't written in stone, however; that much I was sure of. *The point of power was in the present. The future took shape from there.*

Unlike me, Wil was saddled with none of the fundamentalist baggage I was, and wasn't the least bit willing to consider that these catastrophic predictions might actually occur. He considered such information to be entirely negative, and in time began distancing himself from Christine over the issue. In fact, Wil refused to worry about the future at all. His attitude was that he would be exactly where he needed to be, even if some horrible event did happen to occur.

Our differing take on the issue soon became the basis for many heated arguments between us, with me wanting to react in fear by running away, and him wanting to ignore the information altogether. With such polarized reactions, it was impossible to find a middle ground.

As time went by, Wil found it increasingly difficult to avoid being drawn into an argument with Christine whenever she was around. Despite his every attempt to steer clear of any topic that might provoke her, when it came to her beliefs Christine was not the type of person to simply let things be. She aggressively challenged his opinions and accused him of being in denial. She prodded him at every turn, searching for cracks in his resistance. Finally, the stain of her aggressive processing drove a wedge into their relationship.

While I, too, sometimes felt the same strain Wil did whenever Christine was around, more than him I could embrace her company as an opportunity to examine my deepest held beliefs and attitudes. If there was any denial going on, you could always be certain it would surface in discussions with Christine. And to be perfectly frank, despite the occasional discomfort her processing sometimes caused, I admired how intensely committed she was.

Like a moth to a flame, I was morbidly fascinated by the dread Ramtha's predictions revealed in me, and could see clearly where my fundamentalist demons had not yet been fully exorcised. In Christine's presence, it was apparent that part of me still believed in the inevitability of divine retribution, no matter what we might try and do to redeem ourselves.

This guilt-induced fear clouded my true desire to leave New York City for a simpler life on the land, with the irrational fear that I would die in some inevitable apocalypse if I didn't. More than just the fear of simply losing my life was an underlying terror that my very soul would somehow be destroyed in the process. It welled up in my chest and threatened to strangle me in its gloomy grasp. I wanted to run away and hide, knowing full well I would simply carry the fear with me wherever I went. I would remain a prisoner of my conflicting beliefs until I was somehow able to let them go.

Over time, Christine came to reject New York City and every aspect of her life there, including her marriage to a wealthy, Jewish businessman. In this regard, she was like a newly reformed smoker, prone to making harsh judgments against anyone continuing in the lifestyle she herself had only recently rejected, and was determined to leave New York City to avoid being caught up in the chaos Ramtha predicted would occur.

Leaving her former life behind, Christine embarked upon a six-month trip around the country, in part, to visit old friends and relations and partly in search of a suitable place to relocate to. Eventually, she had fallen in love with Sedona, Arizona, a small, resort town situated in the high desert, two and a half hours north of Phoenix, surrounded by some of the most beautiful, red-rock formations in the world. The area was a magnet for every new-age teaching imaginable, including some of the best and the worst. *Hello the good news. Hello the bad. The truth lies between the lines!*

Convinced that she had finally found a community of like-minded souls, Christine returned to New York and sublet her apartment, collected her belongings and returned to Sedona to live. Once there, she had quickly found a small house in one of the fertile areas of the nearby Verde Valley and signed a lease.

Despite the obvious difficulties involved in our relationship, Wil and I were looking forward to visiting Christine in her new home and seeing firsthand the new life she had carved out for herself, far from New York City. Not surprisingly, I was secretly hoping that Sedona might be a place Wil and I could settle into after we had finished our tour in the Winnebago--whenever that might be.

On leaving Santa Fe, we drove for a full day without stopping, reaching the outskirts of Flagstaff, twenty five miles north of Sedona, just as the sun was beginning to set behind the mountains. From there, we headed south along scenic highway 89A. The abundant alpine forest offered a welcomed respite from the arid landscape we had just traversed, and we were grateful for the relief from the heat.

About twenty miles outside of Flagstaff, the thick, pine forest gave way to reveal wide-open skies and breath-taking views of the mountains in the distance. The narrow serpentine road veered sharply to the right and down, and a canyon of incredible beauty opened before us.

I downshifted into low and steered the Winnebago down into the gaping chasm, following the precarious road along a narrow ledge carved into solid rock. At the bottom of the canyon, a stream ran along-side the road, beyond which majestic walls of granite rose up thousands of feet in the air, sparkling in the rays of the late-day sun. The surreal beauty of the place was unlike anything Wil and I had ever seen.

As we made our way along the gently sloping floor of the canyon, the color of the rocks overhead deepened in hue, causing the already lush, green forest to appear even greener than it was. Through the thick underbrush on either side of the road, houses and an occasional resort or inn could be seen tucked in among the rocks. We slowed our pace to a crawl, allowing ourselves plenty of time to appreciate the cool, fresh air and spectacular scenery. Then, rounding a sharp bend in the road and crossing over a narrow bridge, the steep canyon walls fell away and the splendid, blood-red, rock formations of Sedona loomed before us in the distance.

Along the horizon, spectacular buttes rose up in distinct formations, each named for the particular shape it resembled. There was Bell Rock, named for its likeness to the Liberty Bell in Philadelphia, and Cathedral Rock, its towering spires suggesting some ancient, mythical place of worship. My favorite formation was Coffee Pot Rock, in the whimsical shape of a percolator. All around us, the rock face created fleeting, fanciful images: the profile of an Indian; a crouching tiger; constantly transforming like clouds in the lengthening shadows of the day.

"Can you imagine living here?" I gushed.

Wil rolled his eyes and refused to dignify my outburst with an answer. "Let's stop and get a cup of coffee," came his deadpan response.

We pulled into a small coffee shop located directly in front of Coffee Pot Rock, and ordered two cups of coffee and took a quick, cursory look at the map. With only about ten miles to go before reaching Christine's house, we wanted to make sure we had the directions clearly in our minds.

Back on the road, we followed the highway south out of town, and made a left hand turn onto Page Springs Road. Then, rounding a tight curve, we spotted Christine's house on our right. I hit the brakes and wrestled the Winnebago into the narrow, gravel driveway. For the sake of the cats which lay prostrate on the floor of the RV, suffering from the unaccustomed heat, we pulled in under the shade of some nearby cottonwood trees and stopped. Hearing the sound of our engine, Christine ran outside to greet us.

Our reunion was a happy one, filled with hugs and kisses and generous peals of laughter. With so much to catch up on, we hardly touched the simple meal Christine had prepared. Between bites, she gave us a blow by blow description of the myriad challenges she had faced in moving to Sedona alone. That being said, her ready smile and radiant glow made it more than obvious that she was happy with her decision.

"I haven't regretted the move for a minute," she assured us, finishing her story and turning her attention to us. "OK, now tell me everything that's happened to you guys since we last saw each other in New York," she insisted. "I want to hear everything. And I do mean *everything!*"

We started at the beginning and didn't stop until she had been fully brought up to speed. Then, with the exertion of the long trip beginning to catch up to us, we retired to the front porch and settled into the swing, looking silently out over the pasture below, in the direction of the setting sun. The cool, night air reverberated with the sound of crickets and the occasional soft whinnying of a horse. Almost immediately, Wil fell asleep and began to snore.

We stayed with Christine for the next several weeks, resting our road-weary bones and taking time out to become better acquainted with the area. "It's actually a lot nicer living in Cornville than Sedona," Christine explained. "Sedona's energy is so intense that it throws anyone who stays there for more than a couple of days into process. That's why the Indians used it as a healing retreat. They'd go there and let the energy purify their spirits, but after a few weeks they'd leave. They weren't meant to be there, long term."

Wil and I agreed that this might help to explain some of the more interesting characters Christine had introduced us to in the days immediately following our arrival.

A week into our stay, we spoke before a small gathering Christine had organized at the local community center, and hung around afterwards to chat with two women from the audience she had recently befriended. Mona Fore, a psychic, minister and brilliant, but eccentric herbalogist, had moved to Sedona with her dear friend, Jane, and opened a healing center called *The Golden Phoenix*, where for the last two years HIV positive people from all over the country had flocked to partake of a strict regimen of detoxification and indoctrination into the spiritual and psychological aspects of healing AIDS.

The Center was run very much like a boot camp, and many of the techniques employed there were borrowed from the Bhagwan Rajneesh, whom the two women had once been loyal devotees of. After touring the center's rather rustic facilities perched high atop a mesa near the small town of Rim Rock, Wil and I took a stack of brochures and promised we'd refer people to them whenever it was appropriate--something we rarely ever did. While we *were* quick to recommend a holistic approach to healing, we were cautious when it came to recommending specific practitioners. It just didn't seem prudent unless we had experienced their work first hand.

We spent the next few days investigating the local real estate market and familiarizing ourselves with the area, just in case we decided to move there at some point in the future. We also decided that we needed a car, preferably one with four-wheel drive. After all, the pair of clunky bicycles we'd bought in Miami didn't always fit the bill.

A few days later, we piled into Christine's small, red roadster and made the two and a half hour drive to Phoenix, where we plied through almost every automobile dealership on Camelback Road. After a great deal of agonizing, we decided on a Suzuki Samurai, in a color perfectly coordinated with the Winnebago. The small jeep-like vehicle was light and compact, and practical for hauling things around. Now, whenever we arrived in a new place, planning to stay for a while, we could park the Winnebago and run our errands in the Suzuki. No more pedaling around on bicycles for us!

With the addition of the Suzuki, Wil and I had managed to equip ourselves with just about every convenience two people could possibly want or need. We had a fully equipped motor home, a computer, a printer, a VCR, two television sets, two bikes and a Suzuki Samurai. As we pulled out of the dealer's lot onto Camelback Road with our new purchase trailing behind us like a love-sick puppy, a passing motorist, his voice tinged with envy, yelled up at us from out of his car window: "Why don't you guys get a job!" he hollered, indignantly.

Wil and I looked at each other and burst out laughing. "That poor sucker doesn't get it, does he?" Wil chuckled, giving me a knowing look. "This is our job, man! There's just no difference between our work and our play."

He was right, of course. There wasn't an iota of difference, anymore, between our lifestyle and our lives. We loved what we were doing and we were doing what we loved! We had transcended the work-a-day world and were living in a state of grace.

16 Charlie, Louise and Oprah

AFTER STAYING IN SEDONA FOR THE better part of a month, Wil and I were itching to get back out on the road again. We had just buckled up and were pulling out of Christine's rutted, gravel driveway when the phone rang from inside the house, bringing our much anticipated departure to a temporary halt.

"Wait," Christine called to us from the front porch. "Don't go yet. It's probably for you." She turned and went inside to answer the phone, and reappeared in the doorway moments later. "Its Toni, from New York," she mouthed, motioning for Wil to come and take the call. "She said something about a man in Los Angeles who's interested in helping you with the California leg of your trip."

Wil looked at me and arched an eye brow. "Maybe this is the break we've been waiting for," he speculated. "We could sure use some help about now."

He jumped down from the cab and followed Christine into the house. I shifted the Winnebago in park and set the emergency brake, leaving the engine running. After fifteen minutes had elapsed and Wil still hadn't come back outside, I contemplated going in and getting him. Before I could unbuckle my seat belt, he emerged onto the porch and paused to kiss Christine goodbye.

"Be careful," she yelled, as Wil crawled back into his seat and buckled himself in. "Don't forget to let me hear from you guys every once in a while."

Her voice was barely audible over the roar of the engine. I depressed the accelerator and the Winnebago lurched forward and out onto Page

Springs Road, the Suzuki trailing behind it. We were on our way to the
Golden State and the west coast leg of our adventure!

Charlie Swanson, the man who Toni had called about, was a free-
lance producer with a distinct predilection for projects of a metaphysical
nature, particularly those involving gay and lesbian issues. His interest had
been piqued by a recent encounter with Anita, who was in Los Angeles
interviewing his employer, Dr. Laurence Badgley, the naturopathic
physician and author of *Healing AIDS Naturally*, for her documentary,
AIDS Alive. Resonating with the little he had learned about us from her,
he had decided to find out more. Now, a connection had been made and
a face to face meeting was planned for San Diego, later in the week.

"I'm pretty well-connected in the California spiritual community,"
Charlie had boasted to Wil, wasting little time in getting to the point.
"I guess what I really called to find out is if there's any way I could be of
assistance to you on your visit to California?"

Obviously, there were any number of things he could do, and Wil
was more than happy to give him a laundry list of suggestions. By the
time the conversation ended, Charlie had agreed to organize our entire
itinerary in California, using his extensive state-wide connections. The
first in the series of talks he arranged was at the MCC in San Diego, two
weeks from the day of his and Wil's conversation, followed immediately
by another at the Church of Religious Science in Huntington Beach, one
week after that. He was also working on several other engagements, in
and around Los Angeles, and one in San Francisco.

When we met him, Charlie was already involved in a number of
worthy projects, the most noteworthy being a holistic AIDS conference
he was producing for Dr. Badgley in Los Angeles, later in the fall.
Incorporating Wil and me into his plans, he invited us to participate in
a long-term survivor panel, along with a couple of other opinionated New
Yorkers: Michael Callen, the outspoken AIDS activist and founding
member of Act-Up, and our good friend and cohort, Niro Assistent.
He also suggested that we consider including his boss, Dr. Badgley, in
our engagements around the state as a way of giving our message the
added validity of a doctor's endorsement, for those who might otherwise
dismiss it.

"Nothing like the word of a doctor to make people stand up and take notice," he argued. "I think it would be a really smart move on your part."

After our experience in Nashville with the angry young man demanding to see copies of our blood work, we both agreed that Charlie's suggestion made a lot of sense. We didn't want to align ourselves with just any doctor, however, but one who was at least *open* to our ideas. Before giving Charlie the go ahead, we read Dr Badgley's book to familiarize ourselves with his philosophy and reassure ourselves that he was a good match.

"We think it's a great idea," we informed him, after we had finished reading the book. "I think the three of us would make a very powerful team."

From the onset of what would ultimately be a rather lengthy association, Wil and I felt a strong affinity for Charlie and his innate, spiritual sensibilities, not to mention an appreciation for the incredible resource he represented in terms of his ability to further our dream of marketing our message to the entire country. In the days following our first face to face meeting in San Diego, we spent as much time as possible with him, brainstorming various ways of expanding our work and sharing our individual insights into the larger process of planetary transformation. Just like us, Charlie also shared the same strong conviction that AIDS was an integral part of a much larger process than most people currently realized, and that it was important for the gay community to hear such a message.

"Throughout history, gay people have traditionally been the shamans and healers," he argued. "AIDS is a wakeup call for the entire community, to remind us of the role we were meant to play in the larger human drama. The sooner people begin to understand this, the quicker this epidemic will end. I think you and Wil have an important role to play in this, and I want to help you any way I can."

After our talks in San Diego and Huntington Beach, we accepted Charlie's invitation to spend time with him in Los Angeles, until arrangements for our subsequent talks could be finalized. After a leisurely drive up the coast from San Diego, Wil and I threaded our way through the heavy, Los Angeles traffic to the address Charlie had given us, and parked the Winnebago out front. I killed the engine and climbed out and stretched my legs, while Wil clamored up the steps to the house and rang the bell.

Moment later, the door to the craftsman-style bungalow swung open, and Charlie appeared in the doorway. He greeted us enthusiastically and ushered us into a tastefully decorated foyer.

"Let's go upstairs," he suggested, once the usual pleasantries had been dispensed with. There's something I want you to see."

On the way up the stairs, I couldn't help but notice the sensual artwork hanging along the landing. The juxtaposition of blatantly erotic themes, with Charlie's obvious spiritual focus, made for a startling but not entirely unfamiliar contrast. The relationship between sex and spirituality had always presented a paradox to me, and like many people of my generation I was still in the process of sorting it out. The two weren't mutually exclusive, however; that much I was certain of. They were opposite ends of the same street, and you had to embrace them both if you wanted to be healthy, happy and whole. Obviously, Charlie was pretty much of the same mind.

"Oh, those belong to my house-mate," he explained, seeing me eyeing the pictures. "He's the national distributor for all things Tom of Finland. Do you like his work?" I blushed and admitted that I did.

Over the next several days, we visited a number of L.A.'s considerable points of interest, including the usual tourist sites like Grauman's Chinese Theatre and the La Brea tar pits. Charlie also introduced us to a number of his closest friends: an eclectic mélange of psychics, healers and relentlessly positive new age types--all metaphysical in the extreme. Wil and I felt strangely normal by comparison.

Afterwards, it dawned on me what some of my friends in New York had meant when they had politely suggested that I 'belonged' in California. My reality had never been fully anchored in the east coast's stuffy establishmentarianism, and I was much more in philosophical alignment with the left coast. What I *still* hadn't decided was whether their comments had been meant as a compliment or not. Either way, it was hard to deny the truth. Try as I might to master a hard-edged, New York attitude, just when I least expected it my basic naiveté seemed to shine through--much to my chagrin. As much as I aspired to it, I simply wasn't a cynical person.

Our talk, several nights later, in a small church in West Hollywood, drew a modest but enthusiastic crowd of mostly PWA's and their caregivers. As Charlie had predicted, the inclusion of Dr. Badgley into the program seemed to enhance the appeal of our message by providing it with an overall balance that had been lacking before. In essence, Wil and I provided the inspiration while the good doctor provided the medical expertise to back it up--to give it legs, so to speak. Thanks to Charlie, we had managed to create a perfectly balanced presentation of medicine and metaphysics.

The highlight of our stay in Los Angeles came a few nights later at the Hay Ride in West Hollywood Park, the large, weekly support group led by the affirmation diva herself, Louise L. Hay. This huge gathering of mostly gay men with HIV and AIDS, and their supporters, was famous nationwide as both a healing circle and a stellar social event, and had been the inspiration for every other healing circle of its kind in the country, including the one that Wil and I belonged to in New York City.

As one of the primary instigators of the new-age sensibility that had only recently emerged within the HIV/AIDS community, Louise Hay's work had had a major impact on both our lives, and on the lives of many of the people we knew and loved. Louise had been the first person either of us had heard say AIDS could be healed, and that one simple statement had made all the difference in the world.

Before she stepped forward to challenge the status quo, the only message we had ever heard was a relentless drumbeat of *die...die... die*, and that message had come from every quarter imaginable. Her courageous stand single-handedly launched the self-healing movement and established her as its patron saint. For Wil and me, the opportunity of visiting Louise at the Hay Ride in Los Angeles, was comparable to a Catholic visiting the Pope in the Vatican in Rome. We were nervous and excited, and very much in awe.

Midway through the evening, Louise introduced us to the group and asked if we'd like to share a bit about our unusual trip around the country. We obliged, naturally, and spoke briefly about our spiritual philosophy and its impact on our health, and the way our unusual trip had come about.

"We really didn't start out with anything like this in mind when we left New York six months ago," I confessed. "We mostly just wanted to get out of the city and decompress from all the stress. But almost from the beginning, the trip seemed to take on a life of its own and we were swept along for the ride. Before long, invitations to speak started coming in from all around the country and we could hardly refuse the offers. It felt like we had been drafted by the Universe, actually, like we didn't really have a choice. After the Harmonic Convergence, it was as though we had been shot full-force out of some sort of powerful cosmic slingshot."

My last remark drew a smattering of laughter from the friendly crowd. Obviously, more than a few people in the audience could relate to what I was saying. Maybe they hadn't been propelled out onto the road in a Winnebago like Wil and I, but they had been catalyzed into action, in one way or another, by the same compelling sense of urgency. In a sense, we had all been shot out of the same cosmic slingshot, whether we recognized it or not.

At the end of the evening, Louise invited us to join her and her assistant, Joseph, for a bite to eat at a trendy little bistro in West Hollywood. We accepted, naturally, thrilled at the prospect of deepening our fledgling friendship even further. Over pasta and wine, we reminisced about the first time the three of us had met at her workshop in New York, and our recent encounter at the AIDS, Medicine and Miracles conference in Boulder. There was also the trip to Chicago, the previous winter, to tape a segment of the Oprah Winfrey Show with Niro and Anita, and a couple of other long-term survivors from L.A.

The night before the taping, Louise had invited everyone up to her suite to discuss setting an intention for the show. It had been an intimate gathering of like-minded souls, and a consensus had quickly been reached about the thrust of the message we wanted to send: death wasn't the only option for people with HIV and AIDS, but you had to take the situation into your own hands. You had to be willing to make drastic changes in your life.

After everyone had an opportunity to share, Louise brought the evening to a close with a guided meditation, after which we dispersed to our separate rooms for a good night's sleep. The next morning, I had the additional opportunity of spending an hour alone with her in her suite, when by some strange twist of fate no one had been assigned to style her hair for the taping. Taking advantage of the oversight by Oprah's people, I had jumped in and volunteered my services, which ended up being a great way for us to get to know each other better. I thanked her for her courage and told her just how much her stand on AIDS had meant to Wil and me.

"Essentially, you saved our lives," I said, "And a lot of other people's, too."

Unfortunately, the taping, the following morning, proved to be a bitter disappointment for Wil and me. As we waited in the green room, nervously awaiting our cue to go on, the door had burst open and Oprah had swept into the room. She graciously thanked us for coming and then promptly proceeded to drop a bombshell.

"Unfortunately, we've overbooked the show, and only five of you will get to go on stage," she informed us. Never mind the fact there were seven of us in the green room--all there for the same reason--all expecting to appear on the Oprah Winfrey show with Louise.

"You two will have to participate from the audience," she said, indicating Wil and me with a quick sweep of her hand. Then, seeing the crestfallen look on both our faces, she tried to soften the blow. "I'll try to get to you from the audience, if I can," she back-pedaled, tactfully. "I'll see what I can do."

At the time, Wil and I had been bitterly disappointed by the unexpected turn of events. To make matters worse, we had cancelled a trip to the Virgin Islands to be in Chicago, where it happened to be somewhere in the neighborhood of ten degrees below zero--and that was before the wind-chill was factored in. Now, at the last possible minute, we had been bumped from the show and there wasn't a damn thing we could do about it.

"What a drag!" I moaned, as we were seated in the audience. "I can't believe something like this could happen!"

Nevertheless, it had happened. Eventually, we managed to put our disappointment behind us and throw our support to the others who had made it on stage. As the taping progressed, it was obvious that the gist of our message was being delivered anyway, even if we weren't the ones to do it. Though the details of the other panelist's stories and perspectives varied slightly from our own, the underlying message was the same: you have the power to make a difference in your life, and in the course of your disease.

As consolation, during the last commercial break, Oprah came out into the audience and made her way up to where I was sitting on the aisle. Leaning her rather ample thigh against my shoulder in a gesture of support and familiarity, she thrust the microphone in my face.

"When we come back on the air, you'll have about a minute to say anything you'd like," she whispered. "Make the most of it!"

Moments later, we were back on the air. As the closing credits scrolled across the screen, I seized upon my 15 seconds of fame.

"I have a book coming out sometime early next year," I plugged myself, shamelessly. "It's called *Beyond AIDS*, and it's a story about my partner's and my spiritual journey after our diagnosis with AIDS in 1985." Never mind the fact that I hadn't finished writing it yet. As far as I was concerned, when I did finish it--and I would--Oprah owed me another chance to be on her show.

Now, here in Los Angeles, one year later and six months into our road trip, we had once again crossed paths with Louise Hay. Though we had no way of knowing it at the time, she was merely the first of a rather lengthy list of prominent people in the healing arts we would collaborate with in the weeks and months ahead. Encounters with Dr. Bernie Siegel, Deepak Chopra, Dr. Elizabeth Kubler Ross and Marianne Williamson lay waiting in the wings, in the not too distant future. For now, however, we were content to bask in the reflected glory of a lady we considered a bonified hero in the ongoing war on AIDS. As far as we were concerned, it just didn't get any better than this!

⚘

17 Radiant Light Ministries

WITH OUR VISIT TO LOS ANGLES drawing to an end, we were expected next in San Francisco, where we were scheduled to speak at a controversial new-age church by the name of *Radiant Light Ministries*. Both of us were excited by the prospect, having stumbled across it by accident nearly two years earlier during a brief visit to San Francisco on personal business. On the way back to our motel after breakfast, the day we were scheduled to fly back to New York, we had happened upon a large, enthusiastic crowd milling around outside a quaint, Bavarian-styled building on upper Market Street, just off of Sanchez Street in the Castro, and stopped to see what all the commotion was about.

"We're waiting to get into Sunday Celebration," a cheerful young woman explained, when I asked what all the commotion was about. "It's like church, but a whole lot more fun."

Back in our motel room, I had an intuitive hunch that the church we had just stumbled across might be something we'd both enjoy experiencing, and had convinced Wil to go back with me and check it out. He had given in, as usual, and walked the short distance back to where a few stragglers were still milling around outside the building.

"Is this your first time here?" a polite, young man asked us, as we approached the entrance to the building. "You'll need a name tag to get inside."

We gave him our names and waited patiently while he wrote them down.

"Here you go," he smiled, handing us each a square of sticky-backed paper with our name printed on it in bold, blue lettering. "Have a good time. And welcome to Radiant Light Ministries!"

We slapped our name tags on and climbed the steep flight of stairs to the main auditorium on the second floor. Inside, a crowd of at least 300, mostly lesbian and gay men, stood noisily socializing with their friends. We paused in the doorway to the cavernous room, searching for a place to sit.

"Over there," Wil said, indicating a pair of empty chairs, halfway down the aisle and to our right. "Follow me."

We had been in our seats for less than a minute when Reverend Carol Webber, the red-headed, assistant minister, bounded onto the stage and called for the room to settle down. "Welcome to Sunday Celebration," she enthused. "To ground ourselves and get back into our bodies this morning, we're going to do the Radiant Light Roar. I want everyone to stand up and bend over and touch their toes, and let out a big roar on the way up. We're going to do this three times, OK? Are you ready?"

Obviously, everyone was. The words were barely out of her mouth before the entire congregation was up out of their chairs and onto their feet, ready to follow orders. Obviously, they had done this kind of thing before.

Wil turned and gave me a withering stare. "What in the hell is going on?" he snapped, his eyes flashing suspiciously, certain that I had involved him in some kind of dangerous cult.

I shrugged and innocently rolled my eyes. "I don't know," I protested, stifling a giggle. "Just go along with it and see what happens."

We followed the lead of the people around us and bent over and touched our toes, and let out three, deep-bellied roars on the way up. The building shook from the sudden release of energy, and a delicious jolt of energy shot up my spine. Before I could react, the music started and the crowd spilled out into the aisles and began dancing to Madonna's hit, *Open your heart to me*. The floor groaned under the weight of 300 swaying bodies.

After Madonna, several more selections, obviously chosen for the inspirational value of their lyrics, followed in quick succession. Then, finally, the music ended and the celebrants took their seats.

With that, Carol Webber gestured toward the back of the auditorium. "Without further ado, I give you Reverend Matt Garrigan," she announced grandly. Amid searing whistles and wild applause, Reverend Matt Garrigan bounded up the aisle and onto the stage, the crystal earring in his left earlobe sparkling as he swept past. He greeted the crowd and mugged self-consciously several times, before composing himself and launching into a sermon based loosely on the teachings of *A Course in Miracles.*

"He reminds me of a queer version of Marianne Williamson," Wil commented later, as we were discussing the experience in a cab on our way to the airport. "I was actually quite impressed. He's very good at what he does."

Now, scarcely more than a year later, Wil and I were scheduled to stand on the very same podium and share our message of hope and healing. Needless to say, we were grateful and amazed by the impeccable string of synchronicities that had conspired to make such an event possible--the fact that Carol Webber had turned out to be an old friend of Charlie's and had championed his request on our behalf.

Every day, there were more and more signs like this, pointing to the fact that life was a process we could trust. From where I stood, Wil's trust seemed unshakeable, and I was a little jealous of his unquestioning faith. Trust remained a particularly thorny issue for me, having been violated in childhood by a damning religious dogma, and later reinforced by society's overt homophobia, even before I came out of the closet and acknowledged my sexuality.

These early experiences had served to convince me that the only thing I could truly depend on was myself; that I was basically alone in a hostile universe and my survival was up to me. In taking these conclusions to heart, I had operated out of a powerful control mode ever since, until AIDS came along and shattered my shaky premise. I now knew that trust was the primary issue I had come into this lifetime to heal, and that the lack of it had been a major contributor to my immune dysfunction. I had made great strides in healing the issue, but, as this trip had continually shown me, I still had a long way to go.

As the most carefully crafted of any of the events Wil and I had been involved in thus far, thanks to Charlie and the enthusiastic support of a crack Radiant Light team, our lecture at Radiant Light Ministries was an overwhelming success. On the night in question, the Swedish American Hall was packed to capacity with more than 300 enthusiastic supporters.

Those who straggled in late were forced to stand in the back, or sit on the floor in the aisles.

As usual, Wil was the first to speak. After Rev. Matt had finished his glowing introduction, Wil thanked the overflow audience for coming and delved directly into his remarks.

"We have lost sight of the natural order of things," he began, "and healing is first and foremost a completely natural process. It's not something you have to make happen, but something that happens naturally when you stop interfering with the process."

"The Universe isn't indifferent to us, either," he continued. "It isn't a black hole that you fall into and disappear. The odds are stacked in favor of living, not dying. If you cut your finger, you don't have to do anything to make it heal except keep it clean, maybe, and not pick at it. There's a natural intelligence at work inside your body that knows how to heal.

"It's no different with AIDS. You simply need to remove whatever barriers you have placed in the way of healing. And those barriers are not just physical, like taking drugs or smoking cigarettes or having meaningless sex, but emotional and mental, like toxic guilt and anger and limiting beliefs."

When the applause had died away, it was my turn to address the crowd. "Here's the better half of my team," Wil joked, "--the Yin to my Yang--my partner of more than a decade, George Melton."

I sprinted onto the stage and was immediately assaulted by a shock-wave of applause, followed quickly by a succession of long, loud, approving whistles. "Thank you," I blushed. "Especially you guys who whistled." That set off another round of whistles and a smattering of laughter.

I removed the microphone from its stand and walked to the edge of the stage. "Many people have asked me how I *know* what I'm saying is true, and that's a legitimate question," I began. "Of course, as I've said a number of times before, what I'm going to share with you here tonight are *my* truths, first and foremost, and not anyone else's. What I try to do, in sharing my story, is inspire you to explore for yourself how the ideas I talk about intersect with your personal reality."

"Ideas, in and of themselves, don't heal anyone," I continued. "They must be grounded in your being through your own experience if they're to be of any actual value. This is where the importance of a spiritual discipline comes into play. Prayer and meditation, and affirmations and visualization are the tools by which your faith--or your beliefs-- become the reality of your experience."

"One of the primary ways I've tried to accomplish this in my own life is through studying my dreams; you can learn a lot about the nature of reality, and about your relationship to your higher self, through doing dream work." I counseled. "As a student of *The Seth Material*, I started studying my dreams and following some of the suggestions laid out in Jane Robert's book, *Dreams and Projections of Consciousness*."

"The first step was simply this: before going to bed each night, I would give myself the suggestion, *I will remember my dreams*. In a week or so, I was remembering them easily and started writing them down. If you don't write your dreams down--or *earth* them, so to speak--the information slips away very, very quickly."

"At the same time, I started to experiment with my sleep cycles, breaking them down into four-hour intervals, more like a cat sleeps-- whenever they feel the need. This begins to weaken the rigid barriers between your conscious and unconscious, waking and dreaming selves, which Seth says are kept firmly in place by the stark divisions we draw between our waking and sleeping lives. The way time is structured in the civilized world is actually unnatural, you see. In that respect, the animals have a lot to teach us."

"Before long, I was having lucid dreams almost every single night. A lucid dream, for those of you who might not know what that is, is when you're dreaming but you're aware that you are. For most people, this happens early in the morning when you're just about to wake up. You know it's time to get up, but you're having a dream that you like so you stay with it and stretch it out for a bit longer. Well, that's lucid dreaming, and what distinguishes it from most dreams is your awareness that you're dreaming, and your ability to manipulate it at will."

I paused for a moment, before continuing with my train of thought. "This level of dreaming--lucid dreaming, consciously explored--can trigger an actual blending of your higher consciousness and your everyday, physically-rooted perceptions--in other words, your ego and your higher self. It facilitates waking up. And what you're waking up to is an awareness that the physical world you live in and believe is so solid and real, is literally a projection of your own consciousness, just like a dream!"

I was on a roll now, and couldn't have stopped if I had wanted to. "In dreams, you think you have a body, you think you are somewhere, and you think things are happening to you over which you have no control. Yet, the truth is that you're safe in bed and *you're making the entire thing up.* When you finally recognize your dreams for what they are, you become *lucid* within them. And when you finally recognize your physical experience as your own creation, you become *conscious* within it. When you become conscious in your life, you can create it in any way you choose."

When I had finished, Wil joined me on the platform and the two of us took questions from the audience for the better part of an hour. Interest in our message was running higher than ever, and neither of us wanted to bring the evening to a close until every question had been responded to in depth.

"This question is addressed to George," came the voice of a thin, young man, standing at one of the microphones in the aisle. "I was interested in what you had to say about dreaming," he said. "What I want to know is this: how do you actually recognize that you're dreaming? I mean, how do you know?"

"That's a good question," I complimented him on his inquiry. "You recognize you're dreaming the same way you do in everyday life: you pay attention and notice when things don't seem quite right; when some event presents itself that's totally out of the realm of reality as you understand it."

"For instance, in a dream you might find yourself at home in bed, but your boss is sitting at his desk where your chest-of-drawers would normally be. Well, that's a pretty good clue that you're dreaming; your boss's desk isn't normally in your bedroom. But you have to be paying attention, you see. When you notice something like this, say to yourself, *this can't be real, I must be dreaming.* When you do, you'll become lucid within the dream. Your waking self will inject itself into the dream state, alongside your dreaming self."

"But there's an even more important parallel to this in everyday life," I continued. "Again, you have to be paying attention; you have to remain conscious. So let's say you go to your doctor and he tells you that you have AIDS, that it's incurable, and that you'll be dead in six months and there's nothing you can do about it. Well, if you have any spiritual consciousness at all then, first of all, you'll know there's no such thing as an incurable illness. So again, you'll say to yourself, *this isn't right; I must be dreaming.* When you do, you'll have invited your higher self--the part of you that exists outside of time and space, and understands what's *really* going on here--into the situation with you. And it will say to you something like this: *There are no incurable illnesses, George, or whatever you name happens to be. AIDS is simply a message from your inner being, telling you that you need to make changes in your life, that you're on a dead end course and that there is more to you than you are currently allowing yourself to express.*"

"Then, instead of killing the messenger, you might respond to it instead. You might want to ask yourself, *what are the thoughts and feelings and perceptions that have given rise to this unreal experience in my life?* I assure you that if you ask, you will always get an answer."

"Thank you," the young man demurred, relinquishing the microphone to the person behind him. "That makes a lot of sense."

The next question was for Wil. "What is your experience with visualization? Do you think it really helps?" the questioner asked. Wil paused a moment to collect his thoughts, before verbalizing his answer.

"The truth is that you're visualizing all the time," he began. "There's a constant movie going on in your mind, 24 hours a day. So it's not really a question of whether you're visualizing or not, but *what* you're visualizing that really counts. The mental images that you focus on are either helping or hindering your healing process, and you need to be aware of that."

The young man seemed satisfied with the answer, and quickly took his seat. Questions continued for another half hour or so, until finally there was no one else waiting at the microphone. Sensing an opportunity to bring the evening to a closed, we thanked the audience for their attentiveness and relinquished the stage to Rev. Matt. Once again, he thanked us for coming and launched into a brief explanation of how our trip around the country was being financed.

"We want to take a love offering this evening, as a show of our support for the work these two men are doing to bring about the end of disease on this planet," he announced. "I trust you will look into your hearts and be generous with your gifts."

An offering was taken, followed by a brief musical interlude. Then, the treasurer approached the podium and handed Rev. Matt a check. He glanced at it, briefly, and called us back onto the stage.

"I want to honor you with this check for $2,500.00," he announced proudly, handing Wil the slip of paper. "Please accept this as a token of our appreciation for the work you are doing on behalf of the end of AIDS. And give yourselves a hand!" he added, turning to acknowledge the audience for their show of generosity. The room burst into applause.

For Wil and me, accustomed to running a deficit and dipping into our personal savings to keep things going, the generosity of the members of Radiant Light Ministries was a God-send. Their generous contributions brought our financial picture into the black, with enough left over to see us through the next several weeks. Once again, the Universe had offered us tangible proof of its support, just when we needed it most.

18 The Pacific Northwest

WITH NOTHING MORE ON OUR SCHEDULE in California, it was time for some much needed rest and relaxation. With so much of our time spent in the glare of the spotlight, it was important to take periodic breaks to recharge our batteries and rest, particularly if we expected to be in peak form whenever the situation demanded it.

Before leaving the state, we decided to spend a little more time with Charlie, who in the few short months we had known him had become an invaluable member of our team. His vision for our work, and skill in making it a reality, was essential to our continued success, and we wanted to go over some of the ideas he had suggested.

Meanwhile, back in New York, Toni found herself increasingly overwhelmed by the volume of requests that came pouring in from all around the country, and was badly in need of a break. Essentially, the job she had volunteered for had grown beyond anything she was equipped to handle and still maintain her own busy life and career. Like so many other things about our trip, Charlie had come into our lives at the perfect time, offering to take over these duties and act as our full-time agent.

One of the first things he did was to create a press packet for potential sponsors, consisting of a brief biography of the two of us, a basic description of what they could expect from us, and a rough outline of our needs. This greatly reduced the amount of time Wil had to spend on the phone working out logistics with potential sponsors, and minimized the risk of any crucial details being overlooked. For the first time since leaving New York, we had an effective support structure in place. The pressure to keep everything running smoothly no longer fell on Wil. Now Charlie shouldered much of the burden.

With his obvious production skills, it occurred to me one evening during meditation that now might be a good time to seek Charlie's advice about the journal I had been keeping, which was increasingly taking on the appearance of a book. After all, I had announced I had a book coming out over a year ago on the Oprah Winfrey Show, and had even called it by name. It was time to get serious about making my boast a reality.

From the onset of our journey, Wil and I had been besieged by people wanting tapes and written material of our message. To meet the demand, we had duplicated a crude recording of one of our earliest talks, with excellent content but not the slightest semblance of professional production values. After listening to it, an appalled Charlie insisted on upgrading all of our material to a more professional look and quality. He also agreed to look over my manuscript and give me his opinion on its viability as a book.

Before leaving San Francisco, I mailed him a copy of the manuscript, not really expecting to hear back from him right away. Surprisingly, he was back to me in less than a week with a number of constructive suggestions for how I might better present our story.

"I think the manuscript has a lot of potential," he assured me, "but it needs a little work. I'm going to send you my notes, and you can see what you think."

Up until now, my attempts at writing had mostly consisted of personal accounts of my own experience--little more than that. Charlie felt that it was especially important that Wil's side of the story be told, and encouraged me to get to work on it right away. In the meantime, he promised to look around Los Angeles for a potential publisher.

His apparent enthusiasm for the project was immediately infectious. While I *had* fantasized about the possibility of *maybe, someday* publishing a book (doesn't everyone?), for the most part, the dream had always seemed a little beyond the realm of possibility. After all, I wasn't a writer and didn't have any academic credentials in the subject matter I was writing about. I was simply a hair colorist with HIV, who claimed to have had a spiritual awakening. That, and a dollar bill, would get me a ride on the subway.

Furthermore, I had heard horror stories about talented writers who had produced quality manuscripts and were never able to get them published. As such, it hardly seemed plausible that my amateurish endeavor would stand more than a snowball's chance in hell. Despite the odds against me, I found myself helpless to resist the siren call of Charlie's enthusiastic endorsement. In my mind's eye, I could see myself signing autographs for thousands of adoring fans, while hefty royalty checks came rolling in.

With little more than a week left before we planned to leave California, we headed south to be near Charlie, who was busy following up on a number of leads that had come in from the Pacific Northwest. As of yet, nothing solid had been confirmed. I took advantage of the lull in our schedule to work on the revisions Charlie had suggested, and consult with Wil for insight into his side of the story. Taking advantage of the balmy Southern California weather, we parked the Winnebago on a bluff overlooking a small, public beach north of San Diego, taking occasional time-outs from writing to lie in the sun and swim. We were focused on one thing and one thing only: completing the revisions and placing them in Charlie's hands by the end of the week.

To conserve money, we spent a number of nights in a rest stop on interstate 5, halfway between Los Angeles and San Diego. After working on the manuscript at the beach by day, we would head back to the rest stop for the night. The place was incredibly busy, filled with eighteen wheelers and carloads of scruffy people who were obviously living there on a permanent basis, and parking was at a premium. It also seemed to be a popular dropping-off point for illegal immigrants coming into the country from the nearby Mexican border.

After finding a spot as far away from the main area of activity as possible, we'd settle in and pull the blinds, and crank up the generator and tune into the nightly news. Safely ensconced within our cozy little home on wheels, I'd cook dinner and we'd polish off a bottle of wine, before drifting off to sleep, exhausted from the day's activities.

Unfortunately, a good night's sleep was not always easy to come by in such a public setting. On more than one occasion, we were jolted awake at two in the morning by a noisy big-rig parked alongside of us with its engine running; and on another by a heated altercation between an angry couple who had obviously imbibed a little too much alcohol. Despite the obvious drawbacks to the set up, it was hard to argue with the cost.

Any inconvenience was more than made up for by the availability of free parking, clean water, and a place to purge our tanks.

We took the irony of our situation in stride, laughing at ourselves and our ability to adapt to circumstances that not long ago would have been unimaginable. We were amazed at how far we had come in less than a year from our upscale lives in Manhattan, to living in a crowded rest stop in California.

"*To hell with circumstances,*" I thought to myself. "*At least we have each other.*" As far as I was concerned, that was the only thing that really mattered. We could weather anything life happened to throw our way as long as we had each other.

By the end of the week, I had completed the revisions to the manuscript and was ready to hand it back to Charlie for his inspection. With the job done, there was nothing standing in the way of our leaving for the Pacific Northwest. As we pulled away from the curb in front of Charlie's house after dropping the manuscript off on our way back through LA, the phone rang and he ran inside to answer it. The call was from an HIV support group in Vancouver, wanting to know if we would come and visit their fair city.

I waited in the Winnebago with the motor running while Wil rummaged through his calendar looking for the approximate dates we'd be in the area. After a moment or two, he gave Charlie a number of possible dates to choose from.

"We'll be in the area the last week in August through the first week in September," he said. "Anytime in between is good for us. And don't worry about Portland and Seattle. Once you hear back from them, I can iron out the details from on the road."

With another engagement penciled into our planner, we said goodbye and high-tailed it out of Los Angeles, following interstate 5 as it wound its way through the dusty, Central Valley of California. At San Francisco, we crossed over the Golden Gate Bridge and headed for the Marin coast and scenic Highway One. Unfortunately, it didn't take us long to realize just how tricky navigating the serpentine, coastal highway could be in a Winnebago pulling a jeep. Add to that, the ever-present fog that completely blocked our view of the ocean and nearby hills, and you begin to get the picture. We stuck it out for as long as we could, and at the Oregon border crossed over the coastal mountains and headed inland for some sun. Stopping at a scenic overlook to chart an alternate route, we spied Crater Lake on the map and decided to check it out.

We also decided that our current stretch of downtime presented the perfect opportunity for a 3-day fast to detoxifying our systems and lose a little weight. It hadn't always been possible for us to eat properly, lately, and after more than a few, egregious, dietary lapses in California, and too many big gulps from the 7-Eleven, we were both starting to look a little bloated around the waist. Vanity had always been a powerful motivator for the both of us, and we didn't like what we were seeing in the mirror. To prepare for the fast, we stopped at a little market in one of the small towns we passed through along the way, and picked up an ample supply of fresh water and an array of frozen juices. These were to be our only nutritional intake for the next three days.

From there, it was at best a full day's drive to our intended destination of Crater Lake. With no pressing engagements to concern ourselves with, we stop along the way to dangle our feet in the icy-cold stream running beside the narrow two-lane road. It was late in the afternoon when we arrived at the lake, and the sun was just beginning to disappear behind the mountains.

Nestled within the gigantic cone of a long-extinct volcano, Crater Lake shimmered before us in all its unearthly beauty, its mirrored surface perfectly reflecting the cloudless, blue, Oregon sky. Drinking in the surreal beauty of the scene as we moseyed around the edge-rim road, I was reminded of various accounts I had read of different UFO landing sites, and remarked to Wil that the deep waters of Crater Lake would certainly be the perfect place for a UFO to hide.

"You have such an imagination," he smirked, not the least bit convinced of my unusual theory. "The only aliens around here are you and me."

With the light fading fast, we parked near a large outcropping of rocks and hiked to the rim of the crater, and meditated until well after dark. Then, groping our way back down the trail, we fired up the Winnebago and set off in search of a suitable place to camp for the night.

Usually, we would have settled in and cooked ourselves something to eat, before turning in early for a good night's sleep. But tonight was a different story. Tonight was supposed to be the first night of our fast. Unfortunately, it took very little goading from me to convince Wil that fasting was not such a good idea--at least, not at this particular time. The long drive had left us both famished, and we were desperate for something to eat.

Appalled by our complete lack of resolve in the face of a few measly hunger pangs, we rifled through the Winnebago's compact kitchen in search of something to eat. Unfortunately, our efforts failed to produce even a single, edible crumb. We had no one to blame but ourselves, of course. We had deliberately not brought along any food with us as a way of enforcing our fast.

"Whose bright idea was this anyway," I demanded, "to come up here without any food? Was it yours?"

"No, it was yours, bright eyes," Wil growled, daring me to say another word. "What do you propose to do about it?"

By my own best estimate, it was at least fifty miles to the nearest town. Despite the distance and the lateness of the hour, we hesitated for only a nanosecond before pulling up stakes and heading off in search of food, hoping against hope to find a store in the area that might still be open for business. A few miles down the road, we happened upon a small general store just about to close for the night. With visions of a delicious home-cooked meal swirling in our heads, we bolted out of the Winnebago and ran inside, our mouths watering in anticipation of the feast to follow. Unfortunately, the store's shelves were mostly barren.

By this time, we were willing to eat just about anything. In desperation, we bought a pitiful loaf of obviously stale bread--the last one on the shelf--and some moldy lettuce, and combined it with an overripe and bruised tomato I found in the bottom of the fridge, and made ourselves a sandwich. Despite the fact that our little feast had the consistency of card board and basically had no taste, we attacked it as if it were the finest gourmet offering, and washed it down with juice we had purchased for the fast. Later, with our hunger satiated, we made a solemn vow to give up the belief you had to fast in order to be spiritual. Having already given up drugs, promiscuous sex and rock and roll, food was one sacrifice we were just not willing to make. After all, there was only so much a person could live without and be happy.

Putting the fasting fiasco behind us, we headed north through the forests of central Oregon, around Mt. Hood and down into the Columbia River Gorge. The power of the mighty river was immediately evident. On the far banks, in the state of Washington, massive bluffs rose up from the river's edge, dotted with houses built to take advantage of the view.

We stopped for gas and consulted the map, before heading off in the direction of a nearby state park on the river's edge. With Portland only about fifty miles away, and both of us still hoping for the opportunity to speak there, the location was ideal. We could be in the city in a matter of hours, as soon as Charlie gave us the go-ahead.

Unfortunately, our contact in Portland, an employee at one of the local AIDS organizations, kept sending mixed signals about our visit. On the one hand, he seemed eager to have us come and speak. On the other, was an underlying reluctance to finalize the necessary arrangements to make it happen. A few days later, Charlie called with some disappointing news. Due to a spate of recent deaths at the agency, our contact felt that a talk on healing at this particular time might offer false hope or in some way invalidate the recent losses the community had suffered.

"I just don't think a visit would be appropriate, right now," he admitted, finally. "We'll just have to take a pass on your offer, for now."

While neither Wil nor I subscribed to his particular concerns, we were certainly sensitive to the situation. After reviewing the facts, trying to ascertain how best to proceed from here, we decided to let go of the matter while leaving the door open for a future visit. As disappointed as we were by the missed opportunity, we knew that whenever this much resistance was encountered in setting up an event, it was usually a pretty, good indication that the community in question was not yet ready to hear our message. Obviously, if we wanted to speak in Portland, we would have to be patient and wait for the appropriate timing.

We had long since realized that not everyone was ready to embrace our message, and that it was pointless to try and force our way into a community when it wasn't. Besides, our pact with the Universe dictated that we were to only go where there was a willing and receptive audience. We didn't need to waste time or energy on places where there wasn't.

A few nights later, Charlie called to confirm an engagement at the Unity Church in Seattle, the following evening. *Gays and Lesbians in Unity*, with over five hundred active members, was led by a man named Jim Toevs, an up and coming leader in the Seattle, gay community. Since we had spoken in quite a number of Unity Churches already, we felt comfortable with the arrangement and eagerly accepted the invitation.

Sitting by the river watching people wind surf all day, was quickly losing its charm. We were anxious to get back to work.

As he hung up the phone, Wil couldn't help but comment on how quickly the Universe had filled the vacuum left by Portland's cancellation. "You see, George," he said, both reassuring and scolding me in the same breath. "Everything works out for the best when you just let go. It's a waste of time and energy to get your panties in a bunch about every little thing that doesn't go our way."

After breakfast the next morning, we broke camp and drove to Jim's house on Capitol Hill, and parked the Winnebago in the narrow alley behind his house. After a home-cooked meal with him and several members of the board, Jim drove us to the church and introduced us to the waiting crowd. As usual, Wil took the podium first. Continuing with the theme of visualization he had led with in San Francisco, he expanded it a little further.

"If you have AIDS, you undoubtedly know how to visualize," he began. "You don't really need to be taught how. Unfortunately, though, if you're like a lot of people, you're probably visualizing your imminent death and all the horrible opportunistic infections you might come down with--in general, terrorizing yourself to death."

"Now I'm not saying that this is necessarily going to kill you," he back-pedaled, gently. "I don't want you to misunderstand. But what I *am* saying is you need to realize that if you're obsessing on a blueprint for death your doctor has given you, or on one that you've made up yourself--or from things you've seen and heard in the media, or from other people's experiences--then you're magnetizing those scenario to you. You're creating chemical milieus in your body that are creating stress on your organs and depressing your immune system; you're unconsciously participating in your own demise. What you need to do is to become conscious of the mental images you're obsessing on and choose them a bit more carefully."

When it was my turn to speak, I picked up on the theme and ran with it.

"When you notice that you're terrorizing yourself with all those fearful thoughts Wil mentioned earlier, then take a little time to do something completely different," I began. "Instead of visualizing what you're afraid of, spend a few minutes each day visualizing *what you want.*

See your immune system functioning perfectly, with plenty of healthy T-cells gobbling up the virus. Picture your body glowing with health and filled with vitality. And picture the end of AIDS. See yourself on the cover of Time Magazine, celebrating the cure with all your friends. And make sure that you *feel* whatever it is you're picturing because *feelings are the energy that propels your visualizations into form.* The thought, or the male principle, married to the feeling, or the female principle, is the basis for conception. The stronger the emotion, the quicker your visualization will be out-pictured in your experience."

The following morning, we got up early and had a quick breakfast with Jim. From Seattle, it was only a hop, skip and a jump to Vancouver, and we wanted to get an early start. Unfortunately, however, our carefully laid plans hit an unexpected snag.

"Make sure your cats have all their vaccinations," Jim mentioned over breakfast. "Otherwise, you just might not be able to get them back in the country without a hassle."

With our departure temporarily thwarted, we hung around Seattle for another day, waiting for the appointment Jim managed to arrange for us with a local veterinarian. Certainly, the last thing either of us wanted was to take our cats into Canada and be refused reentry into the States, simply because they hadn't received the proper shots. Those scruffy fur-balls we were traveling with were our children, and we were as protective of their safety as you would expect of any doting parents.

Our oldest cat, Reggie, had been given to me by Wil on Gay Pride Day, the first year we were together as a couple. Russell, the younger of the two, was a gift from a mutual friend, and served mostly as a companion for Reggie. Reggie was half Angora and half Persian, with long white hair and a fluffy tail, and the sweetest disposition of any cat I'd ever known. Russell, on the other hand, was a short-haired, black and white mutt with an extremely bad attitude. He was literally the cat from hell!

Owing to Russell's generally vicious demeanor, I had basically disowned him in favor of Reggie, while Wil, ever sympathetic to the underdog, subsequently claimed him as his own. As inseparable parts of our family, we had brought both cats along with us for the duration of the trip. Being the more docile of the two, Reggie was content simply being wherever I was, while Russell was an entirely other matter. More than anything, he longed to be an outdoor cat. With one eye fixed on the door, he was always on the lookout for any little slip-up that might offer him an opportunity to escape. More than once during our trip, he had managed to slip away during an unguarded moment, forcing us to retrace our steps in search of him. So far, we had always found him. But who could say what might happen the next time he ran away?

If the truth be known, I think Russell got some perverse sort of pleasure in knowing we cared enough about him to come looking for him. Perhaps it was his way of getting revenge for all the attention we constantly heaped on Reggie, or perhaps he simply wanted to run free. Whatever his motives, he was skating on thin ice, as far as I was concerned. Compared to my angel, Reggie, Russell was a lot more trouble than he was worth.

Once the cats had been seen by the veterinarian and gotten all the necessary shot, there was nothing standing in the way of our leaving for Canada. The trip to Vancouver marked our first opportunity to speak outside of the United States, and we were pleased with the international character our trip was beginning to take on--even if the foreign country in question was only neighboring Canada. As we crossed the border into British Columbia, Benjamin's prediction echoed in both our ears.

"You will speak all over the world, and people will be healed because of your words."

"I guess ole Benjamin was right, after all," Wil commented, as we crossed through the checkpoint at the border. "I didn't really believe him when he said all that stuff on Fire Island, the night before the Harmonic Convergence, but I guess he was right."

"Neither did I, really," I admitted. "I'd never have believed we'd quit our jobs and leave New York, and travel around the country in a Winnebago talking about healing AIDS. The whole thing's a little ironic, don't you think?"

"Ironic..., moronic..., whatever," Wil replied. "We did what we did because it was what we wanted to do. You don't have to read anything more into it than that."

I didn't happen to agree with his last statement, but it wasn't worth getting into an argument over. For me, looking back at the year gone by since the weekend of the Harmonic Convergence, everything that had happened to us had more of a quality of destiny about it than just simply the sum total of our various choices. We had done what we had done, freely, certainly, but had we *really* had a choice? The answer wasn't simply black or white, true or false. It was both and neither, and all of it and none of it. It was a paradox that defied easy explanation. It was as though, through our vision and intention, we had been put in a cosmic sling shot and rocketed into an alternate reality by the power of the Harmonic Convergence.

We lapsed into silence, lost in our own private worlds of thought. Neither of us spoke for quite some time. Neither of us needed to. Just knowing that we were there for each other was sufficient for us both. Eventually, the skyline of Vancouver appeared through the Winnebago's dirty windshield, gleaming like a pastel mirage in the white-hot light of noon. In the distance, great snowcapped mountains rose up to greet a flawless, blue sky, cradling the city between forested slopes and sea.

Taking in the scene for the first time, Wil let out a slow, deliberate breath. "What a beautiful city!" he murmured. I nodded in agreement.

As pretty as the city was, we had very little time for sight-seeing. Our talk was scheduled for seven that evening, and it was already half past three. We bypassed the heart of downtown and crossed over the Lions Gate Bridge, and settled into a small RV park by the water's edge. Then, after freshening up a bit and changing clothes, we contacted our sponsor and set out in the Suzuki to pay him a visit.

Later that evening, we spoke before a small but attentive group of mostly HIV positive, gay men and their caregivers. The most memorable thing about the experience was the marked contrast between our Vancouver audience and the audiences we were accustomed to in the States. In general, the Canadians were more reserved than their Americans counterparts, and reluctant to participate in the question and answer portion of the program. They were shyer, more like some of the audiences we had encountered in the South and Midwest.

Their marked reticence to betray any actual interest in our message, beyond just the basic fact of showing up to hear us, made it hard to determine what kind of impact we had made. Ultimately, all we could do was trust that we had done our best, and that it would be enough. We took consolation in knowing that at the very least we had spread our message beyond the borders of our own country. To a degree, however small, our message had gone international, just like Benjamin had predicted.

151

On the way back to the States, we again found ourselves reminiscing about the various predictions Benjamin had made at our house during the Harmonic Convergence. Besides telling us that we would travel the world and speak, he had also predicted that we'd be famous--not that it really mattered.

"One day soon, everyone will know your name," he had said, gazing up at us through Mark's dark, luminous eyes. *"The young men will sit at your feet and listen."*

Now, little more than a year later, his predictions were proving to be true. Certainly, our fame, such as it was, had spread across much of the United States--at least among people affected by HIV and AIDS. And now we had been to Canada, and Australia was beginning to beckon.

The uncanny accuracy of Benjamin's predictions for us, personally, gave validity to his many predictions of a global nature, and we speculated about what the future might hold for planet earth. Would AIDS really be part of the biggest revolution in consciousness ever to sweep the planet, as he had proposed? And if so, just what, exactly, was our role in it? We rode along in silence, pondering these and many other questions, as the Canadian countryside rolled by.

Eventually, the border crossing came into view. I eased up on the gas petal and steered the Winnebago into an empty checkpoint, and brought our dusty caravan to a halt. An obviously disinterested border agent asked us a few brief questions about the purpose of our visit, and waved us through without incident. Ironically, he never even bothered to ask about the cats.

19 "Well, Dorothy, were not in Kansas anymore."

CROSSING THE BORDER BACK INTO THE United States, we stopped at the first rest area we came to and checked in with Charlie in Los Angeles and gave him a progress report on our visit to Vancouver. Besides wanting to know if any new speaking requests had come in while we were away, I was curious to know if he had found time to look over the revisions I had made to the manuscript, and if so, what he thought about them.

"You did a great job," he congratulated me, even before I had the chance to ask. "So I went ahead and gave it to a friend of mine who did some basic line-editing on it--you know, checking for spelling and grammar and things like that. When he gave it back to me, I submitted it to the Hay House thinking they might be interested since you and Wil are friends of Louise--but, no dice. They claimed to have their hands full just taking care of her stuff." A loud groan issued from my end of the line.

"I wouldn't be too discouraged, though," he added. "She did agree to write a preface for you, and we still have a lot of other options to explore. Give me another week or so to see what I can come up with, and then give me another call. In the meantime, just forget about it and enjoy your well deserved time off."

The news wasn't exactly what I had been hoping for, but clearly there was nothing I could do about it. "I've gotten my first rejection," I groaned, hoping to elicit sympathy from Wil. "The Hay House rejected my book."

"No worries," he said, brushing the entire matter off as if it were nothing. "Your book is meant to be published, and it will be. You just have to be patient, that's all. You can't expect to get lucky with the very first publisher you approach."

He was right, of course; I would have to be patient. And I would just have to get over feeling that in rejecting my book, the Hay House was rejecting me. This wasn't the first time I had ever been rejected, and it certainly wouldn't be the last. I was an adult. I could take it. I did my best to forget about it, and pushed the entire situation out of mind.

For the next several days, we meandered in the general direction of Seattle, and on Labor Day weekend rendezvoused with Jim Toeves and a group of his friends on Camano Island in Puget Sound. They were restoring an old A-frame cabin that had been left to them in the will of a recently deceased friend, and invited Wil and me to join them for the weekend. We helped clear the overgrown tangle of brush from around the house and erect a temporary tin roof over the rotted original. It was hard work, but it was fun, and the camaraderie was a pleasant change of pace.

On Tuesday, I couldn't stand the suspense any longer, and placed a call to Charlie in Los Angeles. "It's me," I said, trying to sound nonchalant. "I was calling to see if anything had happened with the book?"

"Well, it's an interesting situation," Charlie drawled. "It seems that even if we do get an established publisher to accept the book--and that's a very big if--there could still be a delay of a year or more before it is out and in the stores. I don't think you want to wait that long, do you?"

"No, I was hoping for a lot sooner than that," I sighed. "A year's an awful long time to wait."

"Well, on a more optimistic note, there's always the possibility of publishing it ourselves," he said. "From what I've been able to learn, I'm beginning to think that might just be our best option. Since we talked last, I did some checking into the cost and I estimate the entire job could be done for just over ten thousand dollars. I know that sounds like a lot of money, but I think we could recoup the investment in less than a year. Your personal sales alone would be enough to do the trick, and then some."

A deafening silence emanated from my end of the line. The ten-thousand dollar figure Charlie so casually bandied about plugged directly into my fears about money, and major alarm bells were sounding inside my head. Nevertheless, I did want to get the book out, and I didn't want to wait an entire year. Obviously, Charlie had given the idea a lot of thought, and this was the kind of project he seemed to thrive on. Besides, publishing the book ourselves would take care of all those messy rejection issues I found so difficult to deal with.

"Yeah, maybe you're right," I hemmed. "Let me talk it over with Wil, and see what he thinks. I'll get back to you in a couple of days."

Wil took to the idea immediately, and insisted we move on it right away. Any reluctance on my part was quickly swept aside by his unflagging enthusiasm. In a series of phone calls back and forth with Charlie over the next several days, we hammered out the details of just how best to proceed. Our first order of business was to form our own publishing company to handle the financial aspects of the project, which we christened Brotherhood Press, in honor of the Great White Brotherhood of Saints, and to symbolize the sacred nature of our relationship. Wil and I would put up two thirds of the money, and Charlie would contribute the rest. Finally, a decision was reached about how any eventual profits would be split, and Charlie drew up the necessary paper work and mailed it to us to sign.

With the two of us on the road, the actual work of creating the book naturally fell to Charlie. Our job was to obtain endorsements from well-known people in the healing arts, for promotional purposes and use on the cover. Dr. Lawrence Badgley was an obvious choice, as well as our new friend, Tom O'Connor, the author of *Living with AIDS*, who we had met during our recent visit to San Francisco. We already had the blurb from Louise, and Charlie felt certain he could get one from Dr. Bernie Siegel.

Later, Wil and I sat down together and composed a letter outlining our request for endorsements, and mailed it to each prospective candidate on our list. "It'll be interesting to see who responds," he commented, calmly echoing my own raging curiosity. "It'll be perfect, though--just wait and see."

With a week remaining before we were expected in Salt Lake City, we backtracked to Seattle and headed east through the Cascade Mountains, into uncharted territory. Beyond Spokane, the land was harsh and sparsely populated, and we drove for miles without encountering another vehicle. Unfortunately, because of the relentless fires in Yellowstone, our planned visit to the park was out of the question. We veered off south at Coeur d' Alene, on an alternative route through the Sawtooth Mountains. In deference to the area's reputation as an Aryan Nation enclave, we proceeded with a bit of caution here. Like we had done in Arkansas, neither of us wanted to call undue attention to ourselves or test the limits of the local's tolerance. We'd leave that up to the few gay people who chose to call the area home.

For the sake of blending in, I chose to forgo my ritual blow-dry, which was a real sacrifice for a former hairdresser like me. That, and a couple of days without shaving, and I managed to achieve what I thought was an authentically local look.

"Are you ever going to take a bath again?" Wil asked suspiciously, as he looked me up and down. "Don't you think you're taking this blending in business a bit too far?" Obviously, I didn't think so. It was a real treat foregoing the usual mantinence.

With Labor Day over and done with, the campgrounds, in and around the Sawtooth Mountains, proved free of the usual hoard that filled them to capacity during the busy summer months. Winter had come early to Idaho's high, mountains passes, and the crisp autumn air had a noticeable chill. We soaked up the splendid solitude of the setting and set up camp in a deserted, roadside park.

Volcanic in origin, the countryside teemed with an abundance of natural hot-springs. I thumbed through the *Guide to Nude America* someone had given us as a gift in San Diego, and found a listing for one nearby. With a little encouragement from me, Wil agreed to hike back into the woods the following night to check it out.

The next evening, with no moon to speak of, and the black, forest floor punctuated by nothing more than the solitary beam of our flashlight, we crept along a poorly marked trail to Jerry Johnson Springs and eventually heard the sound of rushing water in the distance. Through a small clearing, we could just make out the faint outline of a stream running through a deep ravine to our right. We scrambled down the rocky embankment to the water's edge and were immediately enveloped in a warm, translucent mist of steam.

Hoping to discover the spring's origin, we groped our way along the slippery bank and stumbled onto a series of man-made, rock pools, stretching from the mouth of a small spring on shore, out into the icy stream. The temperature of the water in each pool varied according to how far it was from the mouth of the spring, and the amount of cold river water mixed in with it.

Unbeknownst to me, Wil had brought along a package of candles and a bottle of Merlot in his knapsack. After making sure that no one else was around, he scrambled over the rocks placing candles strategically along the edge of the pools, and lit each one. When he had finished, he popped opened the wine and retrieved two glasses from his knapsack. Shivering against the cold, I stripped off my clothes and slipped into the large pool furtherest from the bank. The warm water was the perfect antidote to the frigid air.

"To us," Wil saluted, slipping into the pool beside me and lifting his glass in a toast. "To another one of our grand adventures!"

"To us," I echoed the sentiment, taking a deep swig of wine.

Gradually, our bodies would adjust to the temperature of the pool we were in, necessitating a move to the next, slightly warmer one. After an hour or so, we had managed to work our way all the way up to where a stream of heated water gushed directly from a fissure in the rocks. We lay back against the toasty boulders, staring up into a crystal sky lit with a million stars. The cold on our faces was in stark contrast to the warmth of our submerged bodies. We sipped our wine and lay completely still, allowing feelings of gratitude to wash over us in waves. The night grew quiet and took on an uncharacteristic feeling of timelessness.

"You know," I whispered, breaking the silence with the urge to share a sudden revelation. "When we lived in New York, I was hardly even aware of the sky. The buildings were so massive they mostly blocked it out."

I lapsed back into silence and remained that way for several minutes. "I remember the first time I flew out of New York City, after I had been there for an entire year. I was so stressed out that I decided to visit my mother in Florida for a couple of days. Taking off from JFK, all of Manhattan was stretched out below me, and lit up to the nines; the buildings were so small they looked like toys. And suddenly, it hit me how little and insignificant my life in New York actually was in the greater scheme of things. Seeing it that way gave me a new perspective and I realized how important it was to get out of the city every once in a while, and see the open sky and be in nature. You get so wrapped up in the hustle and bustle that you forget what's real and important."

For a long minute, there wasn't a sound to be heard, just the ghostly plumes of steam rising silently off the surface of the water. Wil turned his head ever-so-slightly in my direction, his face illuminated by the soft, warm glow of candle-light.

"Well Dorothy," he said, mocking me softly in his gentle way. "We're not in Kansas anymore. And to be perfectly honest, I seriously doubt that we're ever going back!"

20 Salt Lake City and the Colorado AIDS Walk

W E WERE EXPECTED IN SALT LAKE City at the end of the week where we were scheduled to speak at a Church of Religious Science we had connected with by way of Kennedy Shultz, the charismatic minister of the church in Atlanta. Our host for the visit was a young man by the name of Benjamin Barr, whose sister, Roseanne--a standup comic by trade--had just signed a contract for her very first television sitcom. We parked the Winnebago in the space behind Ben's modest apartment, and showered and changed our clothes.

With the afternoon free, we set off to explore the highlights of the city--chief among them, Tabernacle Square, in the very heart of downtown. I had always been curious about the Mormon Religion and was anxious to pay the site a visit. We spent an hour or so touring the impressive temple complex, and were lucky enough to catch a glimpse of the famous Tabernacle choir as it rehearsed.

On our way out, we made a last minute stop at the bookstore and spoke with a helpful lady behind the counter, who graciously offered me a free copy of the Book of Mormons, after I expressed interest in it. As a serious student of Truth, I was curious to know just what this unfamiliar text might have to say that was different from the other more well-known gospels. Perhaps I might discover a perspective on Jesus that I had previously overlooked.

That evening, before bed, I settled into a comfortable chair and opened the blue, leather-bound book and began to read. A couple of chapters into it, after finishing a story where God had supposedly sent one of his faithful servants out to kill his enemies for him, I slammed the book shut in disgust. The perverse idea that God would have enemies or condone murder, much less get someone else to do his dirty work for him, was simply too much to swallow. It was just a different spin on the same tired old ideas I had been force fed as a child, and I wanted nothing to do with it. I got up from my chair and tossed the book in the trash.

Our schedule over the next several days included an interview on the most popular radio talk show in Salt Lake City, broadcast live during the height of the afternoon rush hour. Over dinner, the evening before, Ben took the opportunity to warn us about the local populace's pervasive antagonism toward anything even vaguely pertaining to homosexuality and AIDS, in hopes of tempering our remarks.

"You have to be careful what you say here," he cautioned. "It could be hazardous to your health." By the time the evening had come and gone, Wil and I were both feeling a bit anxious about the interview, and beginning to think we might have been unwittingly set up by a hostile talk show host out to create controversy at our expense.

The following afternoon, Ben accompanied us to the studios of KALL radio, and introduced us to the man who would be conducting the interview. Luckily, he turned out to be both gay-friendly and relatively open-minded. He got the interview off to a flying start with a line of questioning that set the stage for a rather lively discussion to follow.

"What would you like the good people of Salt Lake City to know about having AIDS?" he asked, innocently enough.

Wil took advantage of the opening to speak about AIDS and the possibility of healing, and the detrimental effect of religious homophobia on the lives of gay people around the world.

"Until very recently, there has been a tremendous vacuum of spirituality in the gay community," he admitted. "For many of us, the issue is still relatively charged. There's often a tendency to confuse spirituality with organized religion, and throw the baby out with the bath water. What George and I try to do is help people understand that spirituality is an essential part of their identity, no matter what their sexual orientation, and separate it from the tangle of organized religion."

"The church is not a very practical place for most gay people to turn for help," I added, launching myself into the discussion. "In fact, for many people--and I speak for myself, here, when I say this--the church has often been the very thing that has most separated us from an experience of our innate connection to God. In my case, I found it was necessary to go outside the structure of organized religion in order to have a spiritual life. In the long run, it's not the structure that really counts, anyway, no matter what the church tries to brainwash you into believing. Only your experience has any actual value when you get right down to it."

When the interview was over, our host leaned up out of his chair and reached across the table to shake our hands. "Thanks for coming," he said, his voice filled with genuine warmth. "And thanks for being willing to share such personal issues with our audience this afternoon. The good folks in Salt Lake could use a little education."

After a string of commercials, the show was back on the air. "Right this very minute, traffic is screeching to a halt all over Salt Lake City," our host crowed. "We've been talking with Wil Garcia and George Melton-- two gentleman with AIDS, from New York City--and boy did they give us an ear full!"

It was hard not to laugh at the image the man's words conjured up, imagining cars running helter-skelter into each other, as shocked commuters threw up their hands in disgust. Certainly, anyone who had been tuned in to the show that afternoon had gotten an earful about AIDS--whether they wanted to or not. Given a chance to shatter the deadly denial of this conservative Mormon community, we had taken full advantage of the opportunity and given it our best shot. How could you not feel good about that?

Later that evening, we spoke to an attentive group of nearly a hundred, mostly HIV-positive men and women, and encouraged them to explore their options. "There is much more out there than just what the medical profession has to offer," Wil admonished the friendly crowd. "But you'll need to take the initiative if you expect to survive. Right now, the medical profession is only prepared to help you die. It's important to find support for your desire to live."

Before leaving town the next day, we taped a brief interview with an attractive young woman from one of the local television stations, for a series she was creating on alternative approaches to healing. Then, after thanking Ben for all of the work he had done on our behalf, we headed south on the main highway out of town. At Provo, we veered off onto a scenic shortcut to Interstate 70, headed in the direction of Denver, and the very first Colorado AIDS Walk. This mostly uninhabited part of Utah was achingly beautiful, despite the obvious harshness of the terrain. Incredible vistas stretched out endlessly in every direction, replete with towering rock spires in every imaginable shape and size.

That night, we slept in a deserted rest area just inside the Colorado state line, as a prelude to negotiating the high passes of the majestic Rocky Mountains. Then, with another full day of driving behind us, and the sun just beginning to slide behind the mountains, we began our final descent into Denver. In the distance, through the Winnebago's dust-caked windshield, the city's skyline gleamed in the late-day sun like an ancient formation of standing stones.

Often, while traveling across immense expanses like these, we couldn't help but marvel at how the early pioneers had managed to make it west at all, considering the conditions they had to endure, fueled by little more than the tenuous hope for a better life. We felt a certain kinship with their struggle, despite the obvious difference that modern roads and a covered wagon more luxurious than anything they could have ever imagined, made in our level of comfort.

Like the journey the early pioneers had taken, our trip, too, had been fueled by dreams--dreams that at times seemed impossibly remote. Often, the sheer arduousness of the task we had undertaken chipped away at our commitment, causing us to want to give up and go back home. We soldiered on, despite occasional bouts of discouragement and homesickness. Come hell or high water, we were determined to change the course of the AIDS epidemic, and this could only be accomplished by changing the way people thought. While our intent was purely spiritual, the actual work of making it happen was decidedly political, and Wil and I were not intrinsically political creatures.

As our exit into downtown Denver presented itself, we took comfort in knowing that we were returning to a familiar city where we had friends waiting on our arrival. "After some of the situations we've been in, this should be a piece of cake," Wil chortled. I smiled a wary response. I couldn't help but worry, in spite of myself. I still hadn't gotten a complete handle on my underlying trust issues.

The Denver community was celebrating its very first AIDS Walk, and Wil and I were slated to be the featured speakers at a brief rally in the park to kick it off. Representative Pat Schroeder and the Governor of Colorado were also expected to put in an appearance, but with only half as much time allotted for their remarks. There was a certain satisfaction to be had in upstaging the power elite on their home turf, and we took full advantage of the opportunity. When it was our turn to speak, we took the makeshift stage together, and emphasized the importance of working together in the fight against AIDS.

As the parade kicked off, we joined our friends from the Colorado AIDS Project for the long walk to the capital building in the heart of the city, where for the remainder of the afternoon, we were entertained with music and dancing and food, as well as the usual educational outreach initiatives and ubiquitous condom giveaways. We took off our shoes and plopped down in the shade of an enormous tree, and chatted with well-wishers and rested our aching feet.

Around 4:30 in the afternoon, the sun slipped behind the dome of the Capitol building, casting a sudden chill over the festivities. We excused ourselves and slipped off to the Winnebago which we had parked behind the Methodist church we had spoken in on our previous visit. As we approached the Winnebago from the rear, Wil noticed that the driver's side window was open and hurried ahead to check it out. As he went to put his key in the lock, he immediately noticed that something was amiss.

"I locked this door myself, I'm sure of it," he muttered. "Someone's been in here while we've been gone."

I caught up with him moments later and found him standing by the door, inspecting it for damage.

"Looks like we've been broken into," he announced, tersely. "No telling what they got away with."

A quick inspection of the Winnebago revealed a number of missing items, most obvious among them the small television set we kept in the living area, up front.

"Go check the closet and see if our money's missing," Wil ordered. "If whoever did this found where we keep our money, we're in big trouble. That's all the cash we have."

Dreading what I might find there, I padded into the bedroom and rifled through the closet in search of the coat in whose pockets we had hidden the love-offerings we had collected. Moments later, I found the overstuffed envelope with the money still inside, apparently undisturbed.

"It's here," I called out in relief. "It doesn't look like anything's missing."

Suddenly, at the exact same moment, both of us remembered the cats. Where were the cats?!? Panicked to think they might have run away, we turned the motor home up-side down, checking all the little places they liked to hide in, and found Reggie rolled up in a ball under the bed, taking a nap.

"If anything happened to you, I don't know what I'd do!" I cried, snatching the startled cat up in my arms and pressing him to my chest. "That mean burglar didn't hurt my baby, did he?" My concern was answered with a decidedly nonplused yawn.

With Reggie accounted for, we continued the search for Russell. After a thorough inventory of all his favorite hiding places, he was still nowhere to be found. We moved outside and carefully combed the surrounding area, calling his name as we went. Wil was concerned that if we didn't find him in the next half hour or so, night would fall and he would be lost for good.

"He's got to be around here, somewhere," he sighed, getting down on his knees and peering underneath the Winnebago. "He's probably scared to death and hiding right underneath our noses. I'd just like to know *where*."

No sooner were the words out of his mouth than he spied Russell crouched behind one of the Winnebago's large front tires. The cat looked up and yawned as if to say, "What took you so long?" I laughed, and went into the kitchen and opened a can of tuna, and came back out and placed it on the pavement by the door. Moments later, Russell poked his nose out from behind the tire and trotted over to the open can. Wil snuck up behind him and scooped him up and put him in the Winnebago. The cat crisis was officially over.

About that time, an elderly gentleman came out of the church and explained what had happened during our absence. Apparently, a random passerby had noticed the open window, and taken advantage of the situation to break in and help himself to our belongings. While he was poking around, both cats had high-tailed it out the door. Russell, the more paranoid of the two cats, had promptly run under the Winnebago and hidden behind a tire. Taking a completely different tact, Reggie had pranced up the steps to the church and down the aisle to the altar, disrupting the service in progress.

Recognizing the cat as ours, several of the parishioners had come outside to investigate, just in time to see a man running from the Winnebago with a television set in his arms. One of the younger men had given chase, and the thief had dropped the set, shattering it to pieces. Unaware that there was another cat on the loose, the kindly parishioners had put Reggie back in the motor home and gone on with their morning service.

Our upset quickly turned to laughter, as a picture of what had happened in our absence took shape. It was easy to imagine Reggie, his fluffy, white tail waving in the air behind him, sacheting his way into the church in the middle of the service, looking for help. This was no dumb cat, this Reggie of mine. Nobody was going to rob his parents and get away with it. Staying calm, he had done the only sensible thing he could do. He had gone into the church to find help.

The robbery in Denver was the first time since leaving New York that anything like this had happened to us, and we felt violated in an unfamiliar way. Our discomfort soon eased, however, as gratitude for the fact that nothing of real importance had been taken took root in our hearts and minds. Our cats had not been lost or injured, and our money had not been stolen. We could easily replace the television with another one from the apartment in New York..

Ultimately, we couldn't afford to let this unfortunate incident get us down. We chose to put the entire episode behind us and forgive the man who had robbed us. The overwhelming abundance in our lives made it easy to feel compassion. After things had settled down, we said a prayer and let go of the situation. Too many things of real importance lay ahead of us to allow ourselves to be sidetracked by something as insignificant as the loss of a television set.

The next morning, we pulled up stakes and headed east, hoping to make New York City in time for my birthday, the day after Halloween. But first, we had a couple of stops to make along the way. Wil had been in contact with a psychologist from Louisville, Kentucky who had expressed interest our work, but as of yet been unable to pin him down on a date. In the meantime, we planned to visit my brother in Nashville, and give the Louisville connection a sporting chance to congeal.

From Ken's house, we placed a call to Charlie to check on the progress of the book, and were surprised with some unexpected good news. The cover design had been completed and the manuscript was already at the printers. If things went according to plan, the first 5000 copies of the book would be rolling off the presses within the week.

"I should have them in my hand by Friday," Charlie crowed. "I can't wait for you guys to see them."

Though we had been anticipating the book being sent to the printer, now that it had actually happened it was a little hard to believe.

"It really is an amazing example of the manifestation process," I said to Wil, still trying to absorb the full impact of the news. "Not too long ago, the book was little more than an idea. Then, we earthed it--we gave words to it, and set them down on paper--and now, six weeks later, we have something tangible you can hold in your hands and share with other people. We actually have a book!"

"I know we did a lot of things to make it happen, but from the very beginning this project seemed to have a life of its own. We supplied the elbow grease, but the details fell magically into place."

Even more remarkable was the fact that the entire process had taken less than six weeks to accomplish--an industry record for sure! A hallmark event such as this called for a major celebration. At our insistence, Charlie agreed to meet us in New York, as soon as the first copies of the book rolled off the presses. Fittingly, the book would debut in the actual place where the events described in it had taken place. Anticipating the reunion, Wil got out his calendar and counted off the days.

With the date of our departure from Nashville looming, our visit to Louisville still remained up in the air. Our prospective sponsor couldn't seem to make up his mind, and hadn't yet made a commitment. Reviewing the situation, we decided to scratch him off our list, again realizing that whenever this much effort was involved and things still hadn't fallen into place, it simply wasn't meant to be.

"There's always the possibility of visiting at a later date," Wil sighed, pointing out the obvious. "Sometimes the timing's just not right. It's better not to go at all, than to go all that way for nothing."

He was right, of course. As much as we would have liked to have spoken in Louisville, it just wasn't going to happen. Like the situation with Portland, we'd have to bide our time and wait for the opportune moment, if and when it came. In the meantime, Charlie and the book beckoned, enticingly. We said goodbye and set out on the final leg of our journey home.

21 Beyond AIDS

T
HE TWO WEEKS WE WERE SLATED to be in New York were a
welcomed respite from our constant travels and the challenges
of living on the road. There was something to be said for being
back in familiar territory once again, surrounded by people who knew
and loved us unconditionally. Leaving Nashville behind, we stopped just
long enough to refuel and grab a bite to eat, and then drove until the twin
towers of the World Trade Center appeared on the horizon, barely visible
through the thick, New Jersey haze.

Our first order of business called for a quick stop at the apartment
to drop off the cats and enough clothes to last for the next two weeks,
followed immediately by a trip to Wil's sister's house in Connecticut,
where we planned to leave the Winnebago for the duration of our stay. It
would be a lot safer parked in a suburban driveway than left unattended
on Manhattan's mean streets. We'd stay in the apartment with Ken and
pick up the Winnebago when we were ready to leave.

With the basic logistics of our stay in place, there were still a number
of important issues needing our attention. Eric Bailes, the friend who
had been handling our finances for us, was moving to San Francisco at
the end of the month, and we needed to know whether he was still willing
to help us, or if we would need to make other arrangements. The biggest
fly in the ointment was the unexpected situation with the apartment.
Since we had last seen him, Ken's health had taken a dramatic turn for
the worse, and he was planning to move back home with his parents.
This left us with only two short weeks to find someone else to sublet the
apartment.

With the fate of the apartment weighing heavily on my mind, how to retain control of it became utmost on my agenda. The apartment symbolized our ability to return to the city at will, and my security-- or so I thought. It was the ultimate ace up my sleeve in case the Universe happened to let me down, and I had no other place to go. Obviously, I still had a way to go in terms of healing myself around the all important issue of trust. But never mind that, for now. We needed to find someone to sublet the apartment right away!

As luck would have it, my best friend, Barry, a fellow member of the power seven, was returning to New York from London where he had been living for the past few months, and was looking for a place to stay. Barry and I had met at the tender, young age of eighteen, the first quarter of our freshman year at the University of Florida, and remained close friends ever since. In the late 70's, when he had moved to New York to pursue a modeling career, he had lived with Wil and me until he had found a place of his own. He had also been the one that had introduced me to the work of Jane Roberts and Seth, and Wil to the work of Louise Hay. Obviously, if he was interested in the apartment, he'd be the logical choice. I ran the idea by Wil, before calling and pitching him the offer.

Naturally, Barry was thrilled at being handed such a simple solution to his housing dilemma and agreed to move in right away--on one condition: he could have a roommate to help with the rent. We agreed, in exchange for the right to stay in the apartment whenever we were passing through the city. That way, the doormen would see us coming and going, occasionally, and be less likely to suspect that we were no longer living there. There was nothing our landlord would have liked better than to find grounds for terminating our lease, due to the relatively cheap rent we were paying, compared to the going rate. Having Barry stay in the apartment constituted a clear violation of our lease. If the doormen were to inform the landlord, we would be out on the streets in a matter of days.

My birthday was a few days later: All Saints Day--the day after Halloween. That evening, Wil and I drove to Kennedy Airport to pick up Charlie who was scheduled to arrive on a flight from Los Angeles, carrying the first few copies of our book. Arriving at the terminal a little before his flight was due to land, we killed time browsing through a nearby sundries shop. Fifteen minutes after it was due in, Charlie's plane eased up to the gate and began disgorging passengers. Moments later, Charlie emerged through the door to the gangway and spotted us in the crowd. He flashed a copy of the book in our direction.

"Did you see that?" I squealed, giving Wil's arm a hard squeeze. "Did you see the cover of the book?"

"I saw it," he chortled, breaking into a wide grin. "It looks pretty good, don't you think? Just like a real book!"

Charlie edged his way through the milling throng, over to where Wil and I were standing. "Your book, sir," he announced in a very formal tone of voice, handing me the slender pink volume. "It's official, now; you're a published author. Now, you can get to work on the next one!"

"The next one!?" I stammered, overwhelmed at the very idea. "I'm not sure I have another one in me. I think I've said just about everything I have to say!"

While Wil waited with Charlie for his luggage to arrive, I set off to retrieve the car, and picked them up by the curb outside the baggage claim area. On the drive back to the city, Charlie filled us in on the specifics of what it had taken to get to New York with the book in time for my birthday.

"It was really touch and go whether they were going to be ready in time," he explained. "The print job took longer than expected, and for a while it didn't look like it was going to get done. I literally picked the books up on my way to the airport to catch my plane."

The next several days proved to be particularly fruitful. For starters, we wanted to pitch the book to the city's two, leading, gay bookstores--Oscar Wilde Books and A Different Light Bookstore--and that involved a trip to the West Village to do the job in person. To our delight, both stores were receptive to our overtures and ordered a full case of sixty books each.

"We'll put a copy right here in the front window," the manager of A Different Light assured us. "That way, everyone will be sure to see it when they come through the door. And give me one of your cards so we have a way to get in touch with you in case we need to order more. I have a feeling we're going to sell a lot of these puppies."

Charlie whipped out a business card and handed it to the manager. "I'll be handling the orders," he said, in his official tone of voice. "You can reach me at this number, day or night. I'll have them in the mail to you by the following day."

"Boy, that was easy," Wil sighed, once we were back outside on the sidewalk. "We've been at this for only a couple of hours and we've already sold two cases. The *real* test will be whether they reorder or not. That's when we'll know if people are actually buying them."

With the two major gay bookstores under our belt, we stopped in a number of smaller bookstores in the neighborhood and repeated the same scenario, introducing ourselves and the book, and meeting with the same success. Each store we approached ordered at least a couple of books, if not more. Our door-to-door marketing strategy was proceeding right on track.

Despite the graciousness with which our efforts were being met, I found myself increasingly unnerved at the prospect of having to ask people to buy the book, and my resistance began to build. In my mind, a rejection of the book would represent a rejection of me, personally, and I felt way too vulnerable to be taking such a risk. Unfortunately, calling it quits was not an option, however. I had to figure out a way to get the job done, while minimizing my exposure.

Ultimately, I made Wil do most of the talking while I lagged behind at a safe distance, waiting to gauge how his efforts were received before joining the negotiations. This way, the book got placed, but at no personal risk to me. Wil was forced to take the brunt of any possible unpleasantness.

"What's wrong with you?" he growled, as we were leaving another store. "I thought we were a team. You don't expect me to do everything myself, do you?"

Unfortunately, he had a point. I wasn't being much help--that was for sure--though it wasn't the first time I had behaved this badly. I had done the same thing on Fire Island, when we were distributing flyers for the fundraiser for AIDS Alive. Like now, I had dragged my feet and forced Wil to do most of the work. Sure, I hated myself for being such a coward, but not enough to confront the source of my unease. When it came to the crunch, I folded every time. I just couldn't seem to get past my deep-seated fear of attack.

On Thursday night, we dropped in on the Healing Circle and introduced our book to the enthusiastic crowd. By the end of the evening, we had managed to sell every copy we had with us, and could have sold more if we had had them. In a different vain, I couldn't help but notice how some of my friends reacted to the idea that I'd actually written a book. One person even pulled me aside and asked if I had written it myself, or if a ghost writer had done it for me. Obviously, it was hard for some people to fathom just how much I had changed in the last nine months, and see me as I was now. They remembered me as a little scatterbrained and slightly self-absorbed, and the change--however small--was undoubtedly confusing.

Rather than be offended by the comment, I chose to find the humor in it. In spite of my rejection issues--and all my other issues--I really was a different person, whether anyone else recognized it or not. Sure, I was a work in progress, but the point was that I was headed in the right direction.

The next week, we caught the New Haven Line from Grand Central Station to Wil's, sister's house in Connecticut, and picked up the Winnebago. With so much flexibility in our schedule, it seemed pointless to put up with the harsh winter weather, when we could just as easily head south to warmer climes. We broke up the long trip to Florida with a return engagement at the Atlanta Church of Religious Science, where this time our talk was open to the entire community.

Fueled by the excitement our last visit had generated, and by the prospect of our brand new book, Kennedy was expecting an exceptionally large turnout. Anticipating strong demand, he ordered several hundred books to have on hand the night of our lecture.

It felt good being back in familiar territory, rather than constantly blazing new trails. Atlanta's strong community, and the ease which with we had been able to make new friends there, made leaving New York a little more palatable, this time. We even entertained the possibility of moving there, once we were ready to settle down. Unfortunately, neither of us had any idea just when that might be. As far as either of us knew, our journey was just getting started.

To be sure, Kennedy was a big part of the attraction. His dry sense of humor, often bordering on the sarcastic, appealed to our New York sensibilities. And he was the type of person that got things done, which we were learning was a bit of a rarity in the spiritual community. Unfortunately, some of our other sponsors had been clueless when it came to the practical aspects of producing an event. Despite their hearts being in the right place, they were often so spacey that their plans failed to achieve any actual traction. Promises were made that frequently never materialized.

As a result, more than once we had showed up in a community, only to discover that no one knew we were coming. By contrast, Kennedy and his crew were particularly well-grounded. When they put on an event, you knew it was going to be a success.

We rolled into Atlanta mid-week, and dropped in unannounced on Kennedy's Wednesday night Science of Mind class. Because of its strong mental approach to spirituality and healing, The Science of Mind, a spiritual philosophy based on the writings of Dr. Ernest Holmes, held a special appeal for Wil, and the visit piqued his interest in becoming a licensed practitioner. After the class disbanded, Wil approached Kennedy with the idea, and purchased a set of tapes so he could study it while on the road.

"That's great," I congratulated him. "I'm studying A Course in Miracles, and now you're studying The Science of Mind. Between the two of us, we've just about got every possible angle covered."

That weekend, the large assembly hall where the event was being held was packed to capacity, and the overflow crowd spilled out into the aisles. At precisely seven thirty, Kennedy ascended the stairs to the podium and called the evening to order. After a brief invocation, he introduced Wil as the first speaker of the evening.

"Some of you have had the privilege of hearing these two, young men speak before," he announced, "and others of you have not. Well, for those of you who haven't had the pleasure, you're in for a real treat. Please give a warm, Atlanta welcome to our first speaker of the evening, Mr. Wil Garcia!" With that, the room burst into a round of applause.

Kennedy retreated to a seat down front, leaving Wil alone to bask in the glow of the crowd's attention. He smiled shyly and waited for the applause to die down, before clearing his throat.

"I'm really happy to be back here in Atlanta tonight," he began. "A lot has happened to George and me since we were here with you last spring, and I'd like to share a little bit about that with you. Since we last saw you, we've been in over twenty cities, and spoken to thousands of HIV and AIDS infected and affected people. I'm pleased to inform you there's a growing understanding that you can be HIV positive and live a long and healthy life. People are beginning to explore their options; not everyone is rolling over and playing dead." The crowd burst into enthusiastic applause.

When the room had quieted down again, Wil spent the next twenty minutes or so delivering a rather upbeat assessment of what we had found in our travels around the country. "There is still a lot of work to be done," he said in closing, "but for the first time, people are beginning to understand that they have choices when it comes to dealing with this disease--that an AIDS diagnosis doesn't necessarily equal death. That's a real improvement over the early days of the epidemic, when hopelessness reigned supreme. *And* it's something George and I have worked very hard to bring to people's awareness."

When he had finished, Kennedy took to the podium again, and introduced me to the primed and waiting crowd. The roar of applause reverberated in my ears, as I made my way on stage. I paused until it had passed, before commencing with the usual pleasantries. Then, with the formalities out of the way, I delved into the central theme of my talk.

"One of the things we in the spiritual community need to be careful about is not to let our desire to have a positive attitude become a denial of what's actually going on," I began. There's a big difference between denying AIDS' power over us--which is the spiritually expedient thing to do--and denying its existence altogether. I've seen a lot of people die over these last few years because they insisted on pretending that AIDS wasn't an issue for them, as though if they ignored it, it would simply disappear. This unfortunate attitude is denial with a capital D, *and it kills*--don't kid yourself. I don't care how much we might try and cover the situation over with spiritual platitudes and affirmations and the like, if we're unwilling to look at what's wrong in our lives it's because we're afraid we're not big enough to handle it--that somehow, by the very act of looking at the problem, it will gain the upper hand."

"Thankfully, the truth is very much the opposite. Our willingness to look at the pain in our lives is an affirmation of our ability to handle it. It's a mistake to look only at the positive and pretend the negative doesn't exist. A truly powerful person--one who *knows* they create their own reality-- is willing to look at everything that comes up in their lives--

especially the things they consider to be negative--knowing that's where the real opportunity for transformation lies."

"Transformation lies at the very heart of the healing process. It doesn't mean that we all recover and go merrily on with our lives, necessarily, but that as a community we no longer need illness to teach us who we are. Through the experience of illness, we remember our perfection."

When I had finished, Kennedy announced a fifteen minute intermission, during which Wil and I signed books and accepted congratulations from a swarm of well-wishers. Then, it was time for the question and answer portion of the program. Wil and I took the platform together, and faced the usual barrage of questions and commentary.

"George, this question is for you," the first, young man at the microphone indicated. "I'm a little confused by what you said earlier about looking at what's wrong in our lives. If we get what we focus on, wouldn't that be counterproductive?"

"It's only counterproductive if you obsess on it," I explained, making sure he understood the distinction. "Then, certainly, you'd be empowering the problem, instead of resolving it. But what I'm trying to address is our failure to be completely honest with ourselves about the motivation for our actions. Because ultimately, it's only one of two things--either love or fear. Love, we all know by now, is what heals us. Fear, on the other hand, attracts to us the very thing we're afraid of. If we ignore what's happening in our lives because deep down inside we're afraid to, then we attract to us the very thing we fear. Does that make sense?"

"Yeah, it makes a lot of sense," the man replied, and quickly took his seat.

The next person had a comment instead of a question. "I just wanted to thank the two of you for the work you're doing, and let you know that it has really made a difference in my life. Before I heard you guys speak last spring, I had resigned myself to dying and was really, really depressed. Hearing your stories jarred me out of my complacency and started me on, what has turned out to be, the most remarkable journey of my life. As a result, I feel better now than I've felt in years, and my blood work has improved, too. Again, thank you for all you're doing. And please, *please*, keep up the good work!"

The man's words reached deep into my heart, and for a moment I had to fight back tears. It was difficult to accept such blatant praise, even though we certainly appreciated the validation. After a few more questions, we thanked everyone for coming and turned the floor back over to Kennedy. He made a few, brief announcements and then brought the evening to a close. By the time the last person straggled out the door, an hour later, every one of our books and tapes had been sold and there was a waiting list for more.

With Atlanta being our first, major outing since the publication of our book, we were elated at how well things had gone, and for the implications it had for our sagging, financial balance sheet. Coupled with the fact that we were rewarded with a handsome honorarium, and we actually came out ahead. Despite successes like this, however--financial ones, to be precise--they were still more the exception than the rule. More often than not, we spoke before small groups of people with AIDS who had been both physically and financially decimated by the experience, and often gave our books away for free. We weren't complaining, mind you. We were more excited by the fact that people were actually reading what we had written, than worried about how much it might cost us. Besides, the universe had a way of evening things out in the long run.

Let me be perfectly clear about one thing. Unless you happened to be a doctor or the head of some major AIDS Agency, working with people with AIDS wasn't really an appropriate line of work for someone looking to make money. While there were tremendous rewards in answering the call to serve, for the most part they tend to be other than financial. We hoped that our book would serve a two-fold purpose: that it would assist our efforts to spread our message to the widest possible audience, and help support our continued travels around the country. In Atlanta, that vision was finally showing signs of becoming a reality. Another piece of the puzzle was falling into place.

When we had first decided to self-publish *Beyond AIDS*, neither of us had the slightest inkling how much work was involved in successfully marketing a book. Like the rest of our trip, we had learned what we needed to know as we went along. Up until this point in time, our only means of distribution was through sales at our lectures and the few small bookstores we had managed to introduce it to along our route. While to a certain extent these efforts had been effective, we desperately needed a major distributor if we hoped to sell the book nationwide. Atlanta represented a breakthrough in this regard.

176

Before leaving town, we met with the head of the purchasing department of *New Leaf Books*, one of the largest, metaphysical book distributors in the country, and obtained an agreement from them to take our book on consignment. At the same time, on the other side of the continent, Charlie was in the process of enrolling two, major, west coast distributors: *Book People* and *Moving Books*. Within days, cases of *Beyond AIDS* went rolling out of Charlie's garage, bound for bookstores all around the country.

With the distribution puzzle falling into place and the Thanksgiving holidays just around the corner, we left Atlanta and headed south to Florida. Over the next, several weeks, we systematically revisited many of the cities we had spoken in before, and added a couple of new ones to our list. In Orlando, we made the cover of the Sentinel's Style section, with a major article about our unorthodox approach to AIDS, and our sojourn around the country. The piece included a large, color photo of the two of us with our arms around each other, gazing affectionately into each other's eyes.

The article was not without its repercussions, however. Not surprisingly, my mother was more than a little embarrassed by all the publicity, and made it perfectly clear that she would have preferred it if we had kept our situation private. Not that she wasn't happy we were both doing well, mind you. It's just that our public stance violated her southern sense of propriety, and exposed a plethora of embarrassing issues she would rather not have dealt with.

Several months later, my brother let it slip that, after we had left town, she had gone out and bought a dozen newspapers with the offending article in them, and given one to each of her friends--anyone whose opinion she valued. It was her way of placing the entire kettle of fish out in the open and saying "like it or not, this is my son; for better or worse, I love him." In her heart of hearts, I think she might even have felt the teeniest, wee bit proud.

We took advantage of being in Florida to visit an old, college chum of mine in Miami, and check in with Anita who was down from New York visiting her mother and step-father. Unfortunately, her health had faltered in the months since our last visit with her, and when we saw her, her face exhibited the familiar sunken appearance that frequently accompanied the more advanced stages of AIDS.

She had started smoking again, and Wil and I suspected she was using drugs as well. Needless to say, it was disheartening to watch someone as powerful as Anita struggle so fiercely and ineffectively against the many difficult challenges she was up against. However, despite her obvious difficulties, she was continuing to work on *AIDS Alive*, and her personal struggle had become the central focus of the film. In addition to hope, it would now explore doubt, disappointment and fear.

As much as we would have liked to, there was nothing Wil or I could do to fix Anita's problems and make them go away. We could only love and support her while she made her own decisions regarding her life and health. I don't for one minute mean to imply that it was for lack of trying that Anita was unable to turn her health around. To her everlasting credit, she had the most powerful will of anyone Wil and I had ever met. Yet, will alone wasn't enough when it came to AIDS, and kicking the litany of powerful addictions she was wrestling with. There needed to be more letting go and an acceptance of the possibility of death. More than anything, Anita was unwilling to give up even a modicum of control. And to make matters worse, she was terrified of dying.

We kissed her goodbye, promising to meet up with her again in New York, and set out for my parent's house in Central Florida, 200 miles away. Christmas was just around the corner and I wanted to spend the holidays with my family. Then, with New Years Eve only days away, we pulled up stakes and headed north to Ocala, to welcome in 1989 with one of my oldest and dearest friends. From Ocala, the highway, like the year ahead of us, seemingly stretched on forever. We drove west along the Florida Panhandle, headed for New Orleans, where we delivered our usual talk and made a quick appearance on a local cable television show. The next day was spent meandering through the narrow streets of the French Quarter, pigging out on spicy Cajun food and beer.

Determined to stick to our schedule, we left New Orleans and skirted the muddy waters of Lake Pontchartrain, and headed west through the swampy bayous. Outside of Baton Rouge, our route took us north though the southwest corner of Mississippi, enroute to the small town of Monroe, Louisiana. The following evening, we spoke to a small but receptive group of people with HIV and AIDS and their supporters, and the next morning, sat in on a board meeting of the only AIDS agency in town.

"We're in a difficult situation here," the president of the board explained. "We're pretty isolated from the rest of the world, and that's why we're so pleased you were willing to go out of your way to visit us here in Monroe. Your mere presence causes people to question their assumptions about AIDS, and gives us hope for the very first time. You've certainly given us an awful lot to think about, that's goes without saying."

We left the meeting feeling good about our decision to visit the city, which to be perfectly honest, we had entertained serious reservations about. The initial invitation, coming from the sister of one of our many friends at the New York healing circle, and the owner of the only new age book store in town, had come with its own distinct warning. Not only were AIDS and homosexuality anathema to the locals, but new-age spirituality was equally suspect. And recently, that sentiment had been hammered home by the brutal murder of a local PWA. Suffice it to say, Wil and I were a toxic brew of all three offending categories: we were gay; we had AIDS, and we were metaphysical to the core. Consequently, we hadn't really known what to expect.

Eventually, we had followed our intuition, overridden our fears, and decided to make the trip--fully expecting the worse. Instead, we had been surprised to find a core group of open-minded, loving people, struggling against impossible odds to serve a suspicious and frightened gay community.

"I'm so glad we didn't back out," I said to Wil, as we headed out of town. "Small, out of the way places, like Monroe, need to hear our message even more than some of the big cities do. They're more out of the loop and isolated from the latest information."

"That's true," he agreed. "And most educators won't go out of their way to visit them. It's just not cost effective. But small towns need information just as much as everyone else, if not more. That's why what we're doing is so unique. With the Winnebago, we can go anywhere we're invited, and at very little cost."

From Monroe, we continued our journey west, and crossed over the Red River at Shreveport, near the eastern border of Texas. A rapid-fire series of return engagements was waiting for us in Houston, Austin and Dallas--except for San Antonio which had expressed no interest in having us return. In Houston, we reconnected with Michael who arranged for us to speak at a fledgling Church of Religious Science. We parked the Winnebago behind the minister's house, and accepted his generous offer to stay in his guest room. It was a nice change of pace, and the bed was unusually comfortable.

The following weekend found us in Austin, speaking before a small but enthusiastic crowd of true believers, and the weekend after that, at an MCC in Dallas. At each stop along the way, we sold our books and tapes, and introduced them to any gay-friendly businesses in the area.

This series of return engagements was a far cry from the first time we had visited Texas, as two unknown commodities from New York, claiming HIV and AIDS could be healed. The seeds that had been planted on our initial visit had sprouted in our absence, resulting in a greater feeling of openness and more acceptance of the possibility of healing. It was just the confirmation we needed to know that our efforts were truly making a difference. It reinforced our commitment and energized our spirits.

Beyond the shift in people's basic attitudes, we couldn't help but notice how differently people treated us now that we had authored a book--never mind that we had published it ourselves. Though nothing of real significance had changed in terms of our basic message, suddenly our every utterance was savored with a distinct, new appreciation. As authors, we were now considered experts in our field.

The change was hardly lost on either of us. And while we were grateful for the unexpected boost in credibility, it was obvious that along with all the attention came the danger of being somehow seen as special in the eyes of those we were trying most to reach. While the celebrity aspect of our work was certainly something we enjoyed, neither of us wanted to be seen as different, or risk creating a situation in which our healing might be considered out of the ordinary, and therefore unavailable to everyone.

As the stakes in what we were doing grew, so too did the challenge of staying centered become all that much more difficult to maintain. Yet, with the increasing difficulty came increased rewards and an acceleration in the pace of our spiritual growth. We were both deeply committed to playing at this new level; the opportunities we were experiencing hadn't fallen into our laps by accident--at least not entirely. They had been created by a burning desire for a deeper understanding of whom and what we were. Ultimately, the road this had led us down would demonstrate whether our metaphysics beliefs were true or not. Either way, we were committed to finding out.

As a result, we were learning to love ourselves more deeply with every passing day, in a way that was real and nurturing, and not just an empty, intellectual concept. Nor was it simply the result of people's flattery, but stemmed from a much more basic source. We were learning through the myriad challenges we faced, just how capable we were as two, creative human beings. We had been forced to look deep within ourselves and draw upon an ever-deepening reservoir of strength. Yes, a person's dream could make a difference in the world. There was a well-spring of unlimited power inside of everyone, just waiting to be tapped.

22 A Miracle in Flagstaff

D ALLAS WAS OUR LAST STOP IN Texas, from which we planned to drive straight through without stopping, to Christine's house in Cornville, just outside Sedona. It was a long stretch of highway, and even with the two of us taking alternating, four-hour shifts at the wheel, it still took over 24 hours to reach Flagstaff, with a half hour's drive to go. As the Flagstaff business district appeared through the Winnebago's bug-splattered windshield, we exited interstate 40 for gas and a bite to eat, before setting out on the last, short leg of the trip.

At a red light near the center of town, we turned and crossed over a jumble of railroad tracks, headed for a Chevron station a block away. Glancing in the rear view mirror to be certain we had cleared the turn, my heart lurched into my throat. The Suzuki had somehow come uncoupled from the Winnebago and was inching its way from behind us, into the oncoming lane of traffic.

"Hold on!" I yelled, startling Wil out of a pleasant slumber. "I think we're in trouble!"

I eased up on the gas and carefully applied the brakes. Moments later, the right-hand corner of the Suzuki's front bumper connected with the left, rear bumper of the Winnebago with a jolt. I braked harder, and in an effort to cause the least possible damage to either vehicle, gently brought our wounded caravan to an unscheduled stop, smack dab in the middle of the road, blocking traffic in both directions.

I set the emergency brake and flipped on the flashers, and bolted out the door after a panic stricken Wil to survey the damage-- expecting to find the worst. A quick inspection of the tow-bar and its couplings revealed the obvious cause of the mishap. Somehow, the large bolt holding the tow-bar to the back of the Winnebago had worked its way loose, causing the two vehicles to become uncoupled. Of the two safety cables that served as backup, one was completely severed, while the other, stretched to its limits, was moments away from snapping too. A single, fragile link of wire was the only thing preventing the Suzuki from breaking free and veering out into oncoming traffic. We had averted a major disaster just in the nick of time!

We quickly freed the two vehicles from each other and pulled them over to the side of the road. Miraculously, the only damage to either vehicle, beyond the pair of severed cables, was a minor dent in the rear bumper of the Winnebago. Despite our good fortune, we were both pretty shaken up by the episode, especially by the thought of what *might* have happened if the last strand of cable had actually snapped. For a moment, we toyed with the idea of blaming each other for the mishap, but wisely decided against it.

For the moment, this near brush with disaster had shaken our faith in the willingness of the Universe to insure our safety and well-being. Throughout our entire trip, we had operated on the assumption that we were overshadowed by divine protection. Yet here, in the space of little more than a month, we had been robbed in Denver and suffered a nearly disastrous accident in Flagstaff. Beyond strictly matters of faith, we still faced the inconvenience of having to replace the damaged cables. Tired and cranky from the long drive from Dallas, the last thing either of us wanted to deal with was a situation like this.

As I sat dejected, looking out of the Winnebago's windshield into empty space, I realized, suddenly, that by some amazing coincidence we had come to a stop directly across from a large U-Haul rental store. Buoyed by the discovery, I calmly called it to Wil's attention. He looked over and saw the U-Haul sign, looked at me again and let out a quiet yelp.

"Follow me," he said, bolting for the door.

As luck would have it, the U-Haul store had everything in stock we needed to repair the damaged coupling. In less than an hour, with a minimum of effort and expense, the severed cables were replaced, the Suzuki was reattached to the Winnebago, and we were off again, with all systems go.

About twenty miles south of Flagstaff, the narrow highway veered sharply to the right, dropping precipitously into the mouth of Oak Creek Canyon. Without a word passing between us, we both recognized the miracle that had occurred only an hour before in Flagstaff. The Universe had not failed to protect us, as we had been tempted to believe at the time. It had merely planned ahead, providing us with the never-failing blanket of safety we had come to depend upon. The Suzuki had come undone on level ground, while we were traveling at a slow rate of speed. Under those conditions, we were able to avoid what might otherwise have been a much more horrendous accident.

If the tow-bar had not come undone when and where it had, it would most likely have broken on this treacherous stretch of steeply winding road, and we would have been helpless to prevent a much greater tragedy. The Suzuki would have snapped free, veered into oncoming traffic, and plunged over the cliff and smashed on the rocks below. Instead, a miraculous collapse in time had interceded on our behalf, rendering the potential disaster, harmless. Even the repairs had been a breeze.

We arrived at Christine's house, bubbling over with gratitude for the miraculous chain of events we had just experienced. "You're not going to believe what just happened to us," Wil exclaimed, bounding out of the Winnebago to greet Christine, who had come running out of the house on hearing us pull into the driveway.

"Yeah, but as usual we were snatched back from the brink, just in the nick of time." I chimed in, cheerily.

"Whoa, one of you guys at a time," Christine exclaimed, overwhelmed by our blast of exuberance. "You can tell me all about it over dinner."

We followed her into the house, where a nourishing meal was spread out on the table. Between bites, we filled her in on the details of the incident in Flagstaff. After we had finished with the story, she sat there shaking her head in amazement.

"I guess you won't be having anymore issues around trust now, will you George?" she remarked, glancing coyly in my direction. "If that doesn't do it for you, then nothing will."

My face turned a bright shade of red. "I guess you're right," I mumbled. "But you know how dense I can be at times." Unfortunately, no one at the table bothered to dispute the point. I sat there embarrassed, with egg on my face.

23 Marianne Williamson and the New York Center for Living

FTER SEVERAL DAYS OF REST AND relaxation, it was time to get back to work. Our schedule called for us to fly to New York City where we were slated to participate in a weekend workshop on AIDS, sponsored as a fund-raiser for the newly formed Manhattan Center for Living. The center, the brainchild of Marianne Williamson and a number of other dedicated individuals from the New York healing community, had been created to serve the needs of people with HIV and AIDS with a full range of services, including support groups, classes on nutrition, massage, energy work, Reiki and more.

By now, Marianne's lectures in New York and LA had attracted the attention of a growing number of HIV-infected and affected people who were anxious to see how the principles outlined in *A Course in Miracles* might be applied to their condition--including me. The upcoming workshop was merely the first of many programs of a spiritual nature planned for the newly created center, and Wil and I had been invited to speak as two individuals who had successfully applied such principles to combating their disease.

We left the cats with Christine and made the two and a half hour drive to Phoenix to catch our flight. It was late spring, and the outside temperature had not yet reached the intolerable levels that summer would eventually bring. Leaving our car in the long-term parking lot, we hopped a shuttle to the main terminal and checked our bags at the curb, and a little over an hour later, were safely in the air.

The five-hour flight to New York offered ample time to reflect upon our destination: New York City! As much as I hated to admit it, I had actually come to appreciate the advantages of simply visiting occasionally, rather than living there full-time. Naturally, we were jazzed about seeing old friends again, and catching up on the local gossip. And as usual, I was looking forward to having my hair cut by a real professional. But most of all, we were excited about spending an entire weekend with Marianne Williamson, of whom we were both enthusiastic fans.

By any account, the workshop was a phenomenal success. For three days, Marianne lectured and prodded, and generally moved everyone there through layers upon layers of resistance. Then, after lunch on the final day of the gathering, she invited Wil and me to join her in front of the room. After a brief introduction, Wil spoke first and basically shared both our stories, from the time of his original diagnosis with AIDS, and mine with ARC, a year later, to our eventual spiritual awakening and current remission in symptoms. Then, it was my turn to speak.

Since Wil had already given the outline of our story, I chose to speak in a different vein, altogether. "The immune system isn't like a heart or a liver or a kidney," I began. "It's not located in a centralized site like your other organs are; it's more elusive than that."

"By its very nature, the immune system is the most psychologically oriented system in the entire human body. It's a physiological reflection of a psychological stance, of how we see ourselves in relationship to the world. To heal ourselves, we're going to have to examine that relationship very, very carefully."

I paused for a moment and looked about the room, taking time to connect with some of the familiar faces in the audience. "AIDS is mainly a disease of the disenfranchised," I continued, "gays, intravenous drug users and women--the very people who most see themselves as victims of the dominant culture. Whether it's at the hands of the church, the government, racism, or the bully down the street, all of us feel threatened, to some extent, and share a deep, intrinsic sense of vulnerability."

"Interestingly enough, AIDS is a disease in which we find ourselves vulnerable to every passing germ and virus; in other words, it's biological vulnerability. And it reflects, perfectly, the way many of us perceive ourselves in relationship to the world--our own personal world view, if you will. To heal ourselves, we need to adopt another way of looking at the world."

The audience sat attentively, quietly digesting every word. I paused and took a sip of water, before continuing with my train of thought. "Where do you find a sense of security in a world that seems to threaten at every hand?" I asked, rhetorically. "How do you learn to trust again?" I paused and gave the audience time to ponder the question.

"To tell the truth, I don't really think there is a basis for trust in the physical world. To try and find security at the level of the body is strictly a waste of time. But there is an answer, I suspect--at least I've found one that seems to be working for me. But it has required me to look beyond the surface of what *appears* to be going on in my life.

For me, spirituality has been the answer; not a blind faith sort of thing, mind you, but an answer based on the oneness that underlies our very existence: a quantum *spirituality*, if you will. I'm learning to trust life again, not because I trust other people, but because I'm learning to trust myself. And that's the only basis for security there is. You must learn to trust yourself by recognizing that you're connected to a power greater than yourself!"

"The only thing that any of us have to be afraid of is the part of ourselves we don't know--the part we're in denial about--because that's the part that can whack us upside the head when we least expect it. And it might look like the government, or the church, or the bully down the block that's the cause of our problems, but it's really only our fearful projections coming back to haunt us."

"Thank you," I said, bringing my remarks to a close. "Thank you very much for your attention."

The room burst into applause. I stood there for a moment, soaking up the energy being beamed in my direction. Out of the corner of my eye, I noticed a vaguely familiar figure of a man get up from where he was seated and abruptly exit the room. I don't know why it caught my attention except that I thought I recognized him, and he seemed agitated and upset.

Later, I learned the reason he had walked out on my talk: knowing me, personally, it was hard for him to take my message seriously. How could someone who had lived the kind of life I had lived, be an authority on matters of spirituality?

For a moment, his reaction saddened me. As far as I was concerned, he had missed the point, entirely. The precise power of my testimony was that it didn't matter what you might have done in the past. You didn't have to be perfect to tap into the healing power of love; it was available to anyone who asked. In judging me, what my friend was really doing was judging himself. In effect, he was saying that because of what *he* had done, *he* was not worthy of being healed. It had nothing to do with me.

Most of my friends understood the implications of my healing in terms of their own, and would dish me affectionately, saying things like, "Well George, if you can do it, anyone can." But all kidding aside, they knew that this was precisely the power of my testimony: I was no genius, and they didn't have to be one, either. In fact, an overly developed intellect could sometimes make the essential step of letting go that much more difficult to achieve.

Over time, I had observed that the people most able to tap into their spiritual center were not always the brightest bulbs in the room. Yet somehow, they seemed more adept at recognizing their own shortcomings and having the humility to ask for help. The so-called brilliant people kept right on trying to figure things out with logic. Yet logic, no matter how perfectly it was executed, wasn't enough when it came to coping with HIV, especially when it was based on the faulty assumption that the body rules the mind. Based on a flawed foundation of belief, logic simply steered you to the perfectly wrong answer, every time. To heal yourself, your thought system needed correction, and this could only come about in response to a humble plea for help.

After Marianne had dismissed us at the end of the day, Wil and I joined Barry and a couple of friends for a bite to eat at a nearby diner. After he had placed his order, Barry cornered me and proceeded to grill me about something I had said earlier.

"You said that AIDS was a result of something called victim consciousness, right?" he asked. "How can you say that, when some of the most successful people in New York were the first to die of AIDS? I don't think you're right about this one," he snapped.

"Remember, things are not always what they seem," I replied. "You have to look a little deeper than whether or not a person was a success as the world measures it, to know what's *really* going on in their lives. You might want to look at where the motivation for their success comes from in the first place."

"A lot of creative people I know--and this includes me--were driven to succeed out of need to prove that they were good enough. They grew up in places where people made fun of them and called them names, then moved to New York City and spent their entire life trying to prove everyone wrong. They needed the money and the clothes and the houses, and all the other status symbols, to make themselves feel worthy: *See what I've got. See how special I am?*"

"Well, from where you and I stand, that might look like success. And on a certain level--a very superficial one, to be sure--I guess it is. But, if you look a little deeper, you can see that in many cases, all that attitude--all that stuff--is simply a defense against a deeply ingrained belief in not being good enough *exactly as you are*. It's a defense to keep from feeling *vulnerable*. Unfortunately, *A Course in Miracles* reminds us that defenses create the very thing they were meant to protect us from, and AIDS, in some cases, is the ultimate result.

Barry cut the conversation short and turned back to the rest of the table. I could see the wheels turning, as he tried to assimilate my comments.

"Having AIDS doesn't make people wrong or bad," I whispered. "It just means that when we're unconscious of what makes us tick--when we're living in reaction to something that happened in the past, rather than living in the *now*--it's easy to attract a situation into our lives that we don't really want. That's why all the great mystics stressed how important it is to *know* yourself--to know how powerfully creative you are, and make conscious choices about what you want in life."

☀

24 Meeting Elizabeth Kubler Ross

W ITH OUR TIME IN NEW YORK drawing to an end, we said
goodbye to Barry and flagged a taxi to La Guardia, and
boarded a plane to Chicago, bound for a gathering of
Massage Therapist at a former Catholic monastery just outside the city.
In keeping with the thrust of the weekend, to educate members of the
massage community to the needs of people with HIV and AIDS, we
shared our stories as usual and emphasized the role massage had played
in our overall healing process.

"It's especially important that people with AIDS not be shunned
or isolated because of their disease," Wil stressed in his remarks. "The
effects of being ostracized are as debilitating as anything the virus can
do. Massage helps counteract the isolation people feel by creating a sense
of connection to others. When someone takes the time to touch you, it
shows they really care."

Ultimately, I think our mere presence at the conference proved to
be as powerful as anything either of us might have said. It put a human
face on a subject, which for many of the participants, had been merely
theoretical until meeting us in person. In coming face to face with two
people actually living with the disease, they could see that we were not
the one-eyed monsters they had half-expected, but human beings with
flesh-and-blood feelings like their own. Being able to look another person
in the eyes, no matter what manner of sickness they were dealing with,
made it impossible not to feel a certain level of compassion.

When the conference disbanded, we caught a taxi to Chicago
O'Hare, just in time to catch the last flight of the day back to Phoenix.

We had been living out of a suitcase for more than two weeks and were more than ready to give it a rest. Unfortunately, our much anticipated sabbatical proved relatively short-lived. On our first night back, Charlie called from Los Angeles with an update on his latest plans. Christine took the call in the kitchen and handed the phone to Wil.

"I've planned a book signing party to introduce you to the movers and shakers in the LA community," Charlie informed him. "And I've got to say, the guest list is looking pretty darn impressive. I've also scheduled a couple of interviews, which need to be done as soon as possible. Do you think you could be out here by the end of the week?"

"We'll leave tomorrow," Wil sighed, seeing our precious down-time evaporate before his very eyes. "We'll be there in a couple of days."

As he hung up the phone, I could tell from the change in his energy that something unexpected had come up. "What is it?" I asked. "Is something the matter?"

"Forget hiking in Boynton Canyon, tomorrow," he informed me, disappointment obvious in his voice. "There's been a change of plans. We're leaving for L.A. first thing tomorrow morning."

Shortly after sunset, we said good night to Christine and turned in early for a good night's sleep. Before crawling into bed, Wil set the alarm for five am. It seemed as though we had barely closed our eyes before we were shaken awake by the sound of the obnoxious buzzer, insisting that we get up and get a move on.

"Wake up sleepyhead," Wil said, giving me a playful shake. "Time to rise and shine!"

"You first," I groaned, pulling the covers up tightly around my neck. "I'll get up as soon as you're out of the bathroom."

Wil slipped his bathrobe from off the hook behind the door, and draped it around his shoulders to ward against the chill. Moments later, the door to the Winnebago slammed shut and the sound of heavy footsteps crunched along the gravel drive. I fell back into a pleasant, semi-lucid sleep.

All too soon, Wil was back again--shaved, showered and raring to go. "It's your turn," he announced, stripping the covers from off the bed. "No more messing around. You've got to get up, now!"

Under protest, I groped my way out of bed and stumbled out of the Winnebago, and headed for the house. Exiting the bathroom, twenty minutes later, the soothing aroma of freshly brewed coffee greeted my newly revived senses.

"I hope we didn't make too much noise," I apologized, padding into the kitchen where Christine sat nursing a cup of coffee. "I tried to be really quiet."

"Oh no, you were fine," she replied, stifling a yawn. "You don't think I was going to let you guys leave without saying goodbye, do you? She retrieved a mug from over the sink and poured me a cup of coffee. "Here," she said, handing me the steaming mug. "You look like you could use this about now."

I added a splash of milk and cradled the mug in my hands for warmth. "This should do the trick," I said, gulping down the warm, brown liquid. "I guess I'd better go and get dressed."

Meanwhile, back in the Winnebago, Wil had finished dressing and was putting things away. The countertops were cleared and he was battening down the hatches in preparation for our departure.

"Here we go again," he grinned, putting the last of the dishes away. "Back on the road again!"

"I'm ready," I chirped, flashing a subdued grin. "Just let me get dressed and we'll be on our way."

A half hour later, we exited Page Springs Road and merged onto a relatively empty interstate 17, heading north in the direction of Flagstaff and interstate 40 West. In anticipation of the sun's imminent ascent, the eastern sky radiated a soft, muted glow of orange.

"This is my favorite time of day," Wil sighed, draining the last drops of coffee from the bottom of his mug. "Los Angeles, here we come!"

As happy as we were to be back on the road again, the six hundred mile trip to Los Angles, against a steady headwind of at least 30 knots, was not exactly our idea of a party. After the blatant beauty of Sedona, the subtlety of the landscape we were traversing mostly escaped our eyes. After wrestling against a relentless head-wind for the better part of the day, we called it quits and settled into a dilapidated RV park for the night, somewhere outside Barstow, California.

The next morning dawned hot and bright, with hardly a trace of wind. Hoping to make up for lost time, we grabbed a quick breakfast at the first Denny's we came to, and hit the road at a clip. Even so, it was late in the day as we pulled to a halt in front of Charlie's familiar house in

LA. The long drive had left us tired and cranky, and we were ravenously hungry, to boot.

"I'll take you to my favorite vegetarian restaurant, just down the hill from here," Charlie said, quickly surmising that neither of us was up for a night on the town. "We can eat and go over our plans for the rest of the week. Then, you two can get to bed early. I want you rested and ready for your interview tomorrow morning. You've both got to be sharp!

Early the next morning, Charlie chauffeured us across town to the apartment of Carolyn Ruben, a writer for the L. A. Weekly, and dropped us off at the curb. "Apartment 2321," he said, pointing to a row of nearby townhouses. "I'll be back for you in a couple of hours."

The interview, which lasted for most of the morning, took the basic form of a conversation and was relatively free of stress. We sipped coffee and shared our unique metaphysical take on the epidemic, and the details of our sojourn around the country.

"That's quite a story," Carolyn commented, after we had finished. "I think I have just about everything I need from you two, for now. I'll call you at Charlie's if I think of anything else."

The book signing party in West Hollywood, the main purpose for our visit to Los Angeles, fell on the following night. Shortly before sunset, we piled into the Suzuki and drove the short distance to a posh hotel on the edge of the Hollywood Hills, where the party was being held.

The top floor banquet room was already crowded by the time Wil and I arrived. Charlie, who had come early to set up the room, saw us standing in the doorway and came bounding over to greet us. "

"Follow me," he said, steering us over to where Dr. Jon Kaiser and Marianne Williamson stood deep in conversation. Marianne, we already knew, of course, having just spent an entire weekend with her, barely three weeks earlier, at the fundraiser for The Center for Living in New York City. Dr. Kaiser, on the other hand, we had never before had the pleasure of meeting.

"Jon has a holistic medical practice in San Francisco, for people with HIV and AIDS," Charlie informed us, after the proper introductions had been made. "He's also writing a book and is interested in talking with you two about your experiences. But that will have to wait, for now. Were running a bit behind, and I need to get started with the program. Are you guys ready?" We indicated that we were.

193

Charlie maneuvered his way over to a small podium at the front of the room, and tapped on the microphone to gain the crowd's attention. When the room had quieted down, he thanked everyone for coming and introduced Marianne Williamson, who opened with a prayer. Next, Wil and I said a few words about our trip around the country, and our newly released book; and as quickly as it had begun, the presentation was over.

Later, as we mingled with the guests, each whom had been given an autographed copy of our book, Sandy Scott, the energetic, blond minister of the West Hollywood Church of Religious Science, steered me into a corner and started pumping me for details about my supposed healing and spiritual beliefs. At first, I was a little taken aback by her aggressive questioning and wasn't quite sure how to respond. Was she really interested in my opinion, or was she trying to make her own point at my expense? I couldn't really tell. I took a moment to center myself, before delving into what turned out to be an engaging give and take.

"I just needed to hear it from the horse's mouth," she confessed later, indicating that I had passed whatever test she had been administering. "You just can't be too careful these days, you know? There are a lot of people out there making a lot of outrageous claims. I just wanted to make sure you guys were the real deal."

A few days later, Charlie received a phone call from Dr. Don Pachuta, a Baltimore physician specializing in the treatment of HIV and AIDS, inviting Wil and me to be his guests at an AIDS conference in Washington D.C. the following weekend. Despite the short notice, we eagerly accepted the invitation, as much for the opportunity of hearing the two keynote speakers, Dr. Bernie Siegel and Dr. Elizabeth Kubler Ross, as for the chance to expose our book to AIDS professionals from all around the country. If Charlie had his way, everyone at the conference would be carrying a copy of our book back with them to their respective communities, to share with their constituents. After all, as he so eloquently reminded us, having a book was essentially meaningless if nobody knew it existed.

That weekend, after an uneventful flight from LA, we checked into the hotel where the conference was being held, and set off in search of the illusive Dr. Pachuta. After scouring the lobby unsuccessfully, we spotted him in one of the adjacent public areas, giving some last minute instructions to a group of volunteers.

"I'm so happy you're here!" he crowed, striding across the room to greet us. "I recognize you both from your pictures, of course!"

I blushed, thinking of the stilted, publicity photo he must undoubtedly be referring to. I might be healing myself, but I was still vain enough to hate the thought I might actually look as bad as the photo would seem to suggest.

"I just had to have you here this weekend," the doctor explained, apologizing for the last minute nature of the invitation. "You two are the embodiment of everything I've been trying to explain to my esteemed medical colleagues, that a person's beliefs have a direct impact on their clinical outcome. Perhaps you'll be able to help me convince them of that this weekend. What do you think?"

"We'll do our best," Wil replied, looking at me for support. Before I could respond, Dr. Pachuta interrupted with some further news.

"Oh, by the way, Elizabeth Kubler Ross is here and would like to meet with the two of you sometime before her presentation, tonight. Perhaps if you're not too tired from your flight, you could go up to her room for a few minutes." He reached into his jacket and pulled out a business card, and handed it to Wil. "Here's her room number," he said. "Be sure to give her a call, first."

Just then, several newly arrived registrants came rushing over to the Doctor. Taking advantage of the distraction, we slipped away to our room to rest. Wil sat cross-legged on the bed, watching as I unpacked the suitcase and put our clothes away. The silence in the room was noticeably thick.

"You seem a little strange," he commented, following me with his eyes. "Is something the matter?"

"Not really," I fudged. "I'm just a little nervous about meeting Elizabeth Kubler Ross, that's all. It's strange having someone so famous want to meet *us*. Usually, it would be the other way around." I turned back to the bed and continued to unpack. "I guess I'm just not used to having the tables reversed like this. It's a little unsettling, that's all."

"You'd better get used to it," Wil said. "It's going to be happening a lot more often now, especially as our book gets more exposure."

I closed the empty suitcase and stashed it in bottom of the closet.

"Well, let's get it over with," I sighed, as if we had been scheduled for an execution. "I'm really tired, and want to take a nap before we go out tonight. Call and see if now is a good time for us to come up, OK?"

A few minutes later, Wil and I were standing outside Elizabeth's room, several floors directly above our own. Wil knocked on the door and listened for signs of activity. Moments later, the door opened a crack and a raspy voice echoed from behind it.

"Come in, come in," the voice beckoned, and an ancient hand motioned for us to enter. "I've been looking forward to meeting you two young men in person."

We stepped inside a small, dimly lit vestibule, and found ourselves face to face with a diminutive woman with a weather-beaten face, dressed in a terrycloth robe, with a cigarette dangling from her lips. The aroma of coffee and nicotine filled the airless room.

"So I read your little book," Elizabeth Kubler Ross began, clasping my hand in hers, "and I was impressed with what you had to say."

I stood there for a moment, not really knowing how to respond to such a gracious complement. An uncomfortable rush of inadequacy welled up behind my face.

"Thank you," I croaked. "That's a real compliment coming from you, Dr. Ross."

"Call me Elizabeth," she replied. "Forget the Dr. Ross nonsense."

I'm not really clear on all the particulars of our conversation that evening, as completely absorbed as I was by my own feelings of inadequacy. And to be honest, I didn't really know all that much about her, either, except that she was famous for her book, *On Death and Dying*, and neither of those subjects was really a forte of mine. To the contrary, I had invested 100% of my energy trying to avoid the subject, entirely. I was completely focused on wanting to live.

"I guess we're going to have to read her books," Wil commented later, back in the safety of our room. "After all, you do realize that she took the time to read ours, don't you?"

"Yeah, I suppose you're right," I said, pulling back the covers on my side of the bed, and giving the pillows a fluff. "But I've got a better idea. Why don't *you* read her books and then tell me what they're about, OK?"

Wil looked at me as though I had lost my mind. I giggled and jumped into bed, and pulled the covers up around my chin. "In the meantime, it's time for some much needed beauty rest," I announced. And with that, I rolled over and went to sleep

A few hours later, refreshed from the nap we had taken, we made our way down to the lobby and threaded our way through the milling crowd, to the ballroom where the opening presentation was scheduled to take place. An elevated stage dominated the center of the cavernous auditorium.

Pausing just inside the door to get our bearings, we spied a pair of empty seats on one of the aisles, to our liking, and quickly settled into them. A short time later, the overhead lights dimmed and Dr. Pachuta strode onto the stage. He waited until the last few stragglers had found their seats, before introducing himself to the pumped up crowd. A litany of announcements quickly ensued. Then, with the formalities out of the way, it was time for the main event.

"I want you to give a very special welcome to Dr. Bernie Siegel and Dr. Elizabeth Kubler Ross," he announced to wild applause. The two people everyone had come to see strolled slowly onto the stage and waved to the audience, before making themselves comfortable on a pair of matching stools. They smiled and chatted with each other until the applause had died away. Then, finally, Dr. Siegel began to speak.

Anyone, who has ever had the pleasure of hearing Bernie Siegel speak, knows how much he loves to talk and how profound and funny he can be. This particular night, he punctuated the seriousness of his subject matter with a joke or two, while effortlessly zeroing in on the central issue at hand. Then, when he had finished with his remarks, he turned the evening over to his fellow presenter, Dr. Elizabeth Kubler Ross.

"I really didn't know why Dr. Pachuta asked me, of all people, to be here and talk with you about AIDS, tonight," Elizabeth began, scanning the room and adjusting her weight on the stool. "When the good doctor called and asked if I would be willing to say something hopeful, I was frankly at a loss."

"Last night, however, just before going to bed, I was sitting in my rocking chair, opening the day's mail, and was just about to call it quits when I spied a small package on the floor. You do know that I live on a farm not too far from here, in Virginia?" she asked, veering off topic for a moment. A murmur of assent arose from the attentive crowd.

"Well, anyway," she continued, getting right back on track, "it got my curiosity up, and so I opened it to see what was inside. To my surprise, there was a little, pink book about AIDS. So I thought I'd better read it and see if it would give me some ideas about what I might say to you this evening."

I nudged Wil to see if he was thinking the same thing I was. He tilted his head ever-so-slightly in my direction, and reached over and squeezed my arm.

"Well, I have to tell you," Elizabeth was saying, "I stayed up most of the night reading this little book, and I couldn't put it down." She slid down from her stool and stooped over and picked up a small, pink book from off the floor, and waved it in the air. "It's called *Beyond AIDS*," she announced, "*and it's the best book on healing I've read in twenty years!*"

The audience strained to catch a glimpse of the book. I gave Wil an elbow in the ribs. "Can you believe it?" I hissed. "Did you hear what she just said about our book!?"

He looked at me and flashed a toothy grin. "Yes I did!" he beamed. "From what she just said, I think she rather liked it!"

We turned our attention back to the stage, where Elizabeth stood holding our book aloft. "Where are those two nice young men?" she asked, gazing out into the audience, using the book to shield her eyes from the glare of the spotlight. "I know they're here, somewhere."

Eventually, she spotted us on the aisle. "Stand up. I want to make sure everybody gets a chance to see who you are," she said, motioning for us to stand.

Dazed, for a moment, by the powerful spot light that was suddenly shining in our eyes, we rose halfway up out of our seats and looked timidly around at the hundreds of curious faces staring back in our direction. The roar of applause thundered in our ears.

"Thank you. Thank you very much," we mouthed, and then hastily took our seats, embarrassed by the rush of so much attention. Not that we minded a little attention, you understand, just that so much of it at one time was a little bit unsettling. Inside, however, we were both bursting with pride!

When Elizabeth had finished speaking, Wil and I were promptly mobbed by a surge of people wanting to congratulate us on the work we were doing, and purchase a copy of our book. To accommodate the demand, we spent the next several hours behind a small folding table Dr. Pachuta had set aside for us in the lobby, thanking well-wishers, signing autographs, and answering dozens of personal questions. By the time midnight rolled around, we had managed to sell every one of the one hundred and twenty books we had brought with us, and people were still clamoring for more. Pleading fatigue, we beat a hasty retreat to the sanctuary of our room.

To make sure that no one who wanted a book left the conference empty-handed, before going to bed, Wil placed a call to Charlie in Los Angeles and explained the situation, and asked him to express another couple of cases, right away. By Dr. Pachuta's closing remarks on Sunday afternoon, we had sold all of these books as well.

Wil and I reveled in the sudden acceleration in our fortunes; for the flattering accolades Elizabeth had so generously bestowed on our book, and for the hundreds of copies we had sold as a result. As an added bonus, we were able to network with representatives of AIDS agencies from all around the country, and many of them expressed interest in having us visit their communities and speak.

The next day, we stopped by Elizabeth's room to thank her for all her help. "Don't mention it," she said, brushing our gratitude aside. "Just make sure to keep in touch with me. At some point I'd like us to do an event, together, in Charlottesville, so my medical students can hear what you have to say. I'm on the board at the University, so I don't think it'll be a problem."

At the end of the conference, we checked out of the hotel and grabbed a cab to the airport, and arrived back in Los Angeles just as the latest edition of the L.A. Weekly, with our recent interview with Carolyn Rubens in it, hit the stands. The article, though written from a more jaundiced point of view than we would have liked, was funny and sharp, and managed to get our message across--not to mention, provide heaps of free publicity for our book.

"If this keeps up, we're going to have to do another printing," I predicted. "About how many copies would you say we've sold, so far?"

"More than 4000," Charlie said, providing the precise statistic.

"Then, let's go ahead and move on it," Wil suggested, jumping onto the bandwagon. "We wouldn't want to run out and miss out on any potential sales."

Over breakfast the next morning, the three of us hashed out the financial details of a second printing. With no set-up costs this time around, Charlie figured that we could print twice as many books, at nearly half the cost of the originals.

"I'll get to work on it, right away," he said, pushing his chair back from the table. "And you guys need to get moving, if you plan to be in Santa Cruz by five o'clock."

We were on our way to San Francisco, by way of the small, beach community of Santa Cruz, where we were scheduled to speak at the John XXIII AIDS Ministry, run by a Catholic priest affectionately known as Father Al. That evening, after the event was over and we were just about to leave, a young woman who was active in the local AIDS community pulled me aside and handed me an envelope with both our names written on it.

"I hope you'll accept this as a token of my appreciation for what you guys are doing," she whispered, gazing warmly into my eyes. "I've been on the front lines of this epidemic for a long time, and I've seen a lot of my friends die before their time. As far as I'm concerned, you guys make as much sense as anything the doctors have to say. I hope, for all our sakes, you'll keep up the good work!"

I thanked her and exchanged a hasty hug, and stuffed the envelope into my pocket and ran to catch up with Wil. Later, as we were driving through the Santa Cruz Mountains, on our way to San Francisco, I remembered the envelope and reached into my pocket to retrieve it.

"A woman gave this to me on my way out the door tonight," I said, tearing open the envelope and extracting what appeared to be a folded check. I unfolded it and glanced at the bottom line. "Oh my God," I gasped. "You're not going to believe this! It's a check for a thousand dollars!

"Alright!" Wil yelled, pumping his fist in the air. "Now will you stop worrying about money?"

"Keep your eye on the road," I shot back testily. "Otherwise, you're going to get us both killed."

Dawn, the following morning, found us parked on a residential street in San Francisco in the Castro. We waited until nine o'clock before putting in a call to Eric, who had just that week signed a lease on a stunning new home on the side of Twin Peaks, with sweeping, panoramic views of the downtown skyline. The house included a small mother-in-law unit on the ground floor, just off the garage, which Eric thought might make a suitable base for Wil and me, in light of our decreased dependence on New York.

While I still entertained fantasies about living somewhere exotic like Sedona or Santa Fe, San Francisco was not completely out of the question. The fact that it was a city, and a very livable one, at that--and had a large, gay population--weighed heavily in its favor. The fact that it was located on the San Andreas Fault did not.

At Eric's insistence, we left the Winnebago at a friend's house in Marin and moved in with him for the duration of our stay. Since his furniture hadn't yet made it from New York, we made do by sleeping on the living room floor, on an air mattress we purchased at Cliff's hardware store. The extraordinary views and charm of a working fireplace compensated for any inconvenience.

Unfortunately, Eric had been sick with a cold and hacking cough for over a week. Apparently, there was a bug going around and he had been unfortunate enough to catch it. A few days later, Wil and I came down with the same nasty bug, which stubbornly refused to respond to any of the several over-the-counter medications we tried to treat it with. Sick as dogs, the three of us were cooped up in the house together for days on end, coughing and sneezing, and generally feeling quite miserable. By the time another week had come and gone, our nerves were shot.

To make matters worse, Eric was increasingly consumed by panic. The flu had sabotaged his plans to begin working, and his insecurity was definitely showing. Sick with fever and uncontrollable fits of coughing, Wil and I were just as edgy--our situation complicated by the crush of events we had scheduled in the days immediately ahead.

We were slated to do a book signing at *A Different Light* bookstore in the Castro, and a number of other appearances at gay-friendly stores in the area. Then, there was the lecture for The Metaphysical Alliance. Not wanting to disappoint any of our sponsors, after all the hard work they had done on our behalf, Wil and I worked out a plan of action we both felt we could live with. First, I would do the book signing at *A Different Light*, while Wil stayed home in bed. Then, I would come home and go to bed, and he would take care of the rest. Both of us would show up for the lecture at the Metaphysical Alliance, after which we'd finally be free to just rest.

A week later, with all of the events behind us, we were both feeling somewhat better; not completely well, mind you, but much better than at any time in the previous two weeks. Unfortunately, the strain of all of us being cooped up in the house together, without a break, had overwhelmed Eric and his nerves finally snapped. To be truthful, Wil and I were as sick of him as he obviously was of us, and were itching to hit the road. One thing was clear: we wouldn't be living in the same house with Eric Bailes; not now; not in the future-- not ever!

As soon as we were physically able to, we boarded a bus to Marin and retrieved the Winnebago, and drove back to Eric's house, scooped up our clothes and the cats, and hit the road running. We didn't stop until we had reached the dusty outskirts of Las Vegas, 500 miles away. Once there, we promptly checked into an RV park on the strip and slept until our lungs had dried out in the dry, desert air.

A few days later, we were both feeling a whole lot better. We pooled our change and hit the casinos for a night of fun. Though we lost all of our money, the evening of mindless entertainment helped us to forget the unpleasantness of the last, few, stressful weeks. The past was the past, and was over and done with--or so we hoped. It was time to refocus on the events at hand.

Before leaving Las Vegas, we spoke to a small AIDS support group at the local MCC, then hit the road running with a succession of stops, beginning with the MCC in Kansas City, followed by events in St. Louis, Cincinnati and Indianapolis. Along the way, we sold our books and tapes, and listened to the testimonies of a growing number of people who had embraced a spiritual journey.

In Cleveland, we caught up with our old friends, Janet and Bellruth, and made a return appearance with our book on *The Morning Exchange*. There was also an informative article about us in The Cleveland Plains-Dealer. Then, as quickly as we had arrived, we were off to Pittsburg for another engagement. Then, finally, with nothing left on our schedule, we packed it in and headed for New York City.

☀

25 Bean Town

O
N ARRIVING IN NEW YORK CITY, we holed up in the apartment for several days, before hopping a plane to Boston for a lecture and personal appearance on the popular, television show, *People are Talking*. Besides Wil and me, the roster of guests included our old friend, Niro Assistant, Dr. Bernie Siegel, who we had met at the conference in Washington a few months earlier, and a newcomer to the scene, Dr. Deepak Chopra, who was there to publicize his very first book. We were excited to be included in such illustrious company, and were looking forward for the opportunity of exposing our message to an entirely new audience of people.

Unfortunately, the show itself proved to be a bit of a disappointment. With so many guests, with so much to say and so little time to say it in, no one got more than a minute or two, at most, to put their respective points across. We took consolation in knowing that we'd have another opportunity the very next night, at a lecture we were scheduled to give at a gay health club and restaurant complex, downtown.

When Wil and I arrived at the venue the following evening, the scene we encountered left little doubt that our reputations had preceded us to Boston. Even before the advertised 7:30 start time, the small auditorium was packed to capacity and a line of people snaked its way out the door. Despite the reassuring turnout, neither of us really knew just what to expect from the conservative Boston audience, and we were a little concerned about how our message might be received.

Home to Harvard, MIT, and a slew of prestigious medical centers, the views of main stream medicine were fairly-well entrenched in the

Boston community, and much of what Wil and I had to say ran counter to conventional thought. To play it safe, we toned down some of our more obvious new-age rhetoric, and couched our message in terms we felt the conservative Boston audience would be more comfortable with.

Wil was the first to speak. "Dr. George Solomon of the UCLA Medical Center, and the father of psychoneuroimmunology, has compiled a list of the ten most common traits of long-term survivors of AIDS," he began, pausing briefly to connect with a number of familiar faces in the audience. "Number one on that list was the patient's ability to say *"no"*, whenever they were asked to do something they didn't want to do. The patients who were able to freely express their feelings, without a lot of guilt, were the most likely to survive."

"The patients who took an active role in the decision making process had a much higher survival rate than the more passive ones," he continued, making his way down the list. "The ones who simply turned their treatment over to their doctor and said *"fix me"*, didn't do nearly as well. It's important to get involved in your treatment, to see yourself as part of a team, and to speak up and ask a lot of questions. If your doctor doesn't like it, then fire him. It's your life we're talking about."

And so it went until all but the last of the ten traits had been listed and explained. "Last, but not least, people who have a support system do better than those who try to handle their situation alone. It's important to reach out to other people and ask for help; a support group is a definite must. But make sure that the support group you're involved with is there to support you in reaching your goals. If they're only there to play *ain't it awful*, then by all means dump them as fast as you can."

With that, he thanked the audience and turned the lectern over to me. Since Wil had already covered the mental/medical angle, I decided to cover the spiritual. After all, science wasn't the only entrenched belief system in this bastion of tradition known as Boston. The Catholic Church had a lot of power, too.

I took a deep breath and centered myself, before taking up a theme I had first explored in Salt Lake City. I addressed my remarks, specifically, to several members of the clergy seated in the audience.

"I remember when I was first coming to terms with my sexuality," I began, measuring my words carefully. "I would be feeling really good about myself, and then I would run into some fanatical Christian who would remind me that the Bible says homosexuality is an abomination. And my self-esteem would come crashing down, as I was reminded that I was just fooling myself in thinking God could possibly love a person such as me--an unrepentant homosexual."

"Unlike some gay Christians, it has never worked for me to try and interpret my way around the offending scriptures, though that's perfectly ok, if that's what you chose to do. Personally, I found that approach a little hard to swallow. I'd read the scriptures; I knew what they had to say. And I wasn't going to try and fool myself by pretending they meant something else."

"Well, anyway, I kept praying about the issue until, one day, I got an answer. This little thought popped into my head out of nowhere-- that's how I get a lot of my answers; they pop into my head from out of nowhere--and it said, *who said the Bible is the divinely inspired word of God?* Instantly, I realized that I had never, ever questioned that belief before; it was so deeply ingrained that for all intents and purposes it was invisible. So no matter how hard I tried to break free of my religious upbringing and learn to love myself for being gay, I would always fail. I would always hit a wall. This one invisible belief invariably stood in the way."

"Needless to say, when I finally recognized this belief, I also realized it wasn't necessarily true. While I do believe that the Bible has a lot of good things to say about how to live your life, it also contains a lot of distortion. After all, it was written by men, and men, at their best, are fallible creatures. I guess you could say that the truth got filtered down though the various author's belief systems and was corrupted in the process. Anyway, once I recognized this, I was free. From then on, I could read the Bible--if I wanted to--and accept only what resonated as true in the deepest part of my being."

Some members of the audience were starting to squirm. I took a deep breath and brought my remarks to a close.

"What the Bible needs, more than anything, is a really good editor, and that editor is *inside* of you. In Christian terms, it's the Holy Spirit- -or the Higher Self, if you're a fan of Shirley Mac Laine. Whatever you do, don't give your power away to a book, no matter who the author is claimed to be. *You* must be your own authority and discover what is true for you."

Early the next morning, Wil and I caught the first plane back to

New York, where a laundry list of personal business was waiting on our attention. By now, it was obvious that in all likelihood we were out of New York for good. Even so, we were reluctant to relinquish the apartment, just in case there was an unexpected change of plans. We agreed to let Barry stay there for as long as he liked, thereby postponing any final decision on the matter.

With much of our time and interest focused in California, it only made sense to move there, at least temporarily, to get the lay of the land. We had made a lot of friends in San Francisco and wanted to give it a try. As a plus, despite our last unpleasant encounter, Eric had offered Wil a part-time job in the small computer firm he had founded. We wouldn't have to worry about a source of income--at least, not right away.

To be perfectly honest, Wil and I had both had enough of New York City. In fact, I didn't care if we ever lived in a city again, not even one as charming as San Francisco. My own fantasies revolved around living in the country in a community of like-minded people, communing with nature and growing my own food. This came partly from a legitimate desire to live in closer harmony with the earth, and partly from a secret fear that Ramtha's predictions might ultimately come true; that at some point in the not too distant future, society would suffer a massive breakdown, and people living in cities would be most vulnerable to the chaos.

Though I liked just about everything about California, I did harbor some concern that at some point it might break off and fall into the Ocean. Despite my fears, I was determined to give it a try. As mobile as Wil and I were, we could easily change our minds if things didn't work out the way we planned. We'd simply rev up the Winnebago and hit the road at a clip.

We packed as many things from the apartment as would fit in the Winnebago, and what we couldn't take with us, we gave away to friends. Neither of us had much attachment to possessions, really. The only thing I regretted parting with was my beloved grand piano. It was a gorgeous piece of furniture, about eighty years old, built in the art nouveau style, with massive, ornately carved legs. The piano had been my first love, and I had bought my very first one when I was only six years old: a termite-riddled, old upright, paid for with the five hundred dollars in pennies I had collected from friends and relatives. Never mind the present one. I could always buy another one when we settled in California.

To save ourselves the expense of hiring a team of professional movers, we packed the back of the Winnebago to its roof line with boxes, and slept on the couch up front. If we were driving to California anyway, there was no point in spending the extra money for movers.

Before leaving town, we made a quick trek to the upper west side to visit Anita, and were shocked when she met us at the front door to her apartment. She was extremely weak and had lost a lot of weight, and her face was drawn and haggard.

"I've had a relapse and I'm shooting drugs again," she confessed, as she led us down a long hall to her bedroom. "I just can't seem to get this monkey off my back. And I don't really believe that I can heal myself, anymore. I know, now, that I'm not going to make it, but it doesn't really matter. I'm tired and I just want this whole damn mess to be over and done with."

We cried and hugged, and cried some more, knowing full-well that this would be the last time we would ever see her alive. There was nothing anyone could say. There was nothing *to* say, really. We simply sat with her and listened as she expressed her anger and frustration.

⁎

26 Elizabeth, UFO's, Star
Seeds and Walk-Ins

O BREAK THE MONOTONY OF THE long, cross country trip, we
scheduled a number of speaking engagements along the way.
Elizabeth had invited Wil and I to speak to a group of medical
students at the University of Virginia in Charlottesville, and naturally
we accepted. The opportunity to expose our views to a group of future
physicians was simply too good an opportunity to pass up, even if it was
a bit of a stretch. After all, the only degree I had was from the Wilfred
Academy of Beauty. Wil, at least, had a degree in engineering from
NYU.

On our way to Elizabeth's farm, we stopped in Washington, D.C.
and spoke to a small AIDS support group, run by Dr. Lark Lands, a
medical doctor and expert on micro-nutritional supplementation. The
crowd was small but appreciative, and we sold a number of books and
tapes.

The next day, we drove the remaining distance to Elizabeth's farm
in Headwaters, Virginia, and took a tour of the healing center she was
constructing on the property. The 350 acre parcel, in a small valley, high
up in the mountains, was cordoned off into three distinct areas: the
center itself, a fully operational organic farm, and Elizabeth's private
domain. A rugged Swiss Chalet dominated the highest point on the
property, along with a smaller cabin she had built to accommodate her
sister's yearly visits from Switzerland.

That night, we shared dinner with Elizabeth and her staff, and accepted her invitation for tea and an after dinner chat at her Chalet atop the hill. The air was crisp and clear as we climbed the quarter-mile distance to the house. Inside the rustic cabin, every room was filled with artifacts Elizabeth had collected over the span of her lengthy career. Dolls of every description, Indian pottery, and a hundred other interesting items were crammed into every available nook and cranny.

"I'm saving these for my AIDS babies," Elizabeth explained, gesturing toward the dolls. Unfortunately, her plans to bring twenty, abandoned AIDS orphans to live with her on the farm, had earned her the ire of her bigoted, nearby neighbors.

"They shot one of my llamas just last week," she lamented, "and tried to burn down the house a couple of times. But they can't scare me. I'm tougher than they are!"

We followed her into the kitchen and waited while she made a pot of tea, before retracing our steps back into the living room. Elizabeth sagged wearily into a rocker beside the fire.

"Have a seat," she said, indicating a pile of pillows on the floor. We did as we were told and made ourselves comfortable, and sipped our tea and stared into the fire. Erie shadows danced along the walls and into the overhead rafters.

For the next several hours, Elizabeth held us spellbound with some of the most fascinating stories Wil and I had ever heard. Whether they were true or not, we couldn't really say for sure. What was obvious, however, was that Elizabeth was a master story teller, and in us she had found the perfect audience. As we sat enraptured at her feet, she regaled us with story after amazing story; of being contacted by alien beings and taken up into the mother ship, and shown a number of futuristic, medical devices.

One of these devises, she explained--a small, black box about the size of a common shoe box--could identify specific disease patterns within a person's energy field, and create the opposing pattern, neutralizing it before it could manifest into physical symptoms. Others were sophisticated laser devices that could cut through flesh without a mark, or close a wound in a matter of minutes. When these technologies were made available to humanity, the aliens had promised, they would revolutionize the practice of medicine.

Elizabeth also described some of her more profound experiences with the spirit world; of her relationship with her spirit guides and a friendly ghost who lived in the farmhouse where we had eaten dinner, earlier. She shared the rewards and challenges of bringing her vision of a healing center to fruition, the frustrating series of setbacks that had continually plagued the project, and the incredible resistance she had encountered from the locals.

"Throughout the whole ordeal, I kept praying for patience," she sighed, showing us photographs of a mud slide that had recently engulfed a major portion of the nearly completed center, causing yet another in a long series of delays. "Yet, the more I prayed for patience, the more things seemed to happen. And then it hit me! I quit praying for patience and started affirming, *I am patient.* After that, things started to run a whole lot smoother!"

With the hour growing late, and Elizabeth beginning to tire, Wil and I excused ourselves and headed back down the hill to the Winnebago, reflecting on the evening as we went. I glanced over at him to see if I could gage his reaction to Elizabeth's claims, knowing from experience that all this UFO business usually made him more than a little uptight.

"Do you think she's crazy?" I asked, attempting to peer inside his head to see what he was thinking. "You have to admit, those stories about being abducted by aliens were pretty far out."

"I don't know," he replied, lapsing into thought. "I don't think she's crazy, really. I just don't know *what* to think!"

With that, I let the conversation die. The truth was that I didn't know what to think about Elizabeth's stories, either. It certainly wasn't the first time I had run into UFO buffs, however. That had happened several years earlier while we were still living in New York; and more recently, again, on our first visit to Denver. After that, the further west we had journeyed, the more this kind of information kept showing up.

Shortly after the Challenger disaster, a friend of mine, Henry Romanowski-- Mr. New York Leather, at the time--invited me to a meeting of UFO buffs in an old, rundown loft in Soho. While I was generally skeptical about such matters, the experience had turned out to be rather enlightening.

After an opening meditation, the young man in charge of the gathering stated, very matter of factly, that he had recently been in touch with the Ashtar Command. Ashtar, he explained, was the leader of a rather formidable band of extraterrestrials who were currently in orbit around the earth, in an enormous spaceship several miles long, and was in charge of facilitating the first, alien contact with earth.

"The Challenger astronauts are now working with Ashtar from the other side." he informed the approving group.

"Preposterous!" my mind had screamed. "These people are completely nuts!"

As the evening progressed, several other people had come forward to share related information; each equally sincere, and each claiming to be either a star-seed or a walk-in-- neither of which I had heard of until this particular night.

Star seeds, it was later explained to me, were extraterrestrials that had incarnated into human form, with full knowledge of their cosmic identity encoded within their DNA. At a certain astrological date and time, the code would be activated and the star seed would remember who they were, and their purpose for being on earth.

A walk-in, on the other hand, was an entirely different matter, altogether. As nearly as I could understand it, walk-ins were humans who, for one reason or another-- because they were homeless or depressed, or suicidal and wanted off the planet--surrendered possession of their body to a waiting entity, in exchange for assistance to the other side. The body's new tenant retained all of the memories of its previous owner, as well as their own cosmic identity and purpose for making the switch.

While all of this was going on around me, internally I was having the most amazing experience. On the one hand, my mind wanted to rebel against what I was hearing, thinking, "UFOs..., aliens..., yeah, right!" At the same time, another part of me understood exactly what was being discussed. Despite these people's stories being couched in terms of UFOs and extraterrestrials, the plain fact was that I resonated with the underlying theme.

Essentially, everyone there believed in a world-wide healing process, initiated through awakening individuals, and culminating in the transformation of the planet. In my new, alien friend's perceptions, this process was being directed by extraterrestrials. In mine, it was directed by my Higher Self. Yet, when I let go of my attachment to the story's form, it was obvious that our experiences were pretty much the same. I left the loft that night, suspecting that I was a star seed.

The day after our fascinating evening with Elizabeth at the chalet, we drove into Charlottesville and gave a talk before a packed house at the University of Virginia Medical School, where Elizabeth sat on the board. After we had finished speaking, Elizabeth commandeered the podium and brought the evening to a close with some well-placed remarks of her own. Later, we checked into a local motel and stayed up well past midnight, finalizing plans for a similar presentation in Los Angeles in the fall.

"I'll see you boys in a couple of months," Elizabeth said, as we were preparing to leave for Atlanta the following morning. She walked us to the Winnebago and gave us each a great, big hug. "You two drive careful, now. And tell Charlie he should plan on making a tape of our talk. I'm sure it would be a big help to a lot of people."

We said we would, and climbed into the Winnebago. I started the engine and pulled slowly out of the parking lot, and headed in the direction of the main highway leading out of town. Connecting with the interstate a few miles later, we headed south along the Blue Ridge Mountains, past Roanoke and Ashville, and down into Charlotte, which was all new territory to us. From Charlotte, it was a straight shot all the way through to Atlanta.

This visit to Atlanta, our third in little more than a year, was shaping up to be considerably different than either of the previous two. This time, we planned on facilitating a one-day, experiential workshop, based on what, until now, we had only talked about in our many lectures around the country.

Needless to say, I was a little cowed by the prospective challenge and was afraid we might muck it up. Facilitating a workshop was a definite stretch for the both of us, considering that all we had done for the last 18 months was share our personal experience. Unlike a lecture, a workshop required certain basic skills--skills I wasn't sure either of us possessed. To pull it off, we would need to effectively communicate our ideas, and illustrate them with experiential exercises. The former, I thought we could handle. Of the latter, I was not entirely convinced.

We spent our travel time to Atlanta developing a framework for the workshop, which we called, appropriately enough, *Beyond AIDS*, in honor of our new book. During our visit to the farm, Elizabeth had been generous enough to offer some helpful suggestions, which Wil immediately used to develop a guided meditation and anger release process. On our recent visit to New York, Anita had proudly given us a copy of the first cut of AIDS ALIVE, which we intended to put to good use. With a little encouragement from Wil, I managed to come up with a workable plan of my own, so that by the time we arrived in Atlanta, the entire layout of the weekend was pretty much fait accompli.

In advance of the workshop, 125 people had paid in full-- which we both felt was a rather favorable sign--and inquiries were still coming in. Thankfully, the entire event went off without a hitch, especially considering how apprehensive we had been in the days leading up to it. People seemed to respond to the more in-depth format and extract whatever they needed from the exercises. As usual, when all was said and done, it was hard to imagine what all the fuss had been about. We had breezed through our latest challenge and learned some important lessons in the process.

It was clear that the workshop was not about us, or how clever we might be as facilitators. Certainly, we needed to do our homework and be prepared for as many eventualities as possible. But to be honest, the participants did most of the work. We simply created the space and focus, and the participants did the rest.

From Atlanta, we hit the road with a vengeance, headed for Sedona and an extended visit with Christine. We were feeling good about ourselves, our lives, and the work we had accomplished. The debut of our workshop had challenged us to stretch beyond the comfortable framework we had been operating in for most of the last eighteen months, and we had successfully met the test. No longer were we limited to simply telling the same old story over and over again, but had a workshop that could assist people in translating the hope our story engendered into more practical expression in their lives. Our work had taken a quantum leap forward. We were riding high on the Cosmic Slingshot, and our lives would never be the same!

☀

Wil at the house on Fire Island, shortly before it was sold. (1986)

The last summer on Fire Island. (1987)

Mark Veneglia and Eric Bailes at the bungalow in the Pines. (1987)

Wil and friend hang the AIDS Alive fundraising banner. (1987)

The flag Mark's designed to send the subliminal message
"People are healing from AIDS." (1987)

Anita in the Pines for the Harmonic Convergence. (1987)

Niro and Anita on the set of the Oprah Winfrey Show. (1987)

Niro, Wil, and Anita in the bedroom of the Winnebago
in Upstate, New York. (1988)

Wil and George on the road
in the Winnebago. (1988)

Charlie at JFK with the
first copy of Beyond AIDS.
(1988)

Mona Fore in Sedona, Arizona. (1988)

Wil and George at the first Colorado AIDS Walk in Denver. (1988)

Wil and George with Elizabeth at her Headwaters, VA farm. (1989)

The cottage in Marin. (1989)

Reiki Master Denise Crundall and husband John. (1992)

George and Phil Donahue backstage. (1994)

George with Louise Hay, Don Pachuta and friends,
in Washington, DC. (2000)

Part Three
Healing into Life
and Death

Like the birth of spring
The blossom of our love bursts forth
And I can smile again
To know that love can never die.
You are home again
With me
To stay
Forever.

George Melton

27 The Cottage in Marin

"**I** SEE A PRETTY LITTLE COTTAGE on the side of a hill, surrounded by lots of trees. And you, George, are working in a garden filled with vegetables and flowers of every kind." It was Christine speaking in soft, even tones, affirming back to me the vision I had just described to her of where I saw Wil and me living in California.

The three of us--Christine, Wil, and I--were sitting in a circle in a sun-dappled meadow in Oak Creek Canyon, surrounded by ancient Ponderosa Pines, playing Mastermind, a manifestation technique we had learned from the Minister of the Church of Religious Science in Houston whose home we had stayed in on our last visit to the city. The sweet scent of burning cedar and the savory aroma of a nearby grill, filled the air. It was a glorious, late spring day.

Proceeding around the circle, each of us took turns describing in as much detail as possible what we wanted to manifest in our lives. Wil and I had moving to California on our minds, and I had a definite picture of just how I wanted our new life there to look. For starters, I didn't want to live in a city anymore. I pictured us living in a small, charming cottage, similar to the one we had rented on Fire Island the last summer we were there-- not too far from San Francisco, preferably with a view and room for a garden.

Wil and I were planning on leaving for California in less than a week, on the final leg of our arduous, cross country move. As I steered the Winnebago through California's monotonous Central Valley a few days later, Wil busied himself with various reference books and maps, trying to figure out where we might set up camp in the Bay Area until we found a more permanent place to live. RV parks, it seemed, were scarce, in and around San Francisco. Faced with having to choose between one near the ocean in Pacifica, and another in Marin, we chose Marin. Crossing the San Rafael Bridge from the eastern side of the bay, we easily located the park just off highway 101, directly on the water in Corte Madeira. Noting the vacancy sign out front, I steered the Winnebago into the driveway and wrestled our dusty caravan to a halt.

"I'll wait here," I said, suddenly feeling much too tired to move. "You go in and check out the situation."

Wil gave me a look and hopped out of the passenger side door. He disappeared into the small office and reemerged several minutes later, and sauntered over to where I was waiting behind the wheel.

"You'll have to pull around to the other entrance," he informed me. "This section is for permanent residents, only. We're on the other side, in lot 121."

Wil walked ahead on foot, while I shadowed him in the Winnebago. Halfway into the narrow, adjacent alley, he gestured toward an empty site to my right. I stopped in the middle of the narrow lane, leaving the engine running, and climbed out to disconnect the Suzuki and move it out of the way. Then, with a little help from Wil, I gingerly backed our 27-foot behemoth into the space we had been assigned.

We spent the next several days settling into our new digs and familiarizing ourselves with the area. Our first course of action was to rent space in a nearby storage facility and empty the Winnebago of all the things we had brought with us from New York. Then, it was off to buy groceries and stock up on supplies. By the end of the week, we were comfortably ensconced in our new home by the bay and feeling pleased with ourselves about how smoothly the move to California had gone.

It didn't take us very long to decide that Marin County was the ideal place to search for more permanent accommodations. Not particularly urban in character, it wasn't exactly suburban either, in any traditional sense. Rather than endless miles of tract housing, so prevalent in much of the rest of the country, the local architecture was rather eclectic, with a bounty of open spaces and hiking trails punctuating the surrounding hills. It was also less than 20 minutes away from San Francisco by car. And since neither of us was bound by the usual rush hour schedules, commuting into the city, whenever we wanted, would be a snap.

Each morning for the next several weeks, we scoured the local classifieds in search of a place to rent, and circled any listings that even loosely met our criteria. Then, we'd set off to investigate each one in person. And each day, we'd return to the Winnebago exhausted and discouraged by what we had seem. Nothing we looked at was even remotely acceptable by the standards we were accustomed to. The houses were either dark or moldy with dated, shag carpeting, or sorely in need of basic repairs. Nothing even vaguely resembled the charming cottage I had visualized for in Arizona.

Finally, after a number of discouraging forays into the surrounding communities, a new listing in the afternoon paper caught my eye. The details leapt up from the page, seemingly illuminated in neon: Mill Valley, Mt Tam area; newly renovated, 600 sq. ft. cottage with a view. $900 a month.

"Wil, listen to this," I squealed, waving the paper in front of his face. "I think this might just be the thing we've been looking for."

Wil looked up from the book he was reading and listened dispassionately as I read the ad aloud. He had been disappointed before and didn't want to get his hopes up, needlessly.

"I don't know," he replied. "Maybe so, maybe not. I'm not really sure." And with that, he gave an annoying little sigh and went back to reading his book.

I found his lack of enthusiasm rather infuriating. I was having one of my famous, intuitive hunches, and was sure that this was the house we were searching for. I wanted his support.

"I'm going to call and see if we can go over and look at it," I insisted, having no intention of letting the matter drop. "We need to act on this right away or it'll be gone, I promise you."

I picked up the phone and dialed the number listed at the bottom of the ad. After a couple of rings, there was a click on the other end of the line and a woman's voice answered.

"Hello?" she said, pausing for me to identify myself.

I cleared my throat and tried not to sound too enthusiastic. "Hi. I'm calling about the cottage that was in the paper today. Would it be possible to come by and take a look at it sometime later today?"

"Let me see," the woman replied. "My husband is over there right now doing some last-minute work on the window trim. You could probably

go over, say in about an hour or so. Would that be good for you? I'll give
him a call if you'd like, and let him know you're coming."

"Hold on a minute," I said, putting my hand over the phone. "She
says we can go over there in about an hour, Wil. What should I tell
her?"

Wil shrugged his shoulder, indifferently. "If you really want to," he
sighed, "but I think it's a waste of time."

An hour later, we piled into the Suzuki and drove the short distance
to Mill Valley. From Highway One, we veered off onto a small side street,
just before a 7-11, and made a right turn onto Marin Avenue, and snaked
our way up an imposing, eucalyptus-covered hill. A half mile later, Wil
spotted the address we were looking for on a mailbox by the side of the
road. I pulled over onto the narrow shoulder and parked. A man and a
woman were standing in the driveway surveying a series of steps leading
down to a small, charming cottage, below. The place was obviously still
very much under construction.

"Ahh, you must be George," the woman exclaimed, as we descended
the gravel steps. "This is my husband, Steve," she said, gesturing toward
the man. "Honey, this is George. And you must be Wil, is that right?"
she asked, giving him a smile.

"That's right," Wil replied, extending his hand, politely.

"Why don't you two go ahead and take a look around," the woman
offered. She indicated the property below with a sweep of her hand. "But
be careful, now. As you can see, we're still finishing up some last-minute
details. You'll want to watch your step."

We made our way through the clutter of tools and lumber, and
climbed onto the newly constructed deck at the side of the house. At
the far end of the property stood a small out-building that appeared to
have once been a garage, beyond which was nothing but open space, as
the hillside behind it fell steeply away.

"Wil, come and see the view," I enthused, leaning on the railing and
taking in a deep breath of cool, fresh air. "Isn't this fabulous!?!"

Wil made his way over to where I was standing and stood there
quietly for a moment, soaking in the beauty of the setting. "Yeah, it's
great," he admitted, finally showing a little enthusiasm. "At least there
aren't any nearby neighbors."

We took our time meandering though the cottage's three, small, interior rooms, checking out important details like water pressure and heat. The small but efficient kitchen had been completely remodeled, and all the appliances were new. Captivated by the house's obvious charms, I could barely contain my enthusiasm. The overall package was almost identical to what I had visualized for in Sedona.

Wil, on the other hand, seemed intent on playing the choosey shopper, as if he had something a bit grander in mind. "It's so small," he complained. "What would you say, about 600 square feet?"

"600 square feet looks pretty big to me, after living in a Winnebago for the last eighteen months," I reminded him. "What do you want, a castle?"

After we had finished inspecting the property, we thanked the couple and promised to get back to them with a decision before the day was out. As far as I could tell, the house was ours if we wanted it. The owners seemed completely amenable to having us as tenants.

On the drive back to Corte Madeira, I could hardly contain my enthusiasm. "That was it! That was the house I pictured in my visualization! Let's call them and tell them we'll take it, OK?"

Despite how convinced I was, Wil still seemed ambivalent about making a final decision. It took my listing the house's various assets, one by one, for his resistance to finally melt.

"Go ahead and call her back," he relented, finally, bowing to my persistent badgering. "If that's where you want to live, then that's just where we'll have to live."

Back at the RV park, I hurried to the pay phone and placed the call to the woman, a deal was struck, and the next day we signed a one year lease. With the house now officially ours, we emptied the storage locker and spent the next several days unpacking and trying to figure out where everything should go. Since there was no place to park the Winnebago on site, we cleaned it up and mothballed it at a nearby storage facility we found listed in the local yellow pages.

Rescuing two wine glasses from the chaos in the kitchen, Wil opened a bottle of champagne and lifted his glass in a toast. "To us," he declared, ceremoniously. "To the completion of 18 months on the road, and a job well done!"

We clinked glasses and downed the contents in a single gulp. Unexpectedly, tears welled up in my eyes--partly out of sadness for the end of such an incredible chapter in our lives, and partly from joy for the new adventure we were embarking upon. For better or for worse, we had accomplished our move to California; New York was now but a fading memory. Fortunately, neither of us had the slightest inkling of the intense series of events that lay ahead of us in the weeks and months to come.

28 *Junito*

NOW THAT WE HAD SETTLED INTO a permanent home after being on the road for most of the last 18 months, we were looking forward to establishing more than just transient friendships in the San Francisco gay community. The San Francisco Healing Circle, run by an HIV-positive, gay man named Greg Cassin, who we had met on an earlier trip to the city, soon became our home away from home. We also became active members of Radiant Light Ministries, the New Thought Church we had stumbled across on the very same trip.

In early July, a call came in from Niro in New York, informing us that she would be conducting a workshop in San Francisco in early August, co-facilitated by a fellow Sanyasan named Amitab. The workshop was scheduled for the University of San Francisco Conference Center, a sprawling mission styled complex perched high atop a hill overlooking the bay. Wil was particularly excited by the news since he had worked with Niro while we were still living in New York, and had achieved a number of important breakthroughs as a result. As soon as our invitations came in the mail, we both signed up to take the class.

The demographics of the workshop yielded an interesting mixture of gay and straight, healthy and physically challenged, as well as a considerable number of Niro and Amitab's Sanyasan friends. Predictably then, many of the techniques they employed over the course of the weekend had a distinctly Sanyasan flavor. Each morning, the session began with a meditation involving the use of various breathing exercises, followed by a half hour of vigorous movement done blindfolded and to the accompaniment of frenetic new-age music. Since this was my first exposure to techniques like these, I reacted with my usual resistance.

"I feel like I'm in some sort of cult," I complained to Wil, exhausted and sweaty after only a few minutes of active shaking. "I really hate this kind of stuff. I really do."

"Be quiet and do it anyway," he fired back at me between shakes, hardly missing a beat. "The mere fact that you don't want to do it is a pretty good sign it's what you need. Your ego's rebelling because it's afraid of what you might find out about yourself."

As usual, he had a point. It would have been so much easier to simply opt out and say I wasn't comfortable with the exercise. Certainly, in politically correct San Francisco, no one was going to force you to go beyond your comfort zone. Unfortunately, I was conscious enough to know that growth wasn't always comfortable for the precise reason that it tended to push you up against your rough edges, and force you to face things you usually tried to avoid. Resigned to my fate, I kept on shaking the best I could ,until finally the music ended and we were instructed to take off our blindfolds and sit by ourselves in silence.

For all my resistance, and the relentless barrage of criticism my ego continued to dish out for the remainder of the weekend, I had to admit that Niro's techniques were remarkably effective. On the final day of the retreat, she led the group in some inner child work which included a guided regression back to the time of our births. As a result of the exercise, Wil made an unexpected breakthrough.

Certainly, this weekend was not the first time Wil had ever worked with his inner child. In fact, both of us knew him quite well. His name was Willie Nerd, an endearing, young boy of five or six. Surprisingly, the unfamiliar infant that Wil discovered during this regression was unfamiliar to either of us, and the issues it represented were particularly significant.

As Niro led the group through the exercise, Wil found himself floating in his mother's womb. What he discovered there was not a younger version of the more familiar Willie Nerd, but a tiny infant named Junito, who spoke only an infantile form of Spanish and was extremely angry. (It's interesting to note that Wil's command of Spanish was rather inept, and he seldom, if ever, expressed his anger) As the regression progressed, the cause of Junito's anger grew increasingly apparent.

Wil had always known that something traumatic had occurred between his parents immediately before he was born, but no one in the family would break their code of silence to tell him what had happened. Not so with Junito. As the meditation progressed, Junito explained that his mother had thrown herself down a flight of stairs while pregnant with him, in an attempt to induce an abortion. She and his father were in the process of getting a divorce, and under the circumstances she didn't feel she could raise another child, alone. Incredibly, while still in the womb, Junito had been aware of the entire chain of events, and was born angry and with a deep sense of not being wanted.

The way in which this initial experience of rejection had played itself out was rather interesting. Wil's sense of abandonment continued to build, as his birth mother gave up custody of him to his father, at around the age of five. From that point on, his behavior grew increasingly unmanageable. He began to act out violently and create chaos at school. Eventually, with the love and patience of his stepmother, Carmen, who in time he came to view as his real mother, his deep-seated anger had subsided and the rejection he felt was buried and forgotten deep in his unconscious mind. To compensate for this unresolved psychic wound, Wil became a major people pleaser.

Ask anyone who knew the two of us and they would most likely describe Wil as *the sweet one*. I was more likely to be described as self-centered and aloof. Wil would go out of his way to make sure even a complete stranger's needs were taken care of, while I was completely self-absorbed. I'm not judging myself by saying this; I'm simply describing things the way they were.

The previously unconscious information that Wil was able to glean through dialoguing with Junito created considerable movement in his life going forward. Rather than being embittered by what he had learned, he chose to feel compassion for his birth mother's predicament. For the first time since I had known him, he reached out to her, beginning with a series of phone calls which eventually culminated in a reunion on a subsequent visit to New York City.

Reconnecting with his birth mother represented a tremendous leap in self-acceptance for Wil, particularly as it related to his Puerto Rican heritage. His family had immigrated to the United States when he was less than a month old, and had settled in the predominately Jewish, middle class, bedroom community of New Rochelle, NY. His parents, like so many other immigrants of the time, had insisted that he speak only English, resulting in his infantile grasp of his native language.

At the tender age of eighteen, in order to please his father, Wil had enrolled in the ROTC program at New York University, and graduated four years later with a degree in electrical engineering. Later, he served a tour of duty as a Captain in the United States Air Force. When his enlistment was over, he began working for Banker's Trust of New York as a stock trader and was eventually hired by Drexell, Burnham, Lambert, the notorious Wall Street brokerage firm, where he was working when we met. Although he was Puerto Rican by birth, Wil was actually more like a nice Jewish boy from New Rochelle.

Unlike Wil, who was very well-educated and completely assimilated, his birth mother spoke almost no English at all and lived a rather ghettoized existence in an ethnic, Brooklyn enclave. For Wil, hurt by what he perceived as her rejection of him at birth, she had come to symbolize the background he was running away from: the Puerto Rican part of himself. As he finally began the long, overdue process of forgiving and reconciling with his mother, he also came to terms with his Puerto Rican ethnicity.

"You know George, at some point we need to have our book translated into Spanish," he remarked, as we were sitting on the deck one afternoon, a week or so after attending Niro's workshop. "AIDS is becoming a real problem in the Latino community, and I think I might be in a position to help."

"You're right," I agreed, looking up from the book on astrology I was reading. "But first, we've got to get ready for our workshop here, next month. At some point, we need to sit down and go over what we did in Atlanta, so we can iron out some of the kinks. But you're right. I think you'd be the ideal person to address the Latino community's concerns. And having a Spanish translation of the book isn't such a bad idea, either."

In the meantime, we had other, more pressing concerns to worry about than translating our book into Spanish. We had a workshop scheduled in early September, for which we hoped to secure the very same room that Niro and Amitab had used for theirs. There was also an upcoming interview with the San Francisco Chronicle, and a smattering of appearances on local television, including a talk show featuring our good friend, Dr. Bernie Siegel.

As such, our work in the AIDS community was expanding to an entirely new level; we were no longer an unknown commodity to anyone involved in the field. The idea that you could survive AIDS, and indeed be transformed by the experience, had finally broken through the seemingly impenetrable strangle-hold of hopelessness surrounding it, and Wil and I had played a major role in bringing that about. But of utmost importance to us, personally, was the one day workshop we had created and debuted to great success on our recent visit to Atlanta. Now, hopefully, we would have the chance to repeat that success in San Francisco.

29 Babysitting Elizabeth

THANKFULLY, THE WORKSHOP IN SAN FRANCISCO was an unqualified success, with over 70 HIV-infected people and their caregivers in attendance. From our clutch of friends at the Healing Circle, we were able to assemble a crack, support team to handle the basic logistics, which left Wil and me free to concentrate on our respective presentations. On hearing of our plans, Marc shipped us a carton of t-shirts he had designed, crafted to send the subliminal message, *People are Healing from AIDS*, which we distributed to every member of the team. Also enclosed were several hundred buttons with the same design, which we gave away as souvenirs.

With autumn approaching, Wil and I were still looking at a full slate of events through the end of the year. Charlie was expected up from Los Angeles and had reserved time in a Sausalito recording studio so that Wil and I could lay down tracks for a meditation tape. People were continually requesting new material from us, and as our producer Charlie was responsible for seeing to it that we produced.

We busied ourselves with our respective contributions. Wil immediately decided on an anger release process, while I set about composing a chakra-clearing meditation. We planned to debut the finished product at our upcoming lecture in L.A.

In his typical, grandiose fashion, Charlie was planning a major production for the L.A. event. He had secured a large downtown church as the venue, with over 1500 seats. At $10 a pop, the profits would go to the Sananda Foundation, a nonprofit organization he had created to promote the use of natural therapies in the treatment of HIV and AIDS.

As the featured speaker of the evening, Elizabeth's fee was to be $10,000, and was non-negotiable. Wil and I agreed to $1,500 dollars apiece-- considerably less than Elizabeth was getting, but still nothing to sneeze at. Three thousand dollars seemed very generous, and we were more than happy with the arrangement.

The trip to Los Angeles gave us an opportunity to take the Winnebago out of moth balls and re-experience the joys of life on the road. We meandered our way down the coast, and stopped overnight in San Luis Obispo, where we spoke to a HIV support group that had contacted us several months earlier. Santa Barbara was next. After lunch at a quaint little Mexican restaurant near the beach, we set out on the final leg of the trip into L.A. It was late in the day, and the sun was just beginning to sink into the Pacific, as we pulled up to the curb in front of Charlie's house.

Making a difference, not making money, had always been Wil's and my primary motivation for our work in the HIV/AIDS community, despite the fact that we were slated to receive a generous honorarium for the L.A engagement. The purity of our motives was one of the many things that kept our enthusiasm fresh and alive, without which we would have quickly lost interest and gone back to New York and resumed our lucrative careers.

It was ironic, then, that the event with Elizabeth exposed us, for the first time, to the fact that not everyone in the healing community was always coming from the same space. Apparently, some people had lost sight of their original motivation and let their egos run amuck.

There were two levels of tickets available for the event in L.A. General admission was $10 a piece, and seating was on a first come, first served basis. Reserved tickets were $50, and guaranteed the holder a seat up front, and the opportunity to meet the speakers at a private reception before the main event. Unfortunately, by commission or omission--I don't really know which--Charlie had failed to inform Elizabeth about the latter. When she finally learned of it, shortly before the event was scheduled to begin, she was furious about the oversight and made her feelings known.

"I never participate in such events," she declared, curtly, cutting

Charlie off in mid- sentence. "How dare you commit me to such a thing without my permission?"

From there, the relationship between Elizabeth and Charlie, apparently a tenuous one from the start, deteriorated even further. With her mind firmly set against anything more he might have to suggest, Elizabeth began nitpicking about the smallest details--the fact that Charlie had gotten a white board with magic markers, instead of a chalkboard with real chalk, and on and on and on.

By the time Wil and I arrived at the church for the preliminary event, Elizabeth was already there and in a horrible snit, and had barricaded herself in a back room and was refusing to come out and meet her waiting crowd of admirers. To make matters worse, she was threatening not to speak, which completely unnerved Charlie for the perfectly understandable fact that he had over 1000 people out front who had paid good money for the privilege of hearing her do just that. The only people Elizabeth would have anything to do with were Wil and me. Under pressure from Charlie, it became our job to humor her until it was time for the event to begin.

I have to admit, I copped out on the babysitting job almost immediately, and let the entire responsibility fall onto Wil's shoulders alone. I was appalled at Elizabeth's behavior, and hadn't the slightest intention of kow-towing to her unreasonable demands. The first opportunity that presented its self, I slipped out of the room to mingle with the guests out front. On seeing me, Charlie rushed over to get an update on the situation with Elizabeth.

"She has to go on," he insisted, desperation showing through a thin veneer of bravado. "We have a contract. I'll sue her if she doesn't!"

"Don't worry," I reassured him. "I don't think that'll be necessary. Wil's got everything under control. But honestly, I couldn't take it in there for another minute. I had to get out of there before she drove me nuts."

"Thank god for Wil," Charlie muttered. "Well, since you're here, I want you to meet a friend of mine. She's over here." He grabbed me by the arm and steered me across the room to where a vaguely familiar figure of a woman stood holding a glass of wine.

"George," he said, "I want you to meet Mother Nature. You know, *it's not nice to fool Mother Nature.*"

"Oh my god!" I exclaimed, as it dawned on me why the woman standing before me looked so familiar. "You're Dena Dieetrich, the actress from the margarine commercial. I'm very pleased to meet you."

I reached over to shake her hand, and inadvertently bumped the glass she was holding, causing a cascade of red wine to spill down the front of her white, silk blouse. "Oh my god, I'm so sorry," I stammered, my face turning a bright shade of red. "Let me get some club soda and see if we can get this out. _Oh God, I'm so embarrassed!_"

Meanwhile, trapped in the room with Elizabeth, attempting to soothe her ruffled feathers, Wil missed out on the comic scenario unfolding in the room out front--one he would have undoubtedly found amusing. He got a kick out of seeing me make a fool of myself, especially when I was trying particularly hard to be suave and debonair. Besides, with what he was going through having to babysit Elizabeth, he could have used a good laugh about then.

A few minutes before the reception ended, Wil managed to coax Elizabeth out of hiding to briefly acknowledge the people who had paid good money to see her, and have her autograph their books. Then, with the time fast approaching for the main event to begin, the three of us, along with the other speaker of the evening--AIDS activist and creator of the AIDS Mastery Workshop, Sally Fisher--filed into the sanctuary and took our seats down front. While it was probably not obvious to anyone else but me, I could tell by the tell-tale twitching of the tiny veins running along his temples, that Wil was still pretty upset.

The rest of the evening proceeded pretty much as planned, considering all the behind the scenes maneuvering that had taken place beforehand. After a brief musical interlude by the young man who had furnished piano background for our new meditation tape, Charlie mounted the stairs of the massive platform and welcomed everyone to the event, and proceeded to give a brief explanation of The Sananda Foundation's mission in the HIV/AIDS community. Then, with the preliminaries out of the way, he introduced the first of the evening's four speakers, Ms. Sally Fisher, who spoke for about fifteen minutes on the importance of activism in the face of AIDS. Next, Wil and I spoke about 20 minutes each.

The climax of the evening was Elizabeth's talk, which lasted for well over an hour. As she climbed the stairs to the podium after a warm introduction by Charlie, no trace of the rancor that had been so prevalent an hour earlier, remained to be seen. In her usual impeccable manner, Elizabeth proceeded to charm the captivated audience with a number of personal anecdotes, in the manner of the best, oral storytellers. Then, when she had finished, the audience rose to its feet and gave her a rousing, standing ovation.

Wil and I hung around afterwards, greeting a steady stream of well-wishers and answering countless, personal questions. In the warm afterglow of a job well done, little thought remained of the evening's earlier difficulties. As people shared their personal stories and the impact our story had had upon their lives, all our efforts--including having to baby sit Elizabeth--seemed worthwhile. Not even her childish tantrums could dampen the exhilaration we felt in knowing that we were truly making a difference.

That night, Wil and I slept in the Winnebago on the street in front of Charlie's house. Then, after a brief meeting with him over breakfast the next morning, we pulled up camp and began the long drive back to San Francisco. In Marin, we put the Winnebago back into storage, and drove the short distance home in the Suzuki. Waiting for us on the answering machine was a message from Charlie, asking us to call him as soon as we got in.

"I wonder what he wants?" I asked, curious about the call. "We just talked to him yesterday, right before we left L.A."

"I don't know, it's probably nothing," Wil sighed, tossing a heavy suitcase onto the bed. "Help me get this bag unpacked and I'll give him a ring and find out."

Later that evening, Wil dialed the familiar number, and Charlie answered after only a couple of rings.

"Oh...Wil," he stammered, seemingly caught off guard. "I need to talk to you about something. This a little awkward for me, so I'm just going to dive right in and ask."

Seeing the curious expression on Wil's face, I quickly surmised that something was amiss, and moved closer to eavesdrop on the conversation.

"Well I don't know, Charlie," Wil was saying. "That's not what we agreed on. I'll have to talk it over with George and get back to you about it later, OK? I'll call you tomorrow. OK. Goodbye."

"What's the matter," I asked, as soon as he had hung up the phone. "Is something wrong?"

"Well...yes," Wil began, choosing his words carefully so as not to upset me anymore than necessary. "Charlie says that because attendance was less than he had anticipated, and because Elizabeth is insisting on being paid the entire $10,000 she was promised, he wants to know if we would be willing to forgo our fee and donate it to the Sananda Foundation. Otherwise, after all the bills are paid, there won't be any money left over."

"You've got to be kidding me!" I exploded. "After we had to hold her hand so she wouldn't throw a tantrum and refuse to go on, he has the nerve to ask *us* if *we'll* donate our fee to Sananda. *She's* the one getting ten thousand dollars for one night's work--not us. Let her donate some of her fee, then, maybe, we can talk about it. Otherwise, no way. We agreed on three thousand dollars, and that's exactly what I expect to be paid!"

Seeing how angry I was, Wil wisely decided to drop the subject and wait for me to cool down. He knew me well enough to know that Charlie's request had plugged neatly into my usual fears about money. And to be honest, he was still pretty upset at Elizabeth too, for her behavior and the unnecessary stress it had placed him under.

He was angry at me, too, though he would never have admitted it, for running out on him and leaving him to deal with Elizabeth by himself. Rather than express his anger, he stored it away, like he always did, where he thought it couldn't reach him--with Junito, in the unconscious part of his being.

Later, when things had cooled down a bit, he delicately broached the subject with me again. "I tend to agree with you that we deserve to be paid the entire fee we were promised," he began. "And since you feel so strongly about it, I think you should be the one to call Charlie and tell him how you feel. I shouldn't always have to be the one to do all the talking for us."

He had a point, to be sure. Increasingly, over the last 18 months, since we had been thrown together for 24 hours a day, I had let most of the responsibility for communicating our needs fall to him, fearing, for some reason, to speak up for myself. I wanted to control things, but I wanted *him* to do it for me. It was a classic passive/aggressive behavior, and it was my way of avoiding having to confront my own deep-seated fear of rejection.

Since Wil's pattern was to always try and smooth things over, he fell quite naturally into the role of my enabler. But as our eighteen-month-long travels had come to an end, this dynamic had become increasingly untenable and was begging to be addressed. Wil was tired of speaking for me; and to be quite honest, I was tired of letting him. We simply didn't know how to communicate what we both knew needed to change.

During the eighteen months we had been on the road in the Winnebago, we had been together twenty-four hours a day, seven days a week. This was completely different from our lives in New York City, where we were both employed at full-time jobs. There, we had been apart for at least ten hours a day, and asleep for another six or seven. That left only seven hours in a day that we actually spent together, except on weekends, of course, when we were rarely apart. Now, after a year and a half of constant togetherness, we were more or less joined at the hip, and it was not a comfortable experience for either of us.

I was sick of being known as WilandGeorge, WilandGeorge, WilandGeorge. Everywhere we went, people knew us as this one, single entity, WilandGeorge. Now that we were no longer on the road full time, I wanted to reestablish some sense of normalcy in our lives; I wanted my identity back. I wanted to be just George, again, not some appendage on a couple known as WilandGeorge.

My growing desire to reassert myself, separate from us as a couple, and my admitted lack of finesse in knowing how to effectively communicate my needs, created an unfamiliar strain in our relationship and plugged directly into Wil's unresolved abandonment issues. It was a difficult period of adjustment for us both, and several times I wanted to shuck it all and run back to Manhattan, where I had a job I understood and knew exactly what was required of me.

Because of the dramatic change in direction our lives had taken, none of the old, familiar signposts held sway anymore. Everything was different now, and we had to create new guidelines to reflect our evolving reality. As exhilarating as this was when it worked--and it did work, most of the time--it was still a constant challenge to keep letting go and trusting. I hadn't completely relinquished the fear that if I didn't control things, nothing would ever work out the way I wanted them to, and was having trouble letting go.

Nevertheless, the next morning I bit the bullet and called Charlie, and calmly explained my feelings about the situation with the money. He listened politely and then reluctantly agreed to keep his original commitment. When the conversation had run its course, I hung up the phone with mixed emotions--on the one hand, feeling empowered at having found the courage to ask for what I felt I was entitled to--and on the other feeling small and greedy for grasping so tightly at money. It seemed as though I was damned if I did, and damned if I didn't. Nothing I seemed to do felt quite right.

☀️

30 An Unpleasant Visit from Christine

OMETIME AFTER MY CONVERSATION WITH CHARLIE about the
money Wil and I were owed from the gig in L.A., I was sitting
on the sofa looking out of the window, when the telephone rang,
jolting me back to the present moment. It was Christine calling from
Sedona to inform me that she was pulling up stakes in Arizona and
heading to Yelm, Washington, to be near Ramtha and enroll in his
School of Enlightenment.

"I don't feel safe living in the desert, anymore" she explained, her
voice betraying a sense of urgency. "I want to establish sovereignty on
my own land, as soon as possible."

Sovereignty was one of Ramtha's most emphasized teachings: the
idea that self sufficiency would provide the only refuge from an imminent,
worldwide, social and economic collapse, triggered by the creation of a
debt too large to repay. According, people living in cities and relying on
credit to finance their lifestyles--most of the American public, actually-
-would bear the brunt of the inevitable suffering to come. To survive,
you would need to own your own land, grow your own food, and be
independent of the regular power grid. Everyone else would become
indentured servants of a global elite--the shadow government, the terrible
beast described in the Book of Revelations as rising up from the sea and
devouring all nations.

"I'll be coming through San Francisco on my way to Yelm," she said,
before signing off, "and I'd like to stay with you guys for a couple of days,
if that's alright with you. Could you give me directions to your house?"

A few days later, Christine arrived on our doorstep with her car packed to the roofline with her belongings. "I shipped the rest of my things on ahead last week" she explained, noticing me eyeballing the over-loaded car, "but it won't get there for another month or so. This is just what I'll need to hold me over until everything else arrives."

I grabbed her bags and motioned for her to follow me down to the house. Wil appeared at the front door and greeted her with a warm, but decidedly reserved, 'hello'. Having been stung by her overzealous processing, one time too many over the years, he had long since decided that the smartest thing to do was approach Christine with a bit of caution.

When I had first told Wil about Christine's impending visit, he had made it abundantly clear that he wasn't in the least bit happy about the undue influence she seemed to exert over me, particularly as it related to Ramtha, who he considered nothing more than an elaborate fraud. I had to admit that he had a point about how Ramtha's ominous teachings invariably plugged into my apocalyptical programming, leaving him to pick up the pieces when the inevitable shit hit the fan.

"Promise me you're not going to let her talk you into going to Yelm with her," he insisted, suspecting that this might be the ulterior motive for her visit. "We have enough things to do around here getting ready for our next trip, without you traipsing off and getting mixed up in that creepy cult in Yelm. Promise me you won't go, OK?"

"I promise," I assured him, not really caring enough, one way or the other, to press the issue further. "If it'll make you happy, I promise I won't go. I don't know why you have to make such a big deal out of it, though."

The morning after Christine arrived dawned hot and bright, without a single cloud in the sky. We planned to spend the entire day together, visiting the local points of interest, leaving Wil home alone at his request.

"You sure you won't go with us, Wil?" Christine asked, as the two of us were heading out the door. "It's such a beautiful day. I'd love to be able to spend it with both of you."

"No, you two go ahead," Wil assured her, shooing us out the door. "I have some things I need to get done around here, and it will be easier if I don't have the two of you to distract me."

"OK then, see you later," I chirped, and headed up the walk with a purposeful gait. "We'll try and be home before dark. Don't eat without us. I'll throw something together when we get back."

Christine and I began our day taking in the panoramic views from atop nearby Mount Tamalpais, and afterwards took a hike through nearby Muir Woods. By the time we had finished, it was close to two in the afternoon and we were famished from the exertion. We jumped into the car and headed for Sausalito and a late lunch at one of the many restaurants lining the famous waterfront. As the Maitre d' seated us at an outside table, San Francisco shimmered in the distance through the slight haze hanging over the bay.

"Isn't it gorgeous here?" I enthused, inhaling the pungent salt air and soaking in the view. "What a perfect day for eating on the deck."

Unfortunately, Christine wasn't one to let even the most innocent remark pass without making something more of it.

"Yes, it certainly is," she demurred, giving me one of her knowing smiles. "But really, George, how can you live on the San Andreas fault when you know what's going to happen here? Why are you choosing to live in a state of denial?"

"Uh oh," I thought. "Here it comes." Experience told me that there was no point in trying to argue with Christine; you couldn't possibly win. And besides, I wondered the same thing too, sometimes, believing what I did about earth changes and the like. Part of me--a large part of me--was terrified that Ramtha's predications might be true, and lived waiting for the proverbial shoe to drop. That part of me definitely wanted to leave California, but didn't have a clue about where to go.

I suppose I could have blindly run away and lived in the woods, like Christine was planning to do, but ultimately I would simply have taken my fears with me, no matter where I chose to go. Instead, it was almost as though my higher self had deliberately moved me to California and sat me atop the San Andreas fault until I understood that I was safe, that I would always be in the right place at the right time, and that I didn't need to waste time and energy trying to protect myself from some frightening, imaginary scenario. If I needed to experience an earthquake, then I would be here when it happened. Otherwise, I'd just happen to be out of town.

"This is where I feel I need to be right now," I mumbled, hating myself for feeling the need to defend my choices. "The people who most need to hear our message are right here in San Francisco. So as much as a part of me would like to leave and live off the land like you, I can't."

I paused and took a sip of wine, before continuing my defence. "You're doing what you need to do--moving to Yelm--and you'll just have to accept that living in California is what's right for me."

Sensing the futility of pressing the issue further, Christine wisely decided to let the matter drop--at least for the time being. "I know," she said, delicately wiping a trace of salad dressing from the corner of her mouth. "Why don't you come to Yelm with me for a couple of days and help me settle in? That way, you could have a look around and see if you like what you see. What do you think? Would you like to do that?"

I looked out over the bay, turning the proposal over in my mind. "I don't know," I hesitated, imagining Wil's outrage. "It does seem like a good idea, though. And I'd like to see what Yelm is like." Then, "OK, maybe I will," I heard myself saying. "Yes, I'll go with you!"

"Terrific!" Christine squealed, raising her glass in a toast to my sudden fit of decisiveness. "We can tell Wil tonight over dinner!"

In the excitement of the moment, dinner seemed like a long way off, and not the least bit intimidating. By the time it had come and gone, however, and the three of us were lingering around the table over coffee, I was seized with an intense dread. Draining the last few drops from the bottom of my cup, I braced myself and launched into the fray.

"Wil," I began, as nonchalantly as I could. "I've decided to go to Yelm with Christine for a couple of days. I hope you won't mind."

There was a long pause in which no one said a word. I started to speak again, albeit a bit more defensively. "I know we have to be in Los Angeles in a couple of weeks, but I'll be back long before then. Besides," I added, trying to put a positive spin on the situation, "I think it will be good for us to have some time apart."

Wil sat there for a moment, obviously too dumb-struck to speak. His face turned a bright shade of red and the little veins on either side of his forehead began to bulge--imperceptibly, at first, and then growing in intensity.

"You promised me you wouldn't go!" he exploded from across the table, rising up out of his chair in a fit of rage. "I specifically asked you not to go up there with those crazies, and you promised me you wouldn't.

What made you change your mind?" he demanded, turning to glare at Christine.

Christine started to react to Wil's reference to Ramtha's followers as 'crazies', but was stopped short by a withering look from me. The last thing I needed was for the two of them to get into it any deeper than they were already.

"You have no right to tell me not to go," I shot back, attempting to justify my broken promise. "Christine had nothing to do with it; it was entirely my idea. And besides, I don't know why you have to act so irrational. I'll be back in less than a week."

Predictably, Wil wasn't buying any of it. He pushed back from the table and stormed out of the room in a huff.

"I think I'll take a little walk," Christine whispered. She folded her napkin and got up from the table. "You guys obviously need some time to work this out."

Later that evening, Wil was more upset than I had ever seen him. "Please don't go with Christine," he pleaded, tears welling up in his eyes. "Just do me this one favor, this one time. Please don't go to Yelm!"

Seeing the emotional state he was in (I had only seen him cry once, in the thirteen years we had been together), I knew that I couldn't possibly go. It didn't matter, anymore, whether I had the right to or not. The man I loved was in overwhelm, and irrational or not, that wasn't something I could easily ignore.

I reached over and put my arms around him, and tried to reassure him. "It's all right," I whispered. "I won't go to Yelm. Don't cry. I'll stay here with you like I promised."

I sat with him until his crying stopped. In the stillness of the late night hour, I heard the screen door hinge squeak, as Christine slipped quietly back into the house.

"I'll have to deal with her in the morning," I thought, dreading the inevitable confrontation. "But for now, I've had just about all the excitement I can take for one night."

While Wil slept soundly, I lay wide awake in bed beside him, my mind crowded with a thousand conflicting thoughts. When I did finally manage to doze off, the slightest little noise or movement from his side of the bed startled me awake. I dreaded having to break the news to Christine, knowing that she wasn't likely to take my change of heart, lightly. In trying to make everyone happy, I had somehow managed to achieve the exact opposite effect. Even I was mad at me.

"When will I ever learn?" I thought in disgust. Would Christine always be able to plug into my fears so easily? Would the irrational fear of punishment, embedded in my DNA like some thick, toxic sludge by my fundamentalist upbringing, always be there to sabotage me, leaving me paralyzed and incapable of acting rationally?

"And what about Wil?" I wondered. It was obvious that my neurotic behavior was beginning to wear on his nerves. How much longer would he be willing to put up with it?

At the first light of dawn, I crawled out of bed and tiptoed through the living room where Christine lay sleeping on the couch, taking special care not to wake her up. Reaching the sanctuary of the kitchen, I put on a pot of coffee and then slipped out onto the deck for some air. The morning was clear and brisk, and my confusion immediately began to clear.

"Good morning," Christine's voice chirped, unexpectedly. She had snuck up behind me without me having noticed. "What a beautiful day for a trip."

"Uh oh," I thought. "She's not going to like it." I cleared my throat and took a deep breath, and exhaled and watched as the steam dissipated in the cold, morning air.

"I'm not going to Yelm with you," I began, timidly. "Wil was really upset last night, and I think I need to stay here with him." I turned away for a moment, then back to face Christine. "I hope you understand," I said, knowing full-well that most likely she wouldn't. "I just can't go with you right now. I just can't."

"What?!?" she exploded, obviously caught off guard by my unexpected change of heart. "You're not going with me? What's this about, George? Why have you changed your mind? You certainly wanted to go last night before you went to bed"

"I didn't really change my mind," I hedged, shaking my head to reinforce my denial. "I'd already decided before you got here that I wouldn't be going. And then yesterday at lunch, I got caught up in the excitement, I guess. It seemed like a good idea at the time."

I paused, knowing that it was probably best not to try and explain myself any further. Anything more I might offer in my defense would simply give Christine more ammunition to use against me, and she had more than enough, already.

"So anyway, I'm not going," I mumbled, averting my eyes. "I just don't want to go, that's all."

Christine was back at me in a flash. "It's not that you don't *want* to," she snapped, "it's that you *can't! Your lover won't let you.* Why don't you grow some balls and stop letting other people run your life, George? Stop giving your power away to that co-dependent relationship of yours."

Her last remark stung hard. For a moment, it felt as though she could see right through me, and that what she saw disgusted her. I stood there feeling ashamed and embarrassed; ashamed for not knowing *what* I wanted, and for caring what someone else might think of me. I turned to go inside, hoping to remove myself from the situation, and ran smack dab into Wil coming through the door in the opposite direction.

"What's the matter, sunshine?" he cracked. "Did you get up on the wrong side of the bed?" He had obviously surmised what was going on, and was trying to inject a little humor into the situation.

I brushed past him without saying a work, and fled to the safety of the bedroom, leaving him to face Christine, alone.

"Well, I see you managed to get your way," she lashed out at him, not bothering to disguise the contempt in her voice. "George isn't going to Yelm because you're afraid to let him go; why don't you admit it? Well, I hope you're happy with yourself!" Then, for good measure, she added one more final dig. "You'd better wake up and smell the coffee, mister. You can't keep on pretending forever."

With that, Wil launched back at her with a scathing counterattack. "And you can't come here poisoning my lover's mind with your paranoid conspiracy theories, either. If you want to believe the world's coming to an end, then fine--believe it. But talk about giving your power away. I don't know anyone you haven't given yours away to!"

Through the thin walls of the cottage, I could hear the muffled sound of angry voices, as Christine and Wil exchanged heated insults on the deck. Finally, the front door gave a squeak and slammed shut again, and Christine stomped into the bedroom where I was hiding.

"I'm leaving,' she announced, her voice brimming with outrage. "I've never been treated so rudely in all my life!" With that, she turned and stomped into the living room and began gathering up her things, and left without saying goodbye.

Standing in the middle of the bedroom amid the deafening silence, I could hear the sound of angry footsteps echoing up the gravel walk. Moments later, a car door slammed, followed by the sound of screeching tires as Christine angrily sped away. Wil came into the bedroom and stood there, looking at me. Neither of us said a word. Neither of us had to. For our own, very different reasons, we were both relieved to see Christine go.

Wil and I never spoke about these events again, the weekend of Christine's fateful visit to the cottage in Marin. Without having to discuss it further, we both seemed to recognize the turning point it represented in our relationship with her, and with each other. From then on, Wil seemed to display less patience with my chronic uncertainty--not because he didn't love me, but because he did. I guess you could say that he loved me enough to stop enabling my neurotic behavior. Recognizing how much I had come to hate the co-dependent aspects of our relationship, even though I didn't always have the will to resist, he loved me enough to no longer allow me the choice. From that point on, I was left to my own devices.

31 The San Francisco Earthquake

A
S THE WEEKS CAME AND WENT, Wil and I fell into the rhythm of a new routine. Eric had founded his own consulting firm in the city and offered Wil a part time job, which he gladly accepted. The new arrangement allowed them to spend more time together--a luxury they hadn't had since we had left New York City, eighteen months earlier. Despite Eric's tendency to get on Wil's nerves (I never knew anyone who's nerves he didn't get on, frankly), they seemed to enjoy each other's company, and the time we were apart provided a boost to our relationship.

The several days a week Wil was working in San Francisco, left me free to pursue my own interests, which at this point involved writing another book. With the success of *Beyond AIDS*, I envisioned myself a writer and planned on producing a series of books with a metaphysical bent. Taking advantage of the cottage's splendid isolation, I spent many lazy afternoons writing ardently about whatever topic popped into my head. When Wil would arrive home, we'd have dinner, he'd share the highlights of his day with me, and I'd read him my latest work.

The small cottage we occupied was situated on a steeply, wooded hillside, with Marin Avenue running by in front at about the level of the roof. For several weeks now, a succession of large trucks had been shunting up and down the narrow, serpentine road in front of the house, hauling materials to and from a large construction site atop the hill. On the afternoon of Tuesday, October 17th, I was lounging on the couch, editing my day's writing, when something extraordinary occurred.

As I sat there, preoccupied with the task at hand, I heard what I thought was a heavy truck coming down the hill, except it sounded as though its brakes were not working properly. A palpable vibration shook the house like a passing freight train might. The cats, both of whom were sleeping on the couch beside me, perked up their ears and jumped to the floor in a panic, leaving an ugly red track of scratches on my thigh. Before I could react to the scratches, I realized that the vibration, which had by now grown even stronger, were not the result of a truck, but an earthquake. All I could think of was getting out of the house before it went tumbling down the hill.

Several weeks earlier, after the unpleasant incident with Christine, I had checked underneath the house to see if it was properly bolted to the foundation, and had found, to my surprise, that it didn't actually have one. The entire cottage was perched precariously on a series of rickety pilings, some of which appeared to be nothing more than tree stumps.

As I scrambled to my feet and headed for the front door, the rapid vibrations snapped suddenly, transforming into a soft, rolling motion. The floor beneath me began to pitch like a boat in rough seas, sending a small table lamp in the living room crashing to the floor. I groped my way into the kitchen and bounced off the adjacent wall into the edge of the counter, bruising my hip in the process, before stumbling out the door onto the deck. With that, the earth gave one final heave and gently settled back into place. I stood there for a moment, watching the eucalyptus tree at the edge of the driveway sway back and forth, and then come to a gradual stop.

"Oh my god," I croaked. "So that's what an earthquake feels like!"

There was a part of me that wanted to panic and make a big deal out of what had happened-- particularly the part of me that had so dreaded living in California for fear that something like this might happen. But truthfully, after carefully inspecting the gas lines beneath the house for leaks, there was really nothing of consequence to be upset about. The earthquake had actually been an amazing experience. And it had happened so fast that now that it was over, it was hard to believe it had ever happened. Of course, it did help that I hadn't been injured, and that the house hadn't fallen down around my ears.

I stayed outside until I was satisfied that nothing else was going to happen, before going back inside to look for the cats, both of whom I found huddled in a corner, together, scared half out of their wits.

Then I remembered Wil. I flipped on the TV and placed a call to Eric's office, and crossed my fingers and prayed that his phone would still be working.

"Hello?" Eric's voice echoed through the static on the line. "Boy, did you feel that earthquake?" he squealed. "It was a real shaker!"

"I sure did! Is everything OK over there?"

Eric assured me that it was. "But I'm not sure about Wil," he added. "He left for home about fifteen minutes before it hit, and I haven't heard from him since."

I found this latest bit of news rather disturbing, and my imagination revved into overdrive, inventing countless possibilities--most of them negative--for what might have happened to Wil. What if he had been on the Golden Gate Bridge when the quake hit? What if he had been injured or even killed?

My eyes were riveted to the first shocking images coming across the television screen from San Francisco. Already, the cameras on the Good Year Blimp, which only minutes before had been covering the opening ceremonies of the World Series, were showing a collapsed section of the Bay Bridge. And there were other pictures even worse: what looked to be an entire section of freeway in Oakland in shambles, its tandem decks pan-caked atop each other with smoke drifting up from between the crushed sections as some of the trapped cars began to burn. A huge fire was raging in the Marina, and numerous plumes of smoke could be seen rising up from all around the city. As the level of destruction began to sink in, I felt sick in the pit of my stomach.

"Where are you Wil?" I muttered, overwhelmed by the recognition of my complete and utter helplessness. "I'll call Eric back," I decided, thinking his familiar voice might help me shake my growing sense of dread. "Maybe he's heard something by now. Maybe the bridge is closed, and Wil's gone back to his house."

I dialed Eric's number again, only to have a recording inform me that phone service into San Francisco was currently unavailable. With this avenue of discovery thwarted, I placed the receiver back in its cradle and stood motionless in the middle of the living room floor. Just then, I heard the familiar sound of the Suzuki's engine, as Wil pulled into the driveway above the house.

I bolted out the door and raced up the gravel walk, reaching the car even before it had come to a complete stop. "Thank God you're all right!" I exclaimed. "I was worried that something terrible had happened!"

The curious thing about the entire affair was that Wil hadn't even been aware there had been an earthquake until he had arrived at the grocery store in Tam Junction, just down the hill from the house, and saw the sign on the door: closed due to earthquake damage. He had been driving down Divisadero Street in San Francisco, on his way to the Golden Gate Bridge, when the quake hit. Because of the Suzuki's rickety suspension, he hadn't really noticed the tremors, and had continued merrily on his way.

Sure, the road seemed bumpier than usual, he told me, but he had chalked that up to the plethora of potholes that marked the heavily traveled thoroughfare. As for the traffic lights being out, he had assumed that had been caused by a routine power outage.

"Really," he explained, in an annoyingly calm voice, "everyone was very polite. At every intersection I came to, people were making four way stops, so traffic wasn't really a problem. I just kept on going until I made it over to the bridge."

"I can't believe it," I snorted. "All this time I'm here at home, running around like a chicken with my head cut off, worrying that something horrible might have happened to you, and you didn't even know there was an earthquake? I believe in creating your own reality, but this is ridiculous!"

For the rest of the evening, Wil continued to rub my face in the fact that he could be in the middle of the biggest earthquake to hit San Francisco in 80 years and not even know it was happening.

"You see, George," he gloated, good-naturedly, "when you trust that you're always where you need to be, you can be in the middle of a disaster and not even know its happening. Don't you think it's about time you got over your fear of living in California?"

Once again, I had to admit he had a point. We had been in California for less than five months, and my biggest fear had materialized. Except it hadn't exactly been the class A disaster I'd been expecting. True, 42 people had been killed by the Cypress Freeway collapse, and some property had been destroyed in the Marina fire. But other than that, the overall damage was rather light when you considered the size and population of the affected area.

"Perhaps I don't need to be so scared of living here, after all," I concluded, after spending time reflecting on the situation. "Perhaps I *can* trust that I'll be in the right place, at the right time. Maybe the world *will* heal itself without having to create a catastrophe to make it happen."

"But then again," my ego interrupted to plant tiny seeds of doubt, "this quake was only a 7.0. Just wait till the big one hits! Then you're going to see some real damage!"

32 Staring into the Face of Death

OR THE NEXT SEVERAL DAYS, WIL and I stayed close to home, banished from San Francisco due to the persistent power outages still plaguing much of the city. The airport, which had been shut down in the quake's immediate aftermath, resumed normal operations within a day, alleviating any worries we had that our flight back east, the following week, would be cancelled. Taking advantage of the unexpected down time, we prepared ourselves for our upcoming series of lectures and workshops in the Midwest and East Coast.

We were on our way to Indianapolis, by way of Lansing, MI and The Fellowship for Today, to facilitate a workshop sponsored by The Heritage House, a Catholic organization run by a former Jesuit priest.

That weekend, as I observed Wil from the sidelines, as he led the group in a guided meditation, it occurred to me that he looked a bit thinner than usual, most obviously in the area around his neck. It seemed less thick than I remembered it; graceful somehow, like a swan. Back in our hotel room after dinner with our host, I questioned him about what I had observed and was surprised by the hostility in his response.

"No, I haven't lost any weight," he snapped, defensively, exhibiting considerably more annoyance than was called for by my simple inquiry. "So why don't you just mind your own business? I'm perfectly capable of looking after myself, thank you very much!"

This was merely the first of several other unpleasant exchanges between us over the course of the next few days, all of which were noticeably out of character with the manner in which we usually interacted. Wil seemed overly annoyed at me for reasons I couldn't quite put a finger on, and this in turn made me edgy and insecure. Reacting to his rebuffs, I went into full control mode, nit-picking about the smallest things--even going so far as to criticize the meditation he had given the day before. At this point, neither of us was very happy with the other, and it showed.

For the moment, we had no choice but to put a discussion of the issues on hold. We had an upcoming interview with the Indianapolis Star and a half-hour segment to tape on the popular morning show, AM Indianapolis. Then, it was off to Pittsburgh where we were slated to participate in a three day retreat sponsored by Persad, the city's premier AIDS service organization.

Taking advantage of the retreat's stunning location just outside the city, on what had once been a private estate, we busied ourselves with separate activities, took long, solitary walks through the blazing fall foliage, and avoided each other as much as possible. We wanted to give each other space, without making it obvious to everyone that we were having personal difficulties. Our fragile truce held until our next engagement in Philadelphia.

From Pittsburgh, we flew to New York and dropped off our excess luggage at the apartment, and caught a train to Philadelphia. That evening, we spoke before a packed house in a beautiful old church in the historic part of town. Afterwards, the shaky truce we had cobbled together in Pittsburg fell apart over dinner.

Gazing across the table at Wil, his face bathed in the soft, golden glow of candle light, I saw something that caused the hair on the back of my neck to stand on end. A shock of adrenaline shot through my system. The face looking back at me was not the face of the man I knew and loved. It was thin and gaunt, with sunken eyes and thinning skin stretched tightly over hollow cheeks. I had seen this look before on the countless faces of people I had known with AIDS. I was staring into the face of death!

Only then did I realize that Wil was seriously ill; it simply hadn't registered on my radar until now. It was frightening to think that something so obvious had been mostly invisible--that I could be with someone 24 hours a day and not actually notice what was going on. Evidently, our constant proximity was part of the problem. We were too close to each other to objectively gage incremental changes in each other's condition.

Looking at Wil from across the table, there was no way I could just mind my own business, the way he had so rudely suggested the last time I had expressed my concern. I would have to confront him whether he liked it or not. He'd just have to have to deal with it, even though chances were that he wasn't going to like it one bit.

"Wil," I began, making a concerted effort to stay calm, so as to avoid provoking an argument. "I don't know what's going on with you, but something is definitely wrong. You've lost a lot of weight; I can see it in your face. And don't tell me to mind my own business, either. You are my business. And its time you faced up to the fact that something's going on with your health."

"I'm alright, really," he mumbled half-heartedly, trying to deflect my concern. "I've just lost a little weight; really, that's all. It's nothing for you to worry about." He looked down at the table and then back up at me. "Anyway, try not to be so negative," he scolded me.

"Listen Wil," I shot back, not in the least bit mollified by his transparent attempt to intimidate me. "Something's wrong, and we need to find out what it is. Now, we're going to be in New York for a couple of days and you can see Dr. Grossman while we're there. I'm sure he'll be able to figure out what the problem is and give you something for it. But you can't afford to mess around with this. You need to see the doctor as soon as we get to New York!"

With that, the tension between us came to a head and our relatively calm discussion degenerated into a full- blown argument, with angry charges and counter-charges flying back and forth across the table. With all the tension, neither of us was in any mood to finish dinner.

"We'll take a check, please" Wil informed the surprised waiter, who had stopped by our table to see if we were enjoying our meal. "The dinner was fine—really. We're just not very hungry, that's all."

Not waiting for the check, Wil pushed back his chair and threw a wad of money on the table, and quickly rushed outside. I grabbed my coat and followed him out onto the sidewalk.

By the time we arrived in New York the next morning, Wil was running a temperature of 102 degrees. I called Dr. Grossman's office and managed to secure an appointment for both of us early the next morning. I figured that as long as Wil was seeing the doctor, it wouldn't hurt for me to get a checkup, either. In the almost two years since we had left New

York, neither of us had seen a doctor more than twice. The omission hadn't been simply a case of denial, however. It was just that at this point in the epidemic, there wasn't really anything allopathic medicine had to offer that was worth spending time or money on--especially not AZT.

After he had finished checking Wil over thoroughly, Dr. Grossman instructed him to get dressed, and invited us both into his office for a chat. Seated behind his rather impressive mahogany desk, he adjusted his glasses and glanced perfunctorily at the chart in front of him.

"I'll be honest with you, Wil," he said, planting his elbows on the desk. "The situation doesn't look good to me. You've lost over 18 pounds since you were here last, and that's not a good sign. I'm not sure what the exact nature of the problem is, but profound weight loss is a very serious matter. In fact, it is often a precursor to more serious illness, or even death." His last words hit like a ton of bricks.

"Here," he said, scribbling on a piece of paper and handing it to Wil. "This is the name of a doctor in San Francisco. I suggest that you see him as soon as you get back home. He'll be able to run the kind of tests you need and find out exactly what's going on. In the mean time, I'll send your records on ahead so they'll be there when you get to his office.

"And try not to worry too much," he added, pushing his back his chair and extending his hand. "If there's anything I can do to help with this matter, feel free to give me a call. I'll be happy to help you any way I can."

Wil spent the next few days propped up in bed, watching television, and reading the occasional magazine.

"Just rest," I advised him, tucking the covers in around his legs to keep him warm. "We have a couple of days before we have to be in Detroit, and you'll need all the strength you can get. Hopefully, you'll feel better by then."

At this point, I was relieved, simply, that Wil had finally seen the doctor, even though he had been unable to tell us anything about the cause of his condition. At least he was facing up to the situation and doing something about it.

In my mind, denial--pretending that nothing was wrong-- was the biggest danger we faced. In staying ignorant, our imaginations would always make things out to be far worse than they actually were.

Experience had taught me that it was always better to confront your fears than to ignore them.

With Wil resting comfortably, I slipped out of the apartment and went for a long walk. Later that evening, Mark called and invited us to a private channeling session at his house the following night. I made excuses for Wil, but promised I'd be there.

On the night in question, I walk the few blocks to Marks apartment, rather than take a cab. "The walk will do me good," I thought. "It'll help clear my head."

Upon reaching Mark's apartment, I hung my coat up and mingled with the other guests, many of whom I knew from our gatherings at the loft, or the healing circle. Then, spying an empty chair in a corner, I plopped down in it to await Benjamin's appearance.

His message that night consisted of a brief discourse on the current state of affairs, after which he opened the floor to questions. Normally, I could never think of anything to ask him and was satisfied just to listen. But this evening was different. When finally he turned his attention to me, remembering his propensity for recommending herbal remedies, I asked if there was anything I could do to help a friend who was running a fever and had lost a lot of weight--making sure not to mention Wil by name. Instead of the simple answer I had expected, the one he gave caused my blood to run cold.

"There is nothing you can do for your friend, brave one," he said, gazing at me softly, through wide, glistening eyes. "Our friend will soon be leaving for the other side."

"Don't be sad," he added, seeing the fear in my eyes. "He needs you to be there for him, to comfort him as he embarks upon his transition." And with that, he turned away and addressed the person sitting next to me.

"And what is it I can advise you with tonight," he inquired of them, seemingly oblivious to the bombshell he had just dropped into my lap. "What is it you would like to know?"

I sat there, too stunned to move, as Benjamin continued around the circle. I couldn't believe what I'd just heard. "Did he just tell me that Wil was dying?" I questioned myself. "'Is that what he just said?"

I looked around the circle, searching each face for some scrap of confirmation that I had heard correctly, but no one seemed to have picked up on it--at least if they had, there was no hint of it from their expressions. Everyone was focused on Benjamin as though everything was completely normal, oblivious to my distress

As soon as I possibly could, I made a feeble excuse to Mark, pleading off with a headache, and grabbed my coat and staggered down the stairs. I decided to walk for a bit, hoping the cold, night air might revive me and pull me back from the brink of hysteria. The further I walked, however, the angrier I became. Before I had gone even a block, my mild distress morphed into a raging, red-hot torrent of exploding furry.

"How dare he tell me Wil is dying!" I screamed up at the darkened buildings, drawing on all the metaphysics I could muster. "How dare he say such a thing? No one can predict another person's future. No one has that much power!"

"I can change this," I decided, "and so can Wil. He can't die! I won't let him!"

I walked the rest of the way home, lost in thought, oblivious to my surroundings. After weighing every option, trying to decide what to do with the information, I concluded that it would be best not to tell Wil anything about it. He wouldn't be receptive to it anyway, and it would only create unnecessary fear. I would work from behind the scenes, coaxing him through his inertia and denial until enough momentum had been achieved to negate the unwanted probability. Catalyzed by the thought of impending disaster, I shifted into full control mode.

By the time we left for Detroit the following Thursday, Wil was feeling better than he had in weeks, despite the fact that he was still running a slight fever. Somehow, we managed to make it through the workshop without incident, and were soon on board a plane to San Francisco.

The next morning, Wil drove into San Francisco for his appointment with Dr. Marcus Conant. After checking him over thoroughly and asking any number of questions about his symptoms, among which was a relatively minor, dry cough, the doctor concluded that in all likelihood Wil was suffering from a slight case of PCP. He wrote out a prescription for Septra and sent him home to rest, with instructions to come back in about two weeks. No X-rays of his lungs were taken.

"The Doctor says I have a slight case of PCP," Wil informed me, on arriving back at the house. "He gave me some medicine to take and said

I should see him again, in about two weeks. In the meantime, he said I just need to take it easy and rest."

"He said you had pneumonia?" I asked, immediately questioning the diagnosis. "Are you sure? I've had pneumonia a number of times, and your symptoms are a lot different than mine were. Was he absolutely sure?"

"Yes, he was sure," Wil retorted, visibly annoyed at my questioning the doctor's opinion. "I'm sure he knows pneumonia when he sees it, George. He is a doctor, after all."

Realizing that perhaps I was being a bit too controlling, I decided to back off, for the time being, and let the matter ride. It was Wil's body, after all, and he had the right to make whatever decisions about its care he believed were best.

"At least he's taking an antibiotic," I reasoned, finding comfort in my own strong belief in their effectiveness, based on numerous personal experiences. "Hopefully he'll be better in a few days and we can work on putting some weight back on. I just need to be patient and stay calm."

Despite my vow of patience, I fully expected to see an immediate improvement in Wil's condition. It was highly disappointing, therefore, upon awakening the following morning, to discover that this was not to be the case, that overnight his fever had gotten noticeably worse.

"Don't worry," he assured me, after I again expressed my concern. "It takes a while before the medicine takes effect. I'll be better in a couple of days. You'll see."

I wasn't happy with his assessment of the situation, but he did have a valid point. It was unrealistic for me to expect him to recover overnight. I'd just have to keep reminding myself to be patient and keep my tendency to try and control everything in check. Wil was going to be fine. There was no reason to get upset.

33 No Lease and no Health Insurance

U NFORTUNATELY, WIL'S DETERIORATING HEALTH WASN'T THE only thing I had to worry about. The next day's mail included an official looking envelope sporting the return address of a high powered New York Attorney's office. I tossed the rest of the mail onto the kitchen counter and tore open the suspicious envelope, and anxiously unfolded the letter inside.

You are hereby notified that you are in violation of your lease agreement for the premises at 60 East 12th Street, Apartment 11L, the letter began, ominously enough. Upon further reading, our lease on the cottage in Mill Valley was given as the primary cause of the proceedings against us. Apparently, under New York City law, a rent stabilized apartment precluded us from holding any other valid lease.

"Oh shit!" I said, loud enough to wake Wil who was napping on the couch in the living room. "Somehow the landlord in New York found out we're living in California, and it looks like we might lose the apartment."

Wil rose up on his elbows and shook his head in an effort to clear his mind. "How in the world do you suppose they found out we have another lease?" he asked sleepily. His question was a good one. I wondered the exact same thing.

At this point, the last thing either of us needed was a situation like this to deal with. I had enough on my hands trying to nurse Wil back to health, without having an eviction notice dumped in my lap, too. Between my fear of Wil actually dying ,and the possibility of losing the apartment, it was beginning to feel as though the very foundations of my life were systematically being knocked out from under me. Everything I counted on was steadily slipping away.

Here we were, living in California, with Wil sick and no steady source of income to speak of, and now my ultimate escape valve--the apartment in New York--was apparently being taken away, too. As I stood clutching the letter, contemplating its ramifications, panic started to well up in my throat.

"I mustn't let Wil see me worry," I decided. "I don't want to do anything that might jeopardize his recovery." I took a deep breath and put on my best game face. I would simply pretend that nothing was wrong, even though on the inside I knew it probably wasn't true.

The hoped for improvements in Wil's health proved painfully slow in coming. Over the next several days, his fever spiked to alarmingly high levels, accompanied by a measure of nausea that made it impossible for him to keep anything down. I busied myself in the kitchen making chicken soup and pudding and jello, anything that I thought he might be able to eat. I was determined to stay busy and keep my mind occupied. I couldn't allow even a single moment through which an unwelcome negative thought might intrude on my peace. Wil wasn't going to die; it was as simple as that. He had healed himself after all--*hadn't he?*

Perhaps this whole experience was just some sort of a test, I thought, or a mistake, maybe. There was no way that Wil could die and leave me out here in California by myself, was there? Anyway, what would I do if he did die? How would I survive? I didn't have any real way of supporting myself.

After several more days of unrelenting fever and nausea, I was beginning to think that it was the antibiotic that was making him sick. After all, I had read that some people were violently allergic to Septra, and had even died from taking it. Perhaps Wil didn't have PCP, after all; perhaps the doctor had made a mistake. He certainly wasn't exhibiting the usual symptoms. Maybe it was the Septra that was making him sick.

"Yes, it's the Septra," I decided. "He just needs to go back to the doctor and get a different prescription."

"Leave me alone!" Wil snapped, when I suggested that he go back to the doctor and have his condition reevaluated. "I'll be alright if you'll just leave me alone! I just need a couple more days for the antibiotic to work, that's all."

Unfortunately, nothing I could say seemed to change his mind. In fact, the more I pushed, the more adamant he became about not doing whatever I suggested. His resistance was strangely incongruent with his usual, rational way of coping, and I was starting to worry that the fever might be affecting his judgment. Here he was, obviously facing a life-threatening situation, and refusing to even acknowledge what was happening. That didn't seem right to me.

Over the next few days, we got into a number of unpleasant, knock-down, drag-out fights-- all of which I lost, unfortunately. Then, after a particularly nasty row, Wil spilled the beans and confessed why he was being so obstinate about not going back to the doctor.

"I can't go back," he confessed, tearfully, looking up at me through dark, sunken eyes. "I forgot to renew my health insurance when the cobra clause ran out in June, so I don't have any medical coverage. If I keep seeing the doctor, it'll bankrupt us. I can't afford to go back, you understand?"

I could hardly contain my shock at this unexpected revelation. It was inconceivable to me how someone as organized as Wil could have forgotten something as basic as maintaining his medical coverage, especially knowing full-well he had AIDS. Even though we both believed we were healing ourselves, wouldn't health insurance still be something you'd hold on to from strictly a financial stand point? Such a grave lapse in judgment was completely out of character, and I couldn't believe my ears.

It's true; I *was* aware that Wil had a powerful streak of denial in him; I certainly wouldn't deny that. Junito was a prime example. Wil was so afraid of acknowledging any negative feelings that Junito had been forced to assume them for him. I could see this same pattern of denial in his spiritual practice too; in his rigid adherence to the more mental aspects of the Science of Mind. In some ways, he was a positive thinker of the worst kind, always affirming some ultimate ideal of perfection while failing to deal with the reality in front of him. Now, when it was a matter of life and death to face up to what was happening with his health, he was refusing to even acknowledge there was a problem.

I was so angry and frustrated by his confession, and by my own impotence to do anything about it, that I removed myself from the situation and went out onto the deck for some air. For weeks, Wil's adamant refusal to act and my iron-willed tendency to control, had been locked in a life and death struggle that neither one of us could win. I threw myself up against the side of the house and beat on it with my fists, kicking and screaming and cursing Wil and God, and anyone else I could think of, in a fit of frustration. I had never felt so angry and powerless in my entire life!

When my rage finally subsided, I was calm enough to go back inside the house and engage Wil in a civil discussion about the predicament we were in. It was clear that I would need to keep a level head if I was going to be of any help.

"I'll call Drexell Burnham in the morning and find out what I can about your health insurance," I said, offering my help as an olive branch. "You're only a couple of months in arrears, at this point. I'm pretty sure we can still get this straightened out."

Wil looked relieved, but didn't say a word.

"I'll handle this, OK?" I reassured him. "You're in no condition to deal with this right now. I'll take care of it. Just try and get some rest."

The first thing the next morning, I called the offices of Drexell Burnham, Wil's former employer in New York, and was quickly transferred through to the benefits department where I explained my situation to the faceless woman on the other end of the line. After listening patiently to my dilemma, she promptly put me on hold, and was back a few minutes later with the information I had requested.

"Your renewal forms were sent to your address in New York City," she informed me, in an efficient, business-like manner. "If they were not forwarded to you at your present address in California, you're still eligible to have your insurance rolled over into a private policy. If you'll give me your new address, I'll send you the forms, and you can return them directly to the insurance company. What is your address please?"

"Thank God," I murmured, and gave her our Mill Valley address. "Thank you, so much. You've been more help than you can possibly know."

The much anticipated papers arrived promptly in the mail a few days later, and Wil and I spent the afternoon gathering up the necessary information and filling out the various and sundry forms. I could tell he was relieved that the problem was being taken care of, although he showed very little emotion and was uncharacteristically withdrawn, Despite his best efforts to disguise it, it was painfully obvious that he was still very, very ill.

To top it off, there was also the small matter of our lecture at the Whole Life Expo in Los Angeles, on the weekend just ahead. Obviously, Wil was in no condition to travel or speak.

"You'll have to go to Los Angeles without me,' he admitted, "and I'll stay here and rest. I'll be alright for a couple of days. Don't worry about me."

But I did worry about him, and I didn't want to leave him home alone in his condition. However, we had signed a contract, and at least one of us was obligated to show up and go through the motions.

On Friday afternoon, Wil drove me to the bus stop to catch the shuttle to SFO. I leaned over and kissed him goodbye, and got out of the car, struggling to keep my composure.

"You'll be fine," he tried to reassure me, seeing how upset I was. "You'll be back before you know it. Don't worry, honey. I'll be fine."

I closed the door and stood there as the Suzuki sped away, watching the frail silhouette of Wil's head disappear into the distance.

"I've got to pull myself together," I told myself. "I'll get through this, somehow. I have to."

In Los Angeles, Charlie was waiting for me by the curb outside the baggage claim area. He loaded my bags into his car and drove straight to the convention center, and stayed with me throughout the entire evening.

"Wil was not able to be here tonight," I informed the disappointed audience at the very beginning of my talk. "He's not feeling very well, and so decided to stay home and take care of himself. He did ask me to remind you of how important it is to respect your limits and learn to say no, whenever it's appropriate. Unfortunately, he needed to say no to being here tonight, and that's what he chose to do." With that, a speculative murmur rippled through the room.

Later, after I had finished my presentation and all of the books and tapes had been sold and signed, Charlie drove me to my hotel and stopped in the circular drive out front, leaving the engine running.

"It doesn't look good, Charlie," I sighed. "He's running a really high fever and has lost a lot of weight. And he won't go back to the doctor, either." I threw up my hands in frustration. "Frankly, I'm afraid we're going to lose him if things don't turn around soon."

Charlie turned to face me in the car. "If there's anything I can do help, don't be afraid to call me," he said. He reached over and rested his hand on my shoulder. "Wil's like a brother to me. You know I'd do anything for him."

I opened the car door and climbed out on the curb, and stood there quietly as Charlie pulled away. *At this point, I'm not sure there's anything anyone can do*, I thought, sadly. The die, I feared, had already been cast.

The next morning, I caught the first flight out of LAX, and was back in San Francisco by nine am. Wil picked me up at the bus stop an hour later, looking even thinner and frailer than when I had left him the previous day. Over the next several days, his condition continued to deteriorate and the last of what little appetite he still had all but disappeared. Frustrated at my inability to halt the relentless slide in his condition, I tried to distract myself from the fear I was feeling by busying myself in the kitchen, preparing anything I thought might stimulate his flagging appetite. Despite my best efforts, the most he managed to swallow was a couple of spoonfuls of jello, before pushing the rest away. From then on, his only form of nourishment came from the little bit of flat coca cola I was able to make him drink.

As a result of not eating, Wil's weight continued to drop, precipitously. With Benjamin's prediction lurking like a black cloud in the back of my mind, along with Dr. Grossman's stern warning about the correlation between weight loss and patient mortality, I was seized with a sense of impending doom.

"Please Wil, you've got to let me take you to the hospital," I pleaded, to no avail. "You haven't eaten in days, you're seriously dehydrated, and you're burning up with fever. You've got to let me get you some help!"

Despite my insistence, Wil remained adamant that he would be alright, and became increasingly withdrawn. "I'll be alright in a couple of days," he insisted, trying to minimize my concerns. "Don't give me anymore aspirin, though. Its more trouble breaking this fever than just letting it run its course."

I tried to argue with him, but my efforts fell on deaf ears. He had made up his mind and he was not going to budge.

Thanksgiving was just around the corner, and I was pretty close to my wits end. I had been cooped up in the house for more than two weeks without a break, and the stress was beginning to take its toll. Receiving a last minute invitation from Greg Cassin for Thanksgiving dinner at his house, I accepted, and the next day, drove into the city, even though I wasn't much in the mood for a celebration

"It'll be a low key affair," Greg had assured me, "with only a few close friends. Getting out of the house will do you good."

Despite everything that was going on at home with Wil, I surprised myself and partook whole-heartedly of the sumptuous spread Greg and his friends had prepared. Unfortunately, not even overindulging in food and wine was enough to deaden the sense of dread hanging over me like a dark, ominous cloud. After pie and coffee, I excused myself and hurried back to Marin, feeling numb and oh-so-hopeless and alone.

On Saturday, Wil's fever finally broke after raging unchecked for a little over two weeks, and the first inklings of an appetite reappeared. I was sure his brains must be cooked by now, but the possibility that the worst was over quickly crowded out any such concerns. I set about trying to rehydrate him, making small cups of broth and giving him Pedialyte and Gatorade--anything I thought might do the trick.

That night, I helped him into a warm bath, then dried him off and wrapped him in a terrycloth robe, and helped him into the rocker in the living room. The flurry of activity exhausted us both, but he managed to smile and thank me, and said he was feeling a whole lot better.

I awoke the next morning feeling optimistic for the first time in over a month. With Wil's fever on the decline, and him finally starting to take in fluids, surely it would be only a matter of getting the proper rest and nutrition before he was good as new.

When Wil awoke a few hours later, I helped him into in the living room and made us both a cup of tea. He took it without saying a word, and drank a few sips before resting the cup in his lap. I busied myself in the kitchen, making breakfast and engaging in small talk. Weak as he was, Wil could only nod or flash a crooked smile to let me know that he was listening. I didn't care, really. I was so relieved that his fever had broken that I hardly even noticed.

Unfortunately, my new-found optimism proved relatively short lived.

As soon as I had finished breakfast and put the dishes away, Wil called to me from the other room.

"I want to go to the hospital," he stammered, in a decidedly uneven cadence. "Something strange is going on. My mouth and my brain don't seem to be working in sync. Call Eric and see if you can get him to come and help."

As startling as this turn of events was, I was relieved by Wil's long, overdue request to go to the hospital. Studying his emaciated figure slouched in the chair in front of me, there was little doubt in my mind that the hospital was precisely where he belonged. His condition had deteriorated to the point where it was obvious, even to him, that extraordinary means would be needed if he ever expected to recover. The situation had progressed far beyond anything either of us could do to fix it ourselves.

I called Eric, and then placed a second call to the doctor in San Francisco and explained the situation to the nurse on duty. She advised me to bring Wil by the office, as a prelude to admitting him to the hospital. Eric arrived at the house, just as Wil was finishing getting dressed. He seemed nervous and unsure of just what to do to help. Seeing his reticence, I immediately took charge of the situation.

With Eric's help, we carried Wil to the car and situated him comfortably in the back seat, and were soon speeding down highway 101 in the direction of the Golden Gate Bridge. We were headed for the offices of Dr. Marcus Conant, just across the street from Mount Zion Hospital. Eric attempted to fill the silence with superficial chit chat, and assurances to Wil that he was doing the right thing. Neither of us dared voice our unspoken fear that the situation might have progressed too far to be reversed.

When the receptionist glanced up and saw Wil's emaciated figure leaning against the counter, supported on either side by Eric and myself, she gave a start and quickly excused herself, and disappeared into the next room. She reappeared a few minutes later, and promptly ushered us into a nearby examining room, where we were immediately seen by one of the several, young interns on staff.

"Your condition is obviously quite serious, so we want to have you admitted to the hospital right away," the handsome young intern said, after hearing a brief account of Wil's recent history. "In the meantime, let's get you hooked up to an IV and get some fluids in you. I'll have the nurse take care of everything else. In the meantime, just lie here and rest."

Everyone, including Wil, was visibly relieved that he was finally going into the hospital where he could receive the kind of attention his condition so obviously required. Despite his long standing resistance to doctors and allopathic medicine, even Wil seemed to understand the obvious necessity of the decision.

"Don't worry," I reassured him, giving his hand a gentle squeeze. "Eric and I will be with you every step of the way. At least, now, you'll be getting the kind of help you need."

Wil flashed a thin smile, and closed his eyes to rest. Eric and I sat quietly nearby, not saying a word, lost in our own separate worlds of thought. Was Wil going to die? Was there anything that could be done to prevent it? Or were we all going to die of this damn disease, no matter how ferociously we might try to ward it off?

After what seemed like an eternity, the attendant stuck his head through the doorway and informed us that Wil's admission to the hospital had been arranged. We eased him into a wheelchair and pushed him back through the crowded reception area, and out into the hall.

Across the street, in the lobby of Mount Zion Hospital, an anonymous attendant in hospital greens was there to meet us in the lobby. He immediately took custody of Wil and promptly wheeled him away in the direction of a nearby bank of elevators. Eric followed right behind them. I was ushered into a nearby office to fill out the necessary paperwork and make arrangements for paying the bill.

"There's a bit of a problem with his insurance," I confessed to the helpful, young woman on the other side of the desk when she asked how I intended to pay. "There was a mix up, of sorts, in converting his cobra to private insurance, and we're still in the process of straightening it out. We should be hearing from the insurance company any day now. There shouldn't be a problem, really. We should be receiving verification, any day."

To my surprise and relief, the precariousness of Wil's insurance status didn't pose as big a problem as I had feared it might. I had half expected to be thrown out of the office on my ear, with Wil following right behind me, the IV still dangling from his arm. Instead, after entering the information I had provided into the computer, the admittance officer asked merely that I keep her abreast of the situation. She glanced up from the monitor and handed me a slip of paper with Wil's room number on it, and directed me to a nearby bank of elevators. As the heavy metal doors slammed shut behind me, my knees buckled and I sagged against the railing in exhaustion.

Thankfully, the elevator's slow ascent gave me a few precious moments to gather my strength and compose myself. When the doors finally parted onto the fifth floor, I stepped out into the hall and was confronted by a choice of rooms in either direction. Checking the slip of paper, I turned and proceeded down a long, nondescript hallway, with doors on either side. Strange hospital smells, sickly antiseptic in nature, assaulted my wary nostrils.

I located Wil's room, halfway down the hall near the nurse's station, and pushed open the heavy, metal door decorated with a bright, red, biohazard sign, and went inside. "Great," I thought, "just what we need. We've been quarantined."

Inside, Wil was resting comfortably in the only bed in the room, with Eric hovering over him, holding his hand. As I entered, a nurse brushed past me on her way out, leaving the three of us alone, together.

Wil looked relieved to see me, even though we had been apart for less than an hour. Apparently, whatever reservations he might have had about checking into the hospital had been overridden by a realization of just how serious his condition was. For the first time since he had fallen ill, he seemed ready to deal with his situation.

Eric stayed for a few, more hours, before begging off with the excuse of an approaching deadline at work. I stayed until the wee hours of the morning and then, at Wil's insistence, agreed to go home and get some rest. I hadn't had any real sleep, to speak of, for weeks, and the fatigue was beginning to take its toll. When I had not been jumping through hoops at the slightest sign of Wil in distress, I had laid wide awake in bed, staring up at the ceiling, unable to sleep, contemplating the unthinkable proposition that my lover might actually be dying.

On one level, I was sure I would be fine, no matter what the outcome of this experience turned out to be. On another, more immediate level, I was overwhelmed at the possibly of having to face the future alone. Wil and I had been a couple for almost twelve years--a good portion of my adult life- and the thought of him not being there was simply unfathomable. *Sure, I could make it on my own,"* I thought, *but do I really want to?* I honestly didn't know the answer.

I drove back home to Marin on automatic pilot, lost in a numbing fog of fear. Gunning the Suzuki up the last, little bit of hill, I turned into the driveway and cut the engine, and stumbled down the steps to the house. It was dark, and I had forgotten to leave the porch light on. It took me a minute to find the key to the front door. On finding it, I jammed it into the lock and pushed open the door and stumbled into the bedroom, and fell into bed fully clothed. I was out like a light the moment my head hit the pillow.

34 The Will

WHEN I AWOKE THE FOLLOWING MORNING, for a moment I almost forgot that Wil wasn't in bed beside me. Then, seeing the empty space where he usually slept, reality came rushing back to slap me in the face.

Determined to stay centered, I took a long, hot shower and fixed myself a bite to eat, and then headed back to the hospital in San Francisco. Thankfully, Wil was much more alert than when I had left him the previous night, and was propped up in bed drinking a small cup of orange juice. His face lit up as I entered the room.

"Wow," I said, planting a kiss on his forehead. "You're looking a whole lot better than when I left you last night. How are you feeling this morning?"

"A lot better," he said, flashing me a crooked grin. "I got a good night's sleep, and the IV fluids really helped. I should be ready to come home in a couple of days."

I was encouraged to see how alert he was, especially after the lethargic state he had been in the night before. Maybe now that he was in the hospital and getting the care he needed, he would be alright. He had just had a minor setback, that was all. Given time, this too would pass.

I stayed with him for the entire morning, keeping myself occupied by reading out-of-date magazines from the reception area by the nurse's station. Wil slept the entire time, which was a good sign, I thought. He needed to rest and conserve as much of his strength as possible.

Eric stopped by around noon and proceeded to chase me out of the room, insisting that I get out of the hospital and go somewhere for lunch.

I protested only briefly, before acquiescing to his demands. With Wil resting comfortably, there was no reason for me to be by his side every single moment. I might as well take advantage of Eric's offer and spend a little time looking after myself.

I retrieved the Suzuki from the parking garage and drove over the hill to the Castro for a bite to eat. Afterwards, I moseyed around the neighborhood, poking my nose into a number of interesting stores. I was determined to keep my mind occupied, knowing that left to its own devices it would undoubtedly manufacture the most negative scenarios imaginable, and that wouldn't help anyone--least of all Wil.

Back at the hospital, there had been a slight change for the worse in Wil's condition. His fever had returned, and he seemed uncharacteristically agitated. It was difficult seeing him like this, particularly since I was powerless to do anything about it. This was undoubtedly the hardest thing I had to deal with. As much as I hated seeing him sick, I hated, even more, being helpless to do anything to help.

Eric hung around well into the evening, before finally taking his leave. Besides trying to support the two of us through this crisis, he had a business to run which he couldn't afford to neglect. As the second night of Wil's hospitalization wore on, his condition steadily deteriorated. He began drifting in and out of consciousness, and his body was wracked with periodic seizures as though he was struggling against an enemy no one else but he could see.

Faced with this unexpected turn for the worse in Wil's condition, my earlier optimism quickly gave way to a growing sense of despair. His disturbing thrashing symptoms, which had grown increasingly intense over time, made it appear as though he was suffering and in pain, though I couldn't really be sure. I was suffering, however--that much was certain. I had never seen Wil this sick and out of control before, and was horrified by the unfamiliar spectacle. He had always been the rock in our relationship, the one that always seemed to have it together and could be counted on no matter what. Now, with him ill and out of control, I was forced to reach deep down inside myself and find the strength to keep it all together for the both of us, which wasn't something I was used to doing.

It was plainly obvious that something was horribly wrong, yet no one seemed to know exactly what it was, or what to do about it. Frustrated by the lack of a definitive diagnosis, I marched to the nurse's station and insisted that he be given something to calm him down and make him as comfortable as possible. At first, the nurse on duty refused to help me on the grounds that the doctor in charge had gone home for the night and that she wasn't authorized to prescribe any new medications.

Finally, however, my persistent badgering wore her down, and she agreed to administer a mild sedative. Moments after the needle was retracted from his IV drip, Wil fell into a fitful sleep, waking up only periodically after that to look around in an obvious state of confusion, before falling back to sleep. I held vigil by his bed for the remainder of the night as the murderously slow hours ticked by, afraid to leave his side even to go to the bathroom.

"Oh God, please let him get well," I pleaded up at the ceiling, hoping for a sign--hoping for anything that might signal an end to this horrible nightmare. "Please God, whatever happens, don't let Wil die! I don't know what I'd do without him."

Thanks to periodic shots of Demerol, Wil slept through most of the night and well into the next morning. Around nine a.m., the doctor in charge arrived for his morning rounds. I cornered him in the hallway and demanded that he do something to find out, once and for all, what was causing Wil's symptoms. I didn't care what he did. I simply wanted anything that could possibly be done, done, to pinpoint the cause of the problem and make it go away.

Over the course of the morning, copious quantities of blood were drawn from Wil's arm, and around noon, he was taken downstairs by a friendly orderly for a spinal tap to check for meningitis. I took advantage of his absence to phone Eric and bring him up to speed on what had transpired during the night, and relate my growing concern that Wil might die without a valid will. A few months earlier, Wil had purchased the computer program, Will Maker, which he had planned to use to put all our affairs in order. In the eventuality that something happened to either of us, we wanted to make sure that whoever survived would inherit everything we owned.

For some reason--probably because neither of us had wanted to acknowledge the unpleasant possibility of one of us dying--nothing had been done to resolve the situation. Now, the unpleasant scenario we had hoped to avoid had become an even uglier probability, and we didn't have the necessary documents to protect ourselves.

A will was especially important for the simple reason that before leaving New York on our trip around the country, we had put all of our individual assets into a single account, in Wil's name for convenience sake. It had made sense at the time, even though I hadn't really been keen on the idea when Wil had first suggested it.

I had acquiesced, finally, after a little, further coaxing from him. After all, he was the one with the background in finance, and who was I to argue? Now, if Wil were to die without a will, and with my money in his account, I could very well lose all my assets. On top of having to deal with the possibility of Wil dying, I now found myself grappling with the possibility of financial ruin.

"Eric, you've got to get down here today with some kind of will he can sign," I insisted. "He's drifting in and out of consciousness, and I'm afraid that if we don't get this done soon, it'll be too late. He might slip into a coma and never come out of it."

"Don't exaggerate, George," Eric chided me, blowing off my concerns. "He was OK when I saw him last night. How much worse could he be today?"

"He's really bad, Eric. I'm not exaggerating. Please, just draw up a will that says everything goes to me, and get down here with it right away. And hurry up!"

I slammed down the receiver and headed back down the hall. Just outside the door to the room, I bumped into the patient advocate who had been assigned to us when we had checked into the hospital.

"I was just coming to see if there was anything I could do for you," he greeted me. "Is there anything you need?"

"I need a lawyer," I blurted out, before I could stop myself. "And I need someone who can witness a will." With that, the entire story of our sorry predicament came tumbling out.

"There's a lawyer that comes through here almost every day," the advocate assured me when I had finished explaining the situation. "I saw him earlier and I think he's still here, if I'm not mistaken. Let me see if I can get hold of him, and I'll get back to you as soon as I do. Don't worry. We'll get this whole thing straightened out before you know it!"

For the moment, the man's calm assurances helped to assuage my anxiety about the situation with the will. I took a moment to compose myself, before going back into the room. Unfortunately, Wil's appearance did nothing to alleviate my fear that he might actually be dying. While he was not as agitated as he had been earlier that morning--whatever was affecting his nervous system seemed to have eased up a bit, at least for the time being--he wasn't fully focused in the same reality as I was, either. He was sitting upright in bed, with strange, wide, luminous eyes, conversing with someone I couldn't see.

"It's Ralph," he gushed, ignoring my expression of dismay. "Ralph's here."

His words sent a shudder running up my spine. Ralph was Wil's cousin who had died of AIDS earlier in the year. The fact that Wil seemed convinced he was talking to him was just one more unwanted indication that he might actually be dying. If he wasn't, then why else would Ralph be here? I couldn't think of another good reason.

"No!" I thought, my control-mode once again kicking into full gear. "He can't die! Not if I have anything to say about it! I won't let him!"

Unfortunately, it was becoming increasingly obvious that the decision whether or not Wil lived or died wasn't mine to make. Over the next few hours, he continued to see any number of other people who had passed on ahead of him, as well as an array of beautiful, geometric patterns and symbols he insisted were on the wall in front of his bed. In a sweet, child-like voice, he described every one of them to me in detail. He also informed me that a parade was going on outside in the hallway, with strange men in orange and red saris playing stringed instruments and drums. And lights too, apparently--lots of beautiful lights.

"George," he whispered, smiling up at me sweetly as I stood beside the bed, fighting back tears and panic. "Love is all there is. Nothing else really matters."

"I know, Wil, I know," I whispered. "And I want you to know that I love you more than anything in the world, and I don't want you to die. Please don't leave me, Wil. Please don't go!"

Now, the tables were turned and it was *his* turn to hold *my* hand and comfort me in my hour of need. Interestingly enough, as far as I could tell, he wasn't afraid at all. In fact, he seemed far beyond the need for any kind of reassurance I might have to offer. The light, so obviously streaming from his eyes and face, had apparently pierced the illusion of death, and he was seeing another life beyond the one we were currently sharing. He was straddling the veil.

I'm sure some people would say that he was demented; that he was hallucinating, or that he was simply out of his mind. I wouldn't be one of those people, however. The best that I could determine, he was sitting serenely in one world--the one he was about to depart from--looking out at the new reality he was poised to embrace. And he wasn't afraid, either. In fact, in the entire time we had been together, I had never seen him so at peace, or more open and accessible.

I stayed by his side for what seemed like an eternity, and held his hand and gently stroked his hair. Then, without my having noticed anyone enter the room, I became aware of Greg Cassin standing beside me, accompanied by a mutual friend of ours from the healing circle, Karen Van Dine. Eric showed up a short time later carrying a small, leather valise containing the hastily drafted will. Suddenly, as if sensing there was still some unfinished business needing his attention, Wil emerged from his semi-lucid state and once again became fully cognizant of his surroundings. He seemed to relish the fact that all of his friends had come to visit him.

"Maybe he's going to be all right," I thought, seeing the sudden improvement in his condition. "Maybe he's going to pull through, after all. Maybe he's not going to die."

Moments later, the patient advocate entered the room, with a tall, thin man in a pin-striped suit trailing behind him. "This is the lawyer I told you about," he explained. "George Melton--Gerald Witherspoon. Gerald will help you with the situation you mentioned to me earlier."

I shook Gerald's hand and steered him into a corner where we could carry on a conversation in private. "My partner is very ill," I explained, "and I need him to sign a will in case he doesn't recover. He's been drifting in and out of consciousness for most of the day, and I'm afraid that if we don't get it done tonight we might not have another chance." I reached into the valise and retrieved the will Eric had created, and handed it to him to inspect.

The lawyer gave the document a quick, cursory read. "Everything seems to be in order," he assured me. "But first, we need to establish that Wil is able to understand exactly what it is he's signing. And we'll need a couple of credible witnesses to that effect."

While the patient advocate went out to find the doctor, I brought Eric up to speed on what was happening. "First, we need to establish that Wil is in full control of his faculties and knows what he's signing," I explained. "You, the doctor, and Mr. Witherspoon will be witnesses to that effect."

A moment later, the door to the room swung open and the doctor entered. He nodded in my direction and proceeded over to the bed where Wil was resting quietly.

"So Wil," he said, reaching out and taking his hand. "How are you feeling this evening?"

Wil gave a weak smile, and indicated that he was feeling a whole lot better. On hearing that, the doctor continued with his line of questioning.

"These gentlemen, here, tell me that they need you to sign some papers for them, and I'm here to make sure you're in the proper state of mind to do it," he said. "What do you think? Do you understand what these documents are?"

"Yes," Wil answered, struggling to raise himself up on his elbows as if to reinforce the fact that he was alert and in control of his mental faculties. "I'm not as out of it as I was earlier in the day."

"Here are the papers George asked me to have you sign," the lawyer interjected, stepping forward to join the doctor by the side of the bed. "It's your last will and testament. I understand that you were planning to execute this, yourself, before you became ill. Is that correct?"

"That's right," Wil replied, nodding his head in the affirmative.

"Your friend, Eric, has drawn up these papers in accordance with your wishes," he continued, "but first, I need to be absolutely certain that you understand what it is you're signing." He gestured in my direction and then continued his line of questioning. "Do you know who this man is, Wil?" he asked.

The room was silent as Wil turned and focused his attention on me. Then, as though a light had suddenly dawned inside of him, his face lit up in the most loving way imaginable, and he answered the question, forthright.

"That's George!" he said, his voice trembling with emotion. "That's my lover, George!"

Next, Gerald went on to explain the exact terms of the will. The document was straightforward and to the point. In the event of Wil's death, his entire estate would go to me. There were to be no other beneficiaries.

When all of the explanations were finished, Wil indicated that he understood the terms of the will and agreed to them. With that, the lawyer took a few steps back and motioned for Eric to take his place. Eric moved to side of the bed and engaged Wil in a brief conversation. A few minutes later, he looked up and indicated that he too was satisfied that Wil understood exactly what he was being asked to sign.

With Wil's competence firmly established in the minds of everyone present, the lawyer presented the papers to Wil for his inspection. He gave them a cursory read and then nodded his head in approval. The lawyer handed him a pen, and he proceeded to sign his name in a very shaky hand; his sprawling signature encompassing nearly the entire bottom of the page.

"There," he beamed, obviously satisfied with what he had accomplished. "I'm glad that's over and done with!"

I took the papers from him and handed them to Eric for safe keeping, until such time as they might be needed. On the one hand, I was relieved that the deed was done and that I didn't have to worry about my financial situation any longer. On the other hand, there was tremendous pain in realizing just why a will had been necessary in the first place.

The previous few weeks had been a rollercoaster of raw emotion, and my nerves were frayed from the relentless onslaught of unhappy news. I felt strangely numb and apart from the situation, as though this horrible nightmare were happening to someone else.

The evening hours continued to tick by slowly. At around eleven o'clock, seeing how tired I was, and that Wil was sleeping soundly, Greg suggested that I go home and get some rest.

"There's really nothing more you can do right now," he assured me. "Karen and I will be happy to stay until you get backin the morning.

It took very little prodding for me to accept Greg's offer to stand vigil in my place. I was exhausted, physically, and desperate to escape the suffocating confines of the tiny hospital room,with its stale air perfumed with the smell of sickness and death. I wanted to forget, at least for a few, precious moments, the horrible reality of my partner's imminent demise.

Greg assured me that he would call me immediately if there was the slightest change in Wil's condition. He took me by the arm and steered me out into the hallway, and pointed me in the direction of the elevators.

"Don't worry," he said, gathering me up in his arms and giving me a slow, hard hug. "Wil's in good hands."

I drove straight home with the windows down, letting the brisk, night air revive my flagging energy, and fell into bed fully clothed without stopping to wash my face. Despite my bone-deep fatigue, I was unable to fall asleep. A merciless torrent of thoughts coursed through my mind, causing my heart to pound in an unnaturally loud way. I could hear the swoosh, swoosh, swoosh of blood coursing through my ears.

Despite the obviousness of Wil's condition, I was not yet willing to let him go, and was determined to figure out a way to save him. I picked up my worn copy of A Course in Miracles from the night stand beside the bed, and turned to the Teacher's Manual in the back. I was looking for a key--any key--for creating a miracle for Wil and myself. After all, didn't it say in the Course that a teacher of God could heal the sick and raise the dead? And wasn't I a teacher of God? If so, then now would certainly be the appropriate time for a practical demonstration.

An hour later, I slammed the book shut in frustration, still not having found the key I was searching for. I rolled over and switched off the light, and pulled the covers up around my neck and fell sound asleep.

35 *"If you could see this differently..."*

W HEN I ARRIVED BACK AT THE hospital the following morning, the scene in Wil's hospital room resembled bedlam. During the night, his physical spasms had returned with a vengeance, and as I entered the room, I could see him up on all fours in bed, struggling against some invisible assailant, crying in that crazy, baby-talk Spanish of his. Greg and Karen were on either side of him, doing their best to keep him from hurting himself. They looked up at me, exhaustion etched on both their faces.

"This started around midnight, not long after you left," Greg said, tersely, "and things got progressively worse from there. We tried to get the nurse to give him a stronger sedative, but she couldn't do it without orders from his doctor. He should be here sometime later this morning."

The surreal nature of the scene plunged me into a renewed state of panic and fear. I had never seen Wil even lose his temper before, much less total control of his body. I wanted to turn and run, and keep on running and never look back, but that wasn't an option. I steeled myself and moved closer to the bed to see if I could help.

"Maybe he will respond to me," I said, trying to sound a not of optimism. "Maybe I can calm him down."

Wil continued to writhe on the bed, babbling incoherently in that funny, pidgin Spanish of his. Suddenly, the realization hit me of just who it was that was speaking. It wasn't the Wil Garcia we all knew and loved, but his inner child, Junito--the angry infant that had first made an appearance at Niro's workshop several months before. Yes, I was certain it was Junito--not Wil--struggling on the bed in front of me, fighting mightily against his long-repressed demons from childhood.

My heart leapt into my throat and then softened as a wave of compassion rolled over me. "Esta bien, Junito," I said, bending down and whispering in Wil's ear in the best, high school Spanish I could muster. I pressed my body up against his, and stoked his head and neck, trying to console him. "Estoy aqui, Junito. Yo te amo. Estas un buen chico. Un chico muy bueno."

Just then, the doctor breezed into the room on his morning rounds. "You've got to sedate him before he hurts himself," I snapped, venting my frustration on the most convenient target around. "He's been struggling like this all night, and if it hadn't been for my friends here, there's no telling what might have happened. The sedative he's been getting isn't strong enough. You've got to give him something stronger!"

"I could give him morphine," the doctor replied, maintaining a professional demeanor. "I think that would do the trick."

I glanced over at Greg, searching his face for a clue about what I should do. "Do it," he said. "Just do it! He needs some help with the pain."

I nodded at the doctor, who immediately excused himself and quietly backed out of the room. He was back a few minutes later with a nurse carrying a syringe, which she used to inject a clear liquid into the IV tube attached to Wil's arm.

"This should allow him to get some rest," the nurse said softly, giving me a reassuring look

True to her words, within moments, Wil's thrashing stopped and he fell into a deep, restful sleep. Greg helped me to shift him into a more comfortable position and then collapsed in a nearby chair. I was much too agitated to relax. I stood vigil by his bedside, busying myself with a thousand little tasks, smoothing the sheets and wiping beads of perspiration from his fevered brow. Having something to do--anything at all--helped to alleviate my unbearable feeling of helplessness.

Around mid-morning, a pair of orderlies arrived and took Wil downstairs on a stretcher for a MRI, and a battery of other tests the doctor had ordered. Eric arrived just in time to see Wil being wheeled out into the hall. Greg and Karen brought him up to speed, and then excused themselves and gathered up their belongings to leave.

"We'll be back tomorrow," Greg assured me. "In the meantime, if there's anything you need, you know where to reach me."

As Eric surveyed the scene before him, he could sense that I was in serious overwhelm and needed his support. "Let me talk to the doctor for you," he suggested, kindly. "I'll arrange for Wil to be put on a morphine drip. That way, we won't have to worry about getting the nurse to give him a shot of Demerol every four hours. We'll just keep him knocked out until they figure out what's wrong with him and know what to do about it."

"A morphine drip?!" I recoiled in horror. "Isn't that's what they give you when their trying to help you die? Well, I'm not ready to give up on him, Eric; I'm just not! I want them to run every test they can think of until they find out what's the matter with him. I'm not going to just stand by and let him die--do you understand me?"

"Don't worry, I won't let them do anything to hurt him," Eric assured me. "I just want to make sure he's as comfortable as possible."

Reassured, somewhat, that a morphine drip wouldn't contribute to Wil's demise, I agree to let Eric speak to the doctor for me. At least he won't be in any pain, I rationalized. The doctor will be able to run whatever tests he needs, and Wil won't be any the wiser for it.

That night, Greg explained Wil's condition to a shocked group of regulars and friends at the San Francisco Healing Circle. They responded magnificently, with an incredible outpouring of love and support. Immediately, a schedule was created for an around the clock vigil to support me at the hospital. Starting the very next morning, there was never a moment when a member of the healing circle was not present in the room with me, bringing food or fetching coffee, helping to change Wil's bed clothes and linens, praying, giving Reiki and massage, or generally doing whatever the situation called for.

The third day of Wil's hospitalization came and went, and still there was no clear indication of the cause of his symptoms. Each time he was taken downstairs for another battery of tests, I crossed my fingers and prayed that, this time, we would finally have a definitive answer. And each time, my hope collapsed into a heap of bitter disappointment, as test after test came back inconclusive. There was nothing in his lungs, nothing in his spinal fluid, and no lesions on his brain.

"The virus must be attacking his nervous system," I speculated, trying to come up with a plausible explanation for his symptoms. "Or maybe the weeks of high fever have simply cooked his brain." That was what I was really afraid of.

On Thursday evening, I bit the bullet and place a call to Wil's parents in New York. I had put the call off for as long as I could, hoping against hope that it would prove to be unnecessary. Unfortunately, it wasn't tuning out that way. When I had finished dialing the number, Wil's mother answered after a couple of short, dull rings.

"Carmen," I began, nervously clearing my throat. "This is George. I'm calling from the hospital in San Francisco." There was noticeable silence from the other end of the line.

"Wil has taken a turn for the worse," I continued, "and no one is really sure what's causing his symptoms. It's pretty serious, though. I think you'd better come out here as soon as possible."

Again, there was silence from the other end of the line. I could hear Carmen's voice in the back ground, calling Wil's father to the phone. Suddenly, Wilfredo, Sr. was on the line.

"What's the matter, George," he demanded, concern evident in his tone of voice. "What's going on out there?"

I quickly explained the gravity of the situation and reiterated my opinion that he and Carmen should come to California as soon as possible. "I can't guarantee you that he's going to recover from this," I said, putting the situation as bluntly as I could. "He could die at any moment."

There was a long pause before Wil's father finally spoke again. "I'll tell you what," he said. "You keep us informed of Wil's condition, and if things don't improve by the weekend, we'll come out there sometime early, next week."

"OK," I relented, feeling much too weary to push the issue any further. I wasn't really sure that Wil would make it through the weekend, but the choice was up to them. "I call you if there's the slightest change in his condition."

I hung up the phone and turned to face Eric who had been standing beside me, ease-dropping on the conversation. "They're not coming until sometime next week," I said, sadly. "I tried to tell them it wasn't a good idea, but they wouldn't listen."

Eric reacted to my words with fury, his face contorting and turning red with rage. "What kind of people won't even come to see their dying son?" he fumed, his body stiffening, his fists clinched. "What kind of family values is that!?"

I tried to calm him down, but gave up in the face of continuing resistance. Whether Eric believed it or not, Wil's parents did love him. That I knew beyond a shadow of a doubt. And they loved me, too. Wil and I had spent every holiday since we had known each other at their house in New Rochelle, and I had always been treated like a son. No, they weren't coming to California because they didn't love him. They weren't coming because it was their way of denying the seriousness of his condition. The reality that their only son might actually be dying was simply too painful to accept.

In large part, Eric's reaction was a projection of his own unhealed, childhood issues. He had been given up for adoption and had never come to terms with the fact that his birthmother had given him away. The knowledge had left him with an enduring lack of self-worth, for which he overcompensated, mightily. Rather than focusing on the fact that his adopted parents had chosen him for a son, he remained stubbornly fixated on having been abandoned.

In fact, this was one of the primary issues that bound Wil and Eric together as friends; they shared similar wounds. And while each of them had dealt with their pain in different ways, it had had a lasting impact on their perception of self worth.

I stayed at the hospital for the entire night, scarcely closing my eyes for even a moment. I couldn't seem to pull myself away from Wil's bedside, except for the minute or two it took me to use the bathroom, or get a drink of water. His slightest twitch or moan sent me into a frenzy of activity trying to ascertain if he was in pain, and if so, what to do about it. I studied his face, trying to imagine where he might be and what he might be feeling. And hoping, always hoping that his condition might miraculously improve.

Early Friday morning, a call came into the nurse's station from Marianne Williamson, in Los Angeles. "I want you to know that our thought and prayers are with you and Wil during this difficult time," her familiar voice intoned, piercing through my haze of fatigue. I mumbled a hollow 'thank you', and mindlessly placed the receiver back in its cradle and headed back down the hall.

I spent the rest of the day cooped up in the room, alternately standing beside the bed or collapsed in a daze in a chair. Although my body was thoroughly exhausted, my mind continued to relentlessly churn in overdrive, trying to figure out a way to keep Wil alive.

If you could see this differently, the words leapt up from the pages of A Course in Miracles, taunting me with their promise, *you could heal the sick and raise the dead.*

"How could I possibly do that?" I wondered. "What is it I need to see?" I wracked my brain, trying to solve the illusive puzzle. "Please God," I prayed, "help me to see this situation differently."

It didn't seem to matter how hard I prayed, no answer was forthcoming. Wil didn't suddenly sit up in bed and say he was feeling a whole lot better, and that he was ready to go home, like I had hoped. He just lay there without moving a muscle, the sound of his breathing growing more and more labored with each passing moment. I wanted to scream and crawl out of my skin. I felt helpless in a way I never had. I wanted to lash out at the people around me, to make them hurt the same way I was hurting. I simply did not know what to do with my pain.

Eventually, my rage turned into tears--a gut wrenching torrent of pent-up, liquid pain that left me limp and exhausted once it had finally passed. I sat crumpled up in the chair beside Wil's bed, numb and uncharacteristically quiet, watching nameless people pass in and out of the room--minute by minute-- hour after hour.

Then, just when my despair was at its deepest, the miracle I had been praying for occurred. Inside my head--or maybe it was my heart; I can't be sure--a wee, still idea quietly insinuated itself into my normal stream of thought.

"George," the idea proposed, "If you could see this situation differently, you'd see the healing taking place here. You'd stop trying to fix Wil and simply be here for him. You'd see how perfect everything actually is."

Startled by this unexpected idea, my eyes blinked open with a start. In a stunning instant of revelation, I understood exactly what was happening to Wil, and what I needed to do. In the only way he knew how, Wil was healing the single, most important issue in his life: his fear of being abandoned.

Here, on the fifth floor of a lonely San Francisco hospital, drugged out of his mind for all intents and purposes, Wil Garcia--Mr. Self

Healing--the guy who always did everything right because he thought
he had to in order to be loved--was doing things in a way most people
wouldn't understand. Not only was he sick, but he was completely out
of control. He was in the most untenable position he could have ever
imagined himself in.

The miracle was this: no matter how ugly his death throes appeared
to those looking on from outside, he couldn't make anyone abandon him.
They simply would not go away. I wasn't going anywhere, certainly, even
though on more than one occasion I had wanted to cut and run. Instead,
I had dug down deep inside myself and bravely stood my ground.

And besides me, there were all those people from the Healing Circle
who had looked to Wil as an example of how to heal themselves from
AIDS. Despite the innumerable questions his predicament must have
raised in their minds, they too stood their ground. No matter how badly
he seemed to be letting them down, he couldn't make anyone leave. No
one abandoned him in his greatest hour of need!

For the first time since that fateful night in New York City, when
Benjamin had predicted Wil's death and I had sworn not to let it happen,
I was at peace. A wave of release washed through me, leaving me limp and
calm in its wake. Up until now, I had wrestled without hope to impose
my will on a situation that wasn't mine to decide, and God knows that
struggle had taken its toll. I hadn't eaten a decent meal or had a proper
night's sleep in days, and had lost 10 pounds as a result-- weight I could
scarcely afford to lose. Now, in the final analysis, there was nothing to
do but be there and watch as events continued to unfold.

Around six in the evening, my friend, Dolores, who had been at the
hospital with me for the entire day, suggested that I go home and get
cleaned up. A quick glance in the mirror at my sunken eyes and stubbled
face, convinced me she was right. Rev. Matt, who just happened to have
stopped by the hospital for a quick visit, volunteered to drive me home.
On the way back to Marin, I shared my recent revelation.

"I know, now, that Wil is going to die." I said, plainly. "God knows I
tried every trick in the book to keep it from happening, but in the end, it
simply wasn't my decision to make. Tonight, I was finally able to see the
situation for what it is: dying is Wil's way of healing himself."

Matt listened without comment, and we finished the rest of the drive in silence. At home, there were at least a dozen messages waiting for me on the answering machine.

"Take your time; do whatever you need to," Matt said, taking a seat on the couch. "I'm not in any hurry."

I pushed the playback button and waited for the tape to rewind. The very first message told me everything I needed to know. "This is Roger from Rolling Homes," a male voice droned. "We sold your Winnebago today. Could you please come by the office tomorrow and sign some papers. The new owners are anxious to close the deal."

I sat down hard on the bed, in a state of disbelief. If I had needed further confirmation that Wil was actually leaving, then this was surely it. We had put the Winnebago up for sale, at my insistence and against Wil's wishes, right after our ill-fated trip to LA. Ultimately, he had let me have my way, as he so often did, knowing how anxious I was to recoup the considerable money we had invested in it.

"You can do it if you want to," he had told me at the time, "but I don't think it's going to sell. You see, I haven't completely let it go."

He had been right, of course. The motor home had sat on the lot for more than a month without a single offer. It couldn't sell, actually, not while one of us was still holding on to it. If there was one thing we had learned during our time on the road together, it was how powerfully creative the two of us were whenever we were in agreement regarding some goal or decision. If we both agreed about something, it damn well happened. If not, nothing did. Now, on the very day I had finally accepted Wil's leaving and had set him free to go, a buyer had seemingly appeared out of nowhere.

"He's really going, Matt," I said, choking back tears. "He's really going to die. How will I ever live without him?"

36 *Death is like taking off a tight shoe*

WITH WIL'S DEPARTURE SO CLEARLY IMMINENT, there was nothing for me to do but accept the inevitable and support him in any way I could. I took a long, hot shower and let the water loosen the tension in my tired, aching shoulders. When the heat had finally done its work, I stepped out of the bath and methodically dried myself off on a clean, rough towel, and padded into the bedroom to get dressed. A pile of dirty clothes was lying on the floor beside the bed. I scooped them up and threw them in the hamper, and rummaged through the closet in search of something to wear. I wanted to look my best for whatever awaited me back at the hospital.

When I had finished dressing and had fed and brushed the cats, Rev. Matt drove me back into San Francisco and dropped me off at the curb in front of the hospital. As his car sped away, I turned and pushed my way through the heavy, glass doors at the entrance to the building, and made my way to the bank of elevators at the back of the lobby. After what seemed like an eternity, an empty car arrived and delivered me to the fifth floor, where the uninviting odor of hospital disinfectant immediately assaulted my nostrils.

In the distance, down the hall, a small crowd of people stood milling around outside Wil's room. Inside, Dolores was waiting for me. As I entered, she looked up from the Reiki she was doing on Wil and smiled.

"It's been like this ever since you left," she marveled, nodding in the direction of the hall. "People have been dropping by all night wanting to know how both of you are doing, and if there's anything they can do to help."

I managed a weak smile. Despite the pain I was in, there was a measure of comfort to be had in knowing that so many people actually cared.

The crush of visitors continued throughout the evening. One group would leave, only to be replaced by yet another set of familiar, somber faces--mostly people we knew from the healing circle, or from Radiant Light Ministries. Then, around two in the morning, there was a lull in what had been a steady stream of visitors since news of Wil's hospitalization had gotten out, and a welcomed quiet settled softly over the room.

Interestingly enough, whether by design or omission, no one had volunteered to stand vigil with me between the hours of two and six that morning. With Dolores having gone home for the night, for the first time since Wil had been admitted to the hospital, I was alone in the room with only him. It was just the two of us, the way it had been for so much of the last, dozen years of our lives.

I must admit that I was glad no one else was there--not that I didn't appreciate all the love and support we had received, from friends and strangers alike. Though it was comforting to know people actually cared, it was exhausting, quite frankly, having them around, constantly. With my heart as heavy as it was, I didn't feel like smiling and making friendly chit-chat.

When Wil had first been admitted to the hospital, I had been especially grateful for all the support people had shown us. With him half out of his mind and thrashing around on the bed like some sort of wild animal, I'd actually been afraid to be alone in the room with him. Now that he was sedated and I had begun to accept the inevitability of his transition, my initial fear had eased and I didn't feel the same way. I sank into a chair beside his bed and drank in the haunting quietness of the early, morning hour. Only the gentle beeping of a chorus of monitors punctuated the eerie silence.

Wil continued to run a fever for the remainder of the night. I hovered beside him, mopping beads of sweat from off his forehead and chest, and talking to him in soft, low tones. I told his how much I loved him, how much our life together had meant to me and that I knew he would be leaving soon. I assured him that I would be OK, even though in my heart of hearts I worried that I wouldn't have a clue how to handle being on my own.

Despite the knot of dread in my gut, I had the presence of mind to realize that the most important thing I could do now as to savor every last moment we had left. There would be plenty of time to grieve and deal with the consequences of my loss when all of this was over.

As I puttered about the room doing my best to stay busy, I noticed that someone had left a wallet-sized, reflexology chart lying on the foot of the bed. Curious, I picked it up and glanced over the small chart illustrating the various pressure points on the hands and feet. Since I had some knowledge of acupuncture and energy meridians, it occurred to me that Wil might benefit from having this done to him. I pulled my chair over to the foot of the bed and propped the card up where I could see it, and began working on his feet.

Around three in the morning, the alarm on Wil's morphine drip sounded, and I immediately rushed out into the hall for help. The night-duty nurse followed me back to the room and made a few adjustments to the machine Wil was connected to, and returned to her duties at the nurse's station. Satisfied that nothing was amiss, I went back to practicing reflexology on his feet.

About fifteen minutes later, the same thing happened again. The buzzer on the morphine drip went off and a small, red warning light on the monitor began to blink, startling me out of the pleasant trance I had drifted off into. Annoyed by what I imagined must simply be another malfunction of the monitor, I again alerted the night nurse, who dutifully followed me back to the room, a second time. Again, she fiddled with the controls for several minutes and continued on her rounds. Once again, I went back to working on Wil's feet.

A few minutes later, the alarm went off for a third time. This time, I was beginning to suspect that the problem might be with Wil, and not the machine he was attached to--and with good reason. Although I didn't fully realize it at the time, Wil's body was beginning to shut down in preparation for ejecting his consciousness at the moment of death, and was rejecting the morphine. As the nurse dutifully fiddled with the machine, a third time, I hovered anxiously by the side of the bed, watching the scene with growing alarm.

To distract myself from the fear that was steadily rising in the back of my throat, I found some tissue and dabbed at the tiny beads of perspiration covering Wil's brow. As I did, he took a noticeably deeper breath than usual, and then stopped breathing altogether. Stunned by this unexpected turn of events, I stared at his perfectly motionless body and held my own breath, waiting for him to resume breathing.

"Come on, breathe," I pleaded in a low whisper. Thirty seconds later, he did just that-- and for the very last time. The moment I had dreaded so deeply had come.

My first reaction was to want to jump on the bed on top of him, and beat on his chest until he started breathing again. I was not going to let him go without a fight. But just as quickly as it had come, the thought passed and I knew that that this wasn't what I was supposed to do. I reached out and gently placed one of my hands over his heart, and the other on his shoulder.

For a long moment, time seemed to stand perfectly still. Then, to my awe and amazement, I saw--partially with my eyes, and partially in an energetic sense-- his soul begin its slow-motion exit from his body. It was as though there were a definitive mass of energy advancing up along his torso in the direction of his head, in front of which his flesh was alive and pink and warm, and behind which his body was only a gray, lifeless shell. I stood, transfixed, and watched as the energy migrated up along his neck and across his face, and disappeared out the top of his head.

At the exact moment I saw his soul leave his body, I felt a tremendous rushing sensation in the center of my own chest, as though my heart were being ripped apart by a huge influx of air. An incredible feeling of expansion continued until all I could feel was rushing wind in the empty space where only moments before my heart had been. It felt as though I had inhaled some sort of powerful popper, only a thousand times more intense.

Instantly, a line from Emmanuel's book popped into my head: *Death is like taking off a tight shoe,* the line went. Indeed, that was precisely what the sensation I was experiencing felt like, and instantly I knew that I was being allowed to share what Wil was feeling at the moment of his death. As his soul cast off the limitations of his physical body, the predominate sensation was one of release. Indeed, *it was like taking off a tight shoe.*

Again, I remembered one of Wil's favorite books, *Life after Life,* about people's recollections of their near-death experiences. Many of those featured in the book had described hovering over their death bed, observing those below them attempting to resuscitate their failing bodies. Intuitively, I looked up at the ceiling, knowing that Wil must surely be there. I stretched out my arms to him, tears streaming silently down my face.

"Go to the light" I whispered. "I'll love you forever. Just go to the light."

After a while, the electrical pulsations in my body began to recede and fade away. I stayed by the side of the bed, holding Wil's hand and stroking his hair, too stunned and overwhelmed by the experience to move. I could see faint, translucent shimmers of light rising off the surface of his body, as each individual cell released the life-force within it.

Then, gradually, his once warm, living, loving, body took on the appearance of a corpse. Before long, I could tell that there was no life left in it. I stood there, anyway, unwilling to leave his side. My lover was dead, yet strangely, I wasn't feeling any pain--only an incongruent sense of euphoria. Wil's death was the most intimate moment we had ever shared together, in the more than a decade we were together as a couple. And it was one I will never, ever, forget.

Eventually, the nurse, who had been standing quietly on the other side of the bed the entire time, gently broke the silence. "I'll take these tubes out of his arms, now," she said, softly. Her voice was kind and filled with compassion. "Stay here for as long as you want. Take all the time you need."

After she had left the room, I phoned Greg at home and roused him out of bed. "He's gone," I told him. "He died about an hour ago. Could you come down here and sit with me for a little while?"

Next, I dialed Wil's mother in New Rochelle. When she finally answered the phone, after several lengthy rings, I realized that she had been crying.

"I know," she said, even before I could get a word out of my mouth. "I know. He was here about three-thirty this morning. I woke up, and he was standing at the foot of my bed. He told me he was leaving." With that, we both broke down into great, heaving sobs.

Interestingly enough, at three-thirty that morning I had been doing reflexology on Wil's feet. Could it be that the reflexology had given him exactly the boost he needed in order to astral project to his mother's house in New Rochelle? As far as I was concerned, that was precisely what had happened.

Twenty minutes later, a sleepy Greg Cassin, with Karen Van Dine in tow, arrived bearing flowers and candles which we lit and placed around the room. As new-age music played softly in the background, we stood around the bed together, alternately laughing and crying, and exchanging stories about our different recollections of Wil. Eventually, the first rays of dawn sliced through the dusty venetian blinds, bathing the room in a soft, golden glow. It was finally time to leave.

I called the nurse and asked if she would arrange for Wil's body to be taken to the morgue. While we waited for the coroner to arrive, I went back and stood beside the bed, stroking Wil's head for what I knew would be the very last time. His hair had grown uncharacteristically long and was starting to form ringlet curls, unlike the short, close-cropped style he had worn most of his adult life.

Eventually, two men in nondescript, grey coveralls--all business and no emotion--appeared with a gurney and a black body-bag. I asked them to wait outside while I gathered up my things and took a final glance around. Taking in every last detail of the scene so as to never, ever forget, I took a deep breath and pushed open the door and walked slowly out into the hallway. I didn't want to see them put Wil's body in that bag. Then, with Greg and Karen supporting me on either side, we headed for the elevator and never looked back, even once.

I was completely exhausted but there was no way I could possibly sleep, even if I had wanted to. I dreaded the thought of going back to the empty house in Marin, alone. When Greg offered to let me stay with him for a couple of days, I gratefully accepted the invitation.

Around ten that morning, I excused myself and went upstairs and placed a call to Charlie in Los Angeles, and gave him the sad news.

"I'll be on the first plane out of here," he assured me. "Don't bother picking me up at the airport. I'll catch a cab to the house."

Despite my fatigue, my mind shifted into automatic pilot. Although Greg and Karen tried to discourage me from going, I was determined to drive out to Walnut Creek and sign the papers on the Winnebago, that very day. With so many of Wil's affairs needing my attention, I immersed myself in the details, hoping to keep my grief at bay.

A series of phone calls ensued to Wil's parents in New York. They, of course, wanted to know where Wil's body had been taken and how they might get hold of it in order to bring it back to New York for burial. I could sense their concern that I might have him cremated, and that was something they found culturally unacceptable. Being Catholic and Latino, they needed a body in order to find closure with his death, especially considering that they had failed to make the trip to San Francisco while he was still alive--even though I had made it abundantly clear in my phone call to them that, in all likelihood, he was dying. Not wanting to accept the seriousness of his condition, then, they were now overwhelmed with guilt and grief.

There was no reason for Wil's parents to be worried; I had no intention of doing anything with Wil's body without consulting them first. Wil had been very explicit in that regard: I was to do whatever his parents needed in order to find closure with his death.

Still, with my feelings as raw as they were, and my mind clouded by grief, I couldn't help but feel they were trying to snatch his body away from me. And while I had every intention of cooperating with them in deference to Wil's wishes, the nagging sense that they didn't really trust me, cut deep. I gave Wil's father the number of the hospital morgue and let the matter go.

Eric agreed to drive me to Marin to pick up the deed to the Winnebago, and then accompany me to Walnut Creek to sign it over to the new owners. Within twenty minutes of arriving at the dealership, I had signed the forms and pocketed a check for $28,000.00, and was back on the road again, headed for San Francisco

Charlie was already at Greg's house by the time Eric and I returned from Walnut Creek, sometime around five in the afternoon. We hugged for a long while, and then pleading fatigue, I trudged upstairs to bed, leaving Greg and Karen to fill him in on the details of the last few days. Sometime around midnight, I awoke with a start. Charlie, who was sleeping on a mat on the floor beside my bed, heard me stir and sat up to see what the matter was.

"I thought I saw an angel," I exclaimed. "He was standing over there by the door!"

Charlie looked in the direction I was pointing. Seeing nothing, he nodded, sleepily, and lay back down and went to sleep. I lay there wide awake, hoping the angelic apparition would show itself again. Nothing further happened, however. Thinking I must have imagined the entire incident, I pulled the covers up tightly around my neck, and closed my eyes and drifted off to sleep.

Around four in the morning, I awoke again,with a searing pain behind my left eye, radiating up past my temple, all the way to the top of my head. As I struggled to sit up in bed, I heard a distinct crackling noise inside my head, like static on a radio. Then, clear as day, a voice-- Wil's voice-- spoke.

"Oh George," he said, as clearly as if he were sitting on the bed next to me. "I wish you could see how beautiful it is here on the inner planes." Then, just as quickly as it had come, the voice was gone. I fell back against my pillow, overwhelmed by a sudden swell of emotion. The pain in my temple lingered for several days.

The next morning brought with it a plethora of mixed emotions. I awoke refreshed, with an unexpected feeling of exhilaration. I had seen an angel in my room--a good enough omen by its self, I thought-- but even more miraculously, Wil had spoken to me from beyond the veil. Even as metaphysically oriented as I was, I hadn't expected anything like that to happen--a sense of him being around me, maybe, but nothing as concrete as an actual voice. Yet I was very clear about what had happened; the experience was neither a dream nor a hallucination. I had heard Wil speak, as clearly as if he had been standing next to the bed.

Then, when I'd least expect it, I'd think of Wil and a wave of grief would well up from my gut, and I would burst into tears. The person I loved most in the world was dead, and I would never feel the tenderness of his smile again, or the warmth of his body next to mine. It was impossible to believe that he was gone and never coming back. The reality was simply too final to comprehend.

That night, Wil's father called to let me know that Wil's body had been shipped to his hometown of New Rochelle, where a funeral would be held in a matter of days. I hung up the phone, sick at the thought of Wil being laid out in a coffin and buried in the cold, hard ground.

I knew everyone would be expecting me to attend the funeral. Yet surprisingly, even to myself, almost immediately I decided not to go. To be perfectly honest, I was pretty much on the brink of joining Wil in the grave myself, due to the crushing stress his illness had caused me, and a long flight to New York seemed like just the thing to push me over the brink.

Besides, I didn't need a funeral to feel a sense of closure with his death; I had been there when it had mattered most. Wil had died in my arms and I had seen his soul depart his body; I had shared his ecstasy at the moment of his death. And if that weren't enough, he had come to me the very next night and whispered of the loveliness of where he now was. No, I didn't need to sit in front of a coffin and weep for the loss of a love. I had already had my moment.

The next morning, I called Wil's parents and explained to them that I wouldn't be attending the funeral. If they were shocked or disappointed at my flaunting convention, their voices never betrayed it.

"You be sure and take care of yourself," Wil's mom admonished me before hanging up the phone. "We'll be in touch with you in a couple of days. We love you very much."

After another night at Greg's apartment, I was ready to face the empty cottage in Marin. A friend from the healing circle offered to stay with me for the night, and I gladly accepted the offer. Back at home, I fed the cats, which were obviously overjoyed to see me, and went into the bedroom to check my messages. The digital screen on the answering machine glowed red, with 26 separate messages. I pushed the playback button and sank down on the bed to listen. There were outpourings of grief and sympathy from all around the country, as well a number of expressions of anger and fear.

As perhaps one of the most visible spokespersons for self-healing in the HIV/AIDS community, there was no way Wil's death could help but have a significant impact. If Wil Garcia--Mr. Self-Healing, himself--couldn't heal himself of the disease and had succumbed to it in the end, what hope was there for the average Joe?

As I pondered the barrage of questions that I'd eventually have to face, my head began to pound. How could I articulate the subtle and miraculous experiences I had shared with Wil in his final moments of life? And what of his message to me from beyond the grave? Undoubtedly, my message would need to change in order to accommodate recent events. But what, exactly, would that new message look like? Where did the inevitability of death fit in with the hope of physical healing? God knows I was at a loss for any answers.

☀

37 *Trying to Find my Footing*

I N THE IMMEDIATE AFTERMATH OF WIL' death, my first instinct was to have Charlie cancel all of our upcoming engagements and to not book any more. After all, with Wil dead, and me at a loss for words, there didn't seem to be any real point in continuing with what we'd been doing. Under the circumstances, why would anyone possibly want to hear what I had to say?

Already, a week before Wil's death, his escalating illness had forced me to cancel our trip to Phoenix to appear with Elizabeth in a reprise of our talk in L.A. While nothing had been said to me, directly, at the time, I had sensed a bit of covert hostility and more than a just little fear when I had called to say that Wil was sick and we wouldn't be able make it. If the expert on death and dying had taken the news of his illness poorly, then what could I expect from everyone else?

In an interesting turn of events, Wil died on the very night we were supposed to be with Elizabeth in Phoenix. When I stopped and thought about it, I had to laugh at the impeccability of his timing. Wil had never really forgiven Elizabeth for her scandalous behavior in L.A., and his death, coming when it had, was like some ultimate form of payback. Now, apparently, the score between them was settled.

A few weeks after Wil's death, I received a phone call from a distraught Dr. Pachuta, about the appearance Wil and I were scheduled to make at the upcoming AIDS Conference he was producing in D.C., early in the spring. Now, inconveniently, one of us was dead. Needless to say, that didn't bode well for the premise of the conference that people could heal themselves of AIDS. After expressing his condolences for my loss, Don got right down to business and negotiated a reduction in my fee. Apparently, with one of us dead, our message was less valuable than it had once been.

It might have been naive of him but I don't think Don realized how insensitive his actions felt at the time. No doubt my feelings were more raw than usual from grief, and I may have overreacted. Whatever the case, I felt betrayed by a person who only a short time earlier had claimed to be my friend. Apparently, for some people, the legitimacy of our message was based solely on the fact that we were alive and well, and that we were doing something right. Realistically, I couldn't really argue with that kind of logic; it certainly had validity. But emotionally, coming when it did, the impact of the conversation on my already shaky morale was devastating.

After a series of phone calls back and forth to Charlie in LA, he persuaded me to at least honor the two engagements Wil and I had scheduled in Florida, in the weeks leading up to the rapidly approaching Christmas holiday. Both of our sponsors there had gone out of their way to reassure him that they were as anxious as ever to have me come and speak. After giving it some thought, I concluded that the best thing I could do was get back out on the circuit as soon as possible. Otherwise, I might never find the courage to do so again.

Thankfully, Charlie agreed to meet me in Miami and provide morale support for my efforts. My flight from San Francisco, a few days later, arrived an hour before his did. In the interest of time, I picked up my bags and boarded a bus to the Alamo rental center, and drove back to the terminal to pick him up. He was waiting for me outside the baggage claim area and flagged me down as I approached. I pulled over to the curb and stopped. He opened the door and climbed into the front seat.

"Boy am I glad to see you!" I exclaimed, in a slightly stricken voice. "I guess I'm a little shakier than I thought. I'm really glad you're here."

"There's nothing to worry about," Charlie reassured me. He reached over and rested his hand on my shoulder. "You're gonna be just fine. These people are not your enemies, you know; they want you to succeed. And they're anxious to hear what you have to say."

That may have been true, but I was not entirely convinced of it. What if the people who had supported Wil and me felt that we had failed them and were simply looking for an opportunity to vent? This was the same reoccurring fear I had struggled with the entire time we were on the road, and now I would have to face the music alone.

"I guess you're right," I said, my voice trailing off to a whisper. *Had Wil failed everyone who had counted on him?* I wondered. *Had we both failed them? Had Wil failed me?* The validity of the last two years of our lives was suddenly up for questioning. Obviously, I had a lot of soul searching to do.

We took the causeway to the beach, past a half-dozen, gleaming, white cruise ships, and found the hotel we were staying in, in a quiet residential neighborhood on the Biscayne Bay side of the island. While I looked for a place to park, Charlie headed for the front desk and checked us in, and waited for me in the lobby. As I emerged through the revolving, front door a few minutes later, I couldn't help but notice the lobby's unusual décor. It was typical sixties, Miami Beach, with terrazzo floors and some questionable aluminum sculptures that must have been considered avant-garde in their day. For a moment, a fleeting smile replaced the worried expression on my face.

After settling into our room, we showered and changed, and set back off across the causeway in search of the Unity Church I was scheduled to speak in. We located it, finally, in a questionable neighborhood off Biscayne Boulevard, halfway between downtown and I-195.

Due to a miscommunication, we arrived at the church well over an hour before the event was scheduled to begin. The minister, who was still in the process of getting dressed, unlocked the door to the parish hall and ushered us inside.

"Welcome to Miami," he said to Charlie, and then turned and offered me his condolences. "You and Wil made quite an impression on your previous visit, and everyone is happy that you're back. He placed his hand on my shoulder in a gesture of support. "I know it probably wasn't an easy decision for you, but I'm really glad you're here."

I smiled and thanked him for his kindness, but inside I was already second guessing my decision. Perhaps I had made up my mind a little *too* hastily, and now that I was here I wasn't convinced that the decision had been a wise one. I felt unusually vulnerable and afraid of being hurt.

The event, itself, was a complete blur. The only thing I do remember was that I planted myself squarely in back of the podium and refused to budge from behind it. The truth was that my heart wasn't really connected to my words, and I stayed in my head for most of the evening, avoiding my feelings and simply going through the motions. Not enough time had passed for me to integrate my experience enough to share it with other people. I felt exposed in front of the audience, painfully vulnerable and completely and utterly alone.

Despite the ineptness of my efforts, no one seemed to notice--or if they did, they were simply too polite to mention it. But *I* knew, and I was unhappy with the entire experience.

"If this is the best I can do, then I might just as well throw in the towel and quit," I thought to myself. My story no longer felt like the truth anymore, but a complete and utter lie.

Wisely, Charlie resisted the urge to try and rouse me from my funk. He retreated outside onto the balcony, leaving me alone to ruminate on my predicament.

"Why did I let myself be talked into coming here?" I moaned, throwing myself on the bed. I curled up into a ball in an effort to make myself disappear. *"What am I going to do?"*

Later, when I had finally fallen asleep, I had a very powerful dream. In it, I was sitting on a couch with Wil, who had his arm around me, and was explaining to him how hard I had taken his death. When I had finished complaining, he had turned to me and said this one simple thing: *"George, if you ever need me, call me. I'll be there for you."*

I awoke a short time later with a distinct impression that our encounter had been more than just an ordinary dream-- that the reality it represented was much more powerful than that. Replaying the experience over in my head, I could still sense Wil's presence in the room with me. It was as though he had actually been there. I even thought I could detect his scent

"That's comforting," I thought, rolling over and pulling the covers up around my neck. "All I have to do is call him. *That's sweet."*

It was a nice sentiment and one that I understood intellectually, but at the moment that was all it was. It didn't change the overwhelming grief I was feeling, and it wasn't going to bring Wil back. Consequently, I didn't really give it much further thought.

The following Sunday, I spoke at a Church of Religious Science in a small retirement community on the shores of Tampa Bay. Unlike my experience in Miami, a week before, the dream in which Wil had told me I could call him and he'd be there, coupled with the passing of another week, allowed me to give a more cohesive, heartfelt talk. For the first time since Wil's death, I was able to speak honestly about the experience, and offer some insight into the larger context of his life and untimely death. My feelings were still raw, however, and at several points in my talk I choked up and had to stop and compose myself--much to my embarrassment.

Thankfully, my raw display of emotion seemed only to endear me to my kindly audience. I flashed back on my experience in Charleston at the beginning of our journey around the country, of how afraid I had been of people knowing I had come down with the shingles, and was reminded once again of how powerful the truth is. It was a familiar lesson, but no less powerful the second time around.

When the service was over, I grabbed a quick bite to eat before pointing my rental car in the direction of my parent's house, where I planned to spend the holidays. Instead of feeling depressed like I had expected I would--after all, it was Christmas and I had just lost the love of my life--I found myself enveloped by an oddly incongruent euphoria, as the extraordinary beauty of what Wil and I had shared together came more clearly into focus.

When my parents had last seen Wil, he had been healthy and vibrant, and full of life. Understandably then, his death came as a real shock and seemed to puncture the wall of denial they had erected around our diagnoses. In many ways, I had been to blame for them not fully understanding the seriousness of the situation we were in. I had been so confident and steadfast in my healing that I had sheltered them from the possibility of a harsher outcome. With Wil's death, the wall of denial came crashing down. For the first time, my parents got a glimpse of the pressures we had been living under, despite our faith and belief.

"You know, we loved Wil very much," my mother confided to me, shortly after I arrived home. She was trying her best to convey her deep sympathy for my loss. "And your father has taken his death especially hard," she added. After that, she never really mentioned Wil's death again. But in acknowledging my loss, she had acknowledged the intimate nature of our relationship, and that was really all I needed at the time.

Like many people, my mother didn't really like to think about death, and certainly wasn't comfortable talking about it. Several times during my visit, I tried to engage her in a conversation about what I had experienced, but each time she had quickly changed the subject. Ironically, within a few short months, she would have to deal with the untimely death of her youngest sister and only brother; and not long after that, the death of her husband, my father. And even then, she rarely spoke about her feelings.

"Why is it that Christians seem more afraid of dying than just about any other group of people I know," I ruminated to myself, sitting on the porch after dinner one night, looking out over the lake behind the house. But of course, I already knew the answer to my question. Who wouldn't be afraid if they believed in the angry, judgmental God of the Old Testament? How could anyone ever hope to live up to the impossible standard he demanded of them? And who likes to think of their loved ones burning in hell for eternity, for a few measly mistakes?

The day after Christmas, I caught a flight back to San Francisco and dropped in on the regular Wednesday night meeting of The Healing Circle. Once again, I found myself surrounded by a sea of unconditional love. Afterwards, I joined some friends for a cup of coffee at a popular pastry shop, just around the corner. In the course of conversation, the dark, good-looking man sitting next to me asked if I'd like to go to a New Year's Eve party with him. At first, I was taken aback by his invitation, considering that my lover had been dead for less than a month. But I surprised myself and told him that I would.

"Why not?" I said, struggling to suppress an embarrassed grin. *Indeed, why not*, I thought to myself. *I'm single, now; I can do whatever I want.* That last thought cut through my heart like a knife, but not enough to convince me not to go.

A few nights later at a private party in a beautiful Victorian high atop Nob Hill, I toasted in the New Year with my new friend, Bill, in what was to be the beginning of an enduring friendship. And, as a result of the wet kiss he planted on my lips at the stroke of midnight, the local rumor mill was set into motion.

A few weeks after the beginning of the New Year, I boarded a plane to Washington to honor my commitment to Dr. Pachuta to participate on a long-term survivor panel, in front of the entire body of the conference. Each of the five members on the panel was allotted ten minutes to introduce themselves and explain what they were about, after which questions would be taken from the audience.

Much to my chagrin, almost every other inquiry was addressed to me. Naturally, people had a lot of questions about Wil's death and wanted to hear what I had to say about it. As each person took their turn at the microphone, I stayed in my heart and responded to their questions as best I could. There were some questions that I couldn't answer, however, and I was learning to say, *I don't know*—especially when it was the truth. And several times over the course of the afternoon, that's exactly what I did.

Later, after the panel disbanded and the audience dispersed, a well-meaning, young woman pulled me aside and commented that she didn't know how I had managed to stay so calm and collected under fire, with so many people attacking me. The interesting thing was that I hadn't perceived any of the questions as an attack. Staying in my heart, I had managed to look past any hostility and see only the pain and fear behind it. And it was to *this* I had addressed my answers. The lessons of A Course in Miracles were becoming second nature to me, and even I couldn't help but notice the change.

Over the course of the weekend, Don managed to redeem himself for the hurt I felt over our unpleasant discussion about money, right after Wil's death. When the conference ended, he invited me to dinner at an elegant restaurant in the loggia of Union Station, along with his partner, Dave, and Louise Hay and a couple of friends. It was a lovely evening; and before it was over they had persuaded me to spend a couple of days at their home in Baltimore, and see their personal acupuncturist for a tune up.

After several days of pampering, it was finally time to leave. I thanked the two men for their hospitality and boarded a train to New York. From Penn Station, it was only a short cab ride to Grand Central Station and the train to New Rochelle. I needed to see Wil's parents. And even though I dreaded the thought of it, I wanted to visit his grave.

Climbing the stairs to his parent's second floor apartment, I rang the buzzer and waited as Carmen undid the lock and invited me in. We looked deeply into each other's eyes, and then fell into each other's arms.

Later, Carmen served me the lovely lunch she had prepared for the occasion--empanadas and plantains with rice and beans, my favorite Puerto Rican delicacies--and then asked me the question I had been secretly dreading.

"Would you like to go to the cemetery," she asked sweetly, searching my face for the answer. I was quiet for a moment, and then let out a long sigh.

"Yes, I think I'd like that."

Wil's father went downstairs to retrieve the car, leaving Carmen and I alone in the apartment. "I know, now, that Wil is OK," Carmen said, sounding very sure of herself. "I went to see the priest the other day and told him all the wonderful things Wil had done to help people with AIDS. And he told me, *your son was a good man.*"

I smiled. I *knew* that Wil was a good man, and I didn't need a priest to confirm it for me. But Carmen did, and that was OK by me. She was Catholic and held deep beliefs with regard to homosexuality and AIDS. If having a priest reassure her that her son was a good man made it easier for her to accept his death, then what did it matter to me? I gave her a hug and helped her on with her coat, and together we walked down the stairs to the waiting car.

We drove past the railway station and crossed over the turnpike to the west side of town. Then, at a narrow, unassuming street, we turned into the ancient cemetery where Wil's body was interred. Naked trees stood bare-limbed like ghostly sentinels, in rows on either side of the road. We drove deep into the cemetery before finally coming to a stop. I opened the door and slowly got out of the car.

"His grave is over there," Carmen said, rolling down the window and pointing to a large, granite headstone in the distance with the name Garcia etched into it. "You go on ahead," she said. "I think I'll wait in the car for a while."

I made my way across the damp, squishy grass, over to where a fresh grave decorated with colorful plastic flowers stood out in bold relief. Ralph's grave was immediately to the right of Wil's. I stood there for a long while, looking at the two graves, one fresher than the next, and grief started to rise up in my throat.

"At least they're together," I thought, finding some comfort in the idea.

It had been raining for several days and the newly turned earth atop Wil's grave had started to settle a bit and crack. As I stood there, mesmerized by the harsh reality of what I was seeing, all I could think of was Wil lying underneath all that wet dirt, cold and all alone. I covered my face with my hands and fell on my knees in the mud, tears streaming down my face.

"Wil, oh Wil!" I wept. "I miss you so much! Why did you have to die? *Why?*"

Carmen got out of the car and came over to where I was kneeling in the mud. She put her hands on my shoulder. "Get up now, baby" she said, smoothing my rumpled hair. "Don't cry anymore. Wil wouldn't want to see you like this; he'd want you to be strong. You don't want him to see you like this now, do you?

Her voice was kind but firm. She took hold of my arm and pulled me to my feet, and wiped the tears from my checks. We stood there for a little while longer, holding on to each other, staring at Wil's grave, lost in our own private worlds of grief. Finally, Carmen broke the silence.

"Let's go, son," she ordered. "You're going to catch your death of cold out here. Let's go home and I'll make you a nice, warm cup of coffee."

I took her hand and together we walked back to the car and climbed inside. As it pulled away from the curb, I craned my neck to look out the back window, staring at Wil's grave receding in the distance. I needed to see it one last time. I didn't know if I would ever be back again.

38 On the Road to San Jose

I DECLINED CARMEN'S INVITATION TO STAY the night and caught the 9:15 express train back to New York City. There were any number of things needing my attention, and I wanted to get an early start.

It was just before midnight when I arrived back at the apartment, and Barry was already in bed. I unlocked the dead-bolt and tiptoed into the living room, and crashed on the couch in my clothes so as not to wake him up. A good night's sleep proved elusive, however. I slept only sporadically and was plagued by a series of disturbing dreams. By the time I awoke the next morning, Barry had already left for work, and I had the entire apartment to myself. For a few fleeting moments, it was as though the last eighteen months had never happened.

I showered and dressed, and packed a small, leather briefcase with a copy of Wil's last Will and Testament, his death certificate, and a letter from my lawyer, and walked to Union Square and caught the Lexington IRT, downtown. I was headed to the Citibank branch at number one Wall Street where Wil's retirement account was on deposit. I intended to cash it in and take the money back with me to San Francisco.

As I passed the Stock Exchange, a headline from the New York Post caught my eye from a nearby news stand. DREXALL BURNHAM LAMBERT FOLDS, the headline screamed in bold, black type face. I stopped and bought a copy of the paper, and scanned the front page story. It was hard not to notice that on the very day I was in New York to liquidate Wil's last remaining assets, the company where he had earned them was meeting the same fate. The synchronicity was pretty obvious.

I gulped back a wave of sadness and hurried on my way. The headline,

310

coming on the heels of my visit to Wil's grave the day before, made the reality of his passing impossible to deny. The inescapable truth was that my lover was dead; the company he had worked for was bankrupt; our lease on the apartment in New York was being rescinded; our house on Fire Island had been sold; my high flying career was over; and with them, any passion I had for living. Everything I had ever valued had been systematically stripped away. The only thing I had left to console myself with was the money--just the cold, hard cash.

On returning to the empty house in Marin the following week, the cold, stark reality that Wil was never coming home again registered even harder. In the strange euphoria surrounding his death, it was almost as though somewhere in the back of my mind I thought he would be coming back again--that this was simply some kind of a test, and when I had passed it he would reappear.

"It's OK, Wil, you can come home, now," I kept thinking. "I understand the lesson. I've got it, now." But of course, he didn't come back. He wasn't ever coming home again--*not ever*.

Every morning, I'd wake up to the inescapable reality of an empty space on the side of the bed where Wil used to sleep. The indention his body had formed in the mattress lingered for a while, but slowly, over time, even that began to fade. A desperate loneliness replaced the high I had been living on, and I felt as though I would suffocate on the emptiness that rose up to engulf me. I'd find myself walking aimlessly around the house at all hours of the day and night, looking for physical traces that he had ever been there--for anything that might bring him back to me in some small way.

I rummaged through the closets, searching for an article of clothing he might have hung back up without laundering, hoping for a trace of his scent. I slept with his pillow clutched in my arms and between my legs; I wouldn't wash the sheets. As time passed, even these meager reminders that Wil had once been a living, breathing, human being became harder and harder to come by. He was steadily slipping away.

I was angry, too; angry at having been abandoned in California without a job or a steady source of income. Hadn't Wil promised me when we had left New York on our trip around the country that he'd take care of me when we got to California? Well, how was he going to do that now that he was dead? I cursed him and God, too, for abandoning me--especially after everything that I had done. Hadn't I given up a lucrative career to answer the call to serve? Hadn't I paraded around the country proclaiming you could heal yourself of AIDS? What a cruel joke! What a fool I had been! So this was the reward for following your heart, was it?

"Well fuck you, God; and fuck you too, Wil," I screamed at no one in particular.

To compound my anger and heighten my already soaring level of insecurity, the bill for Wil's hospital stay arrived in the mail in early February. The total for the four short days he was there was just over fourteen thousand dollars, and that was without actually being treated for anything specific.

There was still no word from his insurance company about his policy conversion, and I was worried about the financial implications of the bill. Had the application we had filled out together even made it to the insurance carrier before he died? And if not, would an insurance company reinstate benefits to someone who was already dead? Even though I wasn't legally responsible for Wil's debts, I felt responsible just the same, for making sure that his estate was settled with the same integrity he had lived his life by. Wil had always paid his bills on time, and by God, somehow, this final one would be paid, too. I'd see to it if it was the last thing I did.

Another month passed, and by now I was simply numb. Perpetual grief had formed a thick callous over the gaping wound in my heart. and for all intents and purposes I was emotionally dead--a walking zombie; a shell of my former self. Then, just when I'd least expect it, I'd think of Wil and my heart would break open and bleed. I'd think of him; I'd feel this clutching sensation in my chest, which would remind me that he was gone, and I'd burst into tears. It happened again and again, week in and week out, month after excruciating month.

To kill the pain, I sought relief in sex with as many partners as I could find. It was an old pattern of mine from before the advent of AIDS, and under the circumstances it was certainly understandable. Not that the relief lasted very long, really. It was merely a temporary fix for an unyielding condition. San Francisco was pretty accommodating in this regard; it wasn't hard to find my drug of choice. There were gay bars filled with lonely men on just about every other corner.

Days would find me sorting through our stuff and carting Wil's clothes off to the Community Thrift Store. I found a small apartment in the city, down the block from Bill, and moved into it with the cats. Weekends found me lurking in the corner of some dark, south of Market Street bar, looking for a friendly stranger to keep me warm, and help me forget the pain I was in. Yet, despite my less than exemplary behavior, the Universe simply would not let me go.

I'd be cruising a handsome stranger and the same damned thing would happen, every time. Seeing my interest, he would swagger over to where I was standing and introduce himself. And every time the conversation would go something like this: "You're George Melton, aren't you?" the nameless stranger would ask, and I'd nod my head that I was. And always the story would be the same--different bars and different strangers, but always the same story.

"You know, I saw you speak a couple of years ago when I was living in Denver (or L.A or New York or wherever- you get the point), and it changed my life. Boy, am I glad to see you!"

And inevitably, right there, in whatever dingy south of market leather bar I happened to find myself in, much as I resisted it, the conversation would turn to God and spirituality and healing. And on a few rare occasions, I got lucky, too--I got laid. Yet, no matter how hard I tried to forget who I was or to run away from what I had become, I couldn't do it. The Universe simply would not let me go.

After months of anonymous trysts, I finally gave up on the south of Market scene. I was becoming used to the idea of being alone, and the pain didn't seem as intense as it had in the immediate aftermath of Wil's death. In fact, there were many things about being single I found quite rewarding. I had let Wil take care of me for so long that I had almost forgotten how good I was at taking care of myself. Now, without him there to do things for me, I was left to my own resourcefulness. And I was beginning to think that this was one of the things he must have intended when he had left: *he had loved me enough to set me free to rediscover myself.*

I know that for a long time I harbored some guilt about Wil's death. I felt that in some way, perhaps, I had been the cause of it. It had become obvious to me in the months since he had passed that he had decided to die--albeit unconsciously--the weekend of Christine's ill-fated visit to

Marin, when I had threatened to accompany her to Yelm. As far as I was concerned, Wil had been murdered by Junito--the unconscious part of his being--the angry, inner child that had symbolized his unhealed issues around abandonment.

When I had threatened to leave with Christine that fateful weekend, Junito had undoubtedly sworn his revenge: *"You won't abandon me, I'll leave you first,"* he must have said to himself. From then on, it was simply a matter of time.

Somehow, my actions that weekend had set into play a dynamic that ultimately resulted in Wil's death. Yet, if Junito had decided to die without Wil being conscious of it, in the process of leaving, the very issue that had triggered his departure had been healed.

In dying, Wil had healed his abandonment issues. No matter how frightening his death throes might have appeared to those who had witnessed them, he couldn't make anyone go away; he couldn't make anyone abandon him. Not just me, but the entire healing circle had kept vigil at his bedside to the bitter end.

Eventually, my anger at Wil subsided; and along with it, my anger at God. I began to see the perfection in my situation, which had been obscured by the immediate trauma of my loss. I was a new me, now, with a new life, in a new city, with a new circle of friends. I had been to hell and back and come out a better person for it.

I wasn't afraid any longer. The chronic fear of attack that had plagued me for our entire trip around the country--indeed, for my entire life-- had been healed by my face to face confrontation with death and Wil's subsequent communications from beyond the grave. If death had no reality, then what could there possibly be to fear? I immersed myself in writing and once again began accepting invitations to speak.

After I had all but given up hope for a satisfactory resolution to the problem, Wil's insurance company posthumously reinstated his benefits and paid his hospital bill in full. But even with all of these small miracles, every once in a while when I'd least expect it, I'd think of Wil, I'd feel a clutching sensation in my chest, and I'd start to grieve all over again.

In November, I was invited to speak at the Metropolitan Community Church in nearby San Jose. The morning of my talk, I got up early and drove the Suzuki down the peninsula on an unusually empty interstate 280. The rising sun revealed another glorious California day, streaking the sparse, high clouds with a warm blush of early morning color. To my right, the watershed surrounding the San Andreas Fault shimmered in all its pristine beauty.

As I sped along, soaking in the quiet grandeur of the morning, my thoughts inevitably drifted to Wil. In the past, we had always done events like this together. Now, however, everything was different. I was alone. I was getting used to it, certainly, but at times like this I still felt his absence, deeply.

As I thought about him this particular morning, I felt an old, familiar, clutching sensation in the center of my chest where my heart was located. And for a moment--only a moment--my eyes began to well up with tears. But then, I caught a glimpse of Wil's smiling face in the sunlight refracted off the Suzuki's windshield. And when I saw him, his hand reached out to me from the glass and touched me on the chest where my heart was located, and he said, *"George, I'm right here. I've been here all the time!"*

With that, my chest exploded and I was laughing and crying at the same time, so much so that I had to pull over to the side of the road. *"He's been here all the time!"* I reveled in the realization. *"He's right here in my heart. He's been there all the time!"*

Hadn't he told me in the dream that night in Miami, that he would be there if I ever needed him? That all I needed to do was call? And how do you call a person who's moved on to another dimension? How do you connect with someone who's no longer in physical form? Why, you think of them, silly; you simply think of them. And in the instant that you do, you're connected by an unbreakable bond of love.

In the months since Wil's death, I'd think of him and I'd feel the same clutching sensation in my chest that I felt that day on the road to San Jose--his energy would be that strong. Yet my mind wouldn't allow the reality of his presence to register; the experience was simply too foreign for me to grasp. I could only associate the feeling with loss. Now, in a single instant of revelation, everything had changed.

I laughed as I remembered how many times I had called out for Wil in the course of the last year, and he had answered, only to be met by a torrent of hot, steamy tears. How frustrated he must have been. Mr. Metaphysics--Mr. Self-Healing-- Mr. George Melton-- the man who thought he understood all there was to know about life and death and healing and God, was too dense to even recognize his own lover when he was standing right in front of him. The irony was too precious for words.

In that one glorious instant of clarity, my long year of grief came to an end that sunny California day on the road to San Jose. It ended the moment I realized that Wil had never left me. Certainly, I couldn't deny that his body was gone. But *he* was not. And he has never gone missing again!

Today, more than twenty years later, he lives within my heart where he has always been, and will continue to be, until the great day comes when we finally meet again face to face. How I look forward to that glorious reunion. But in the meantime, I'm in no rush to make it happen. I am at peace with myself, and I still have a lot of living to do. But if, by chance, I awake one morning and the stars are aligned just so, then maybe, just maybe, I'll take one more ride on the Cosmic Slingshot. For truly, it was the most amazing ride of my life!

Epilogue

I DIDN'T HAVE TO WAIT VERY long for another ride on the Cosmic Slingshot. The opportunity presented itself less than a year later in the form of a fortuitous encounter with the most powerful teacher I have ever had the privilege of working with.

In 1990, Reiki Master, Denise Crundall, was devoting much of her time and energy teaching Reiki, and the principles of self- healing, to the growing HIV/AIDS community in her native Australia. While her efforts had been largely successful, she remained thwarted by an attitude on the part of some of her students that said, in essence, *"Yes, what you are teaching makes sense, but you're not gay, you don't have AIDS, and you don't really know what its like."*

Taking her frustration into meditation, she asked for help in overcoming her student's resistance. Not long afterwards, someone placed a copy of my little, pink book, *Beyond AIDS*, into her hands, with Wil's and my smiling faces on the cover. She read it, and recognizing the commonalities in what we were teaching, made a mental note of it and sat the book aside, and promptly forgot all about it.

In December of 1990, Denise and her husband, John, were conducting a Reiki seminar at The Center for Living with Dying, in San Jose, CA. That weekend, my picture surfaced again on the cover of Parade Magazine, as part of an ongoing article about long-time survivors and the various approaches they were using to beat the odds. The article, written by Bernie Gauser, a producer from New York City who had worked on Anita Wexler's film, AIDS Alive, happened to mention that I resided in San Francisco. She and John decided to pay me a visit. They found my phone number in the directory and called to see if they could stop by to meet me on their way to the airport. The call piqued my curiosity, so naturally I said yes.

This began a collaboration that would span the next decade. Before leaving, John and Denise invited me to speak at a conference they were producing in their hometown of Melbourne, Australia, and share my experiences with Wil during his transition. In lieu of an honorarium, they offered to produce my workshop, The Power of the Healer Within, in a number of the other major cities in Australia. The offer proved impossible to resist, even though I was terrified at the prospect of speaking on the topic of death and dying. After all, I had spent the last five years of my life trying to avoid dying at all cost.

My association with Denise and John represented an enormous shift in my understanding of healing, which expanded to include both healing into life and death. Over the next several years, I returned to Australia two more times to present my workshop and participate in Reiki retreats. Denise became my primary spiritual mentor, as well as a dear friend.

For the next seven years, I reciprocated by producing yearly Reiki trainings for her and John in San Francisco. As a result, a permanent Reiki Clinic was established in the Castro, run on a donation basis and staffed by volunteers who had taken the classes. Over time, Denise's work in California expanded to include Reiki Centers in San Jose, Santa Barbara and San Diego, as well as Toronto, Canada.

In addition to my involvement with Reiki, I continued to lecture and present my workshop throughout the US and Canada, and remained an active presenter at the AIDS, Medicine and Miracles Conference until the middle of the decade. In 1992, Wil's dream of a Spanish translation of Beyond AIDS became a reality, and I subsequently appeared on the Phil Donahue show with Niro Assistant.

In 1997, with the advent of effective drug therapies, and the changing face of the epidemic, I resigned my commission as the poster boy for the self-healing movement, satisfied that the message Wil and I had worked so hard to deliver had been heard, and that the AIDS community could be better served by people more closely resembling its changing demographics. In 1998, I returned to work as a hair colorist at a prestigious salon in San Francisco, where I continued to be employed for the next seven years.

Over the years, I have lost contact with many of the people who made Wil's and my incredible trip around the country possible. Many of them are mentioned in this book, but there are countless others who unfortunately shall remain nameless. Marianne Williamson, of course, went on to write almost a dozen books based on the teachings of A Course in Miracles, and establish herself as a veritable force of nature within the pantheon of contemporary spiritual voices. Louise Hay is a brand unto herself. A decade after Wil and I stood her up in Phoenix, Elizabeth Kubler Ross suffered a stroke and died several years later, at her home in Arizona. The healing center she had envisioned and struggled so hard to create, never came about.

Mark Veneglia lives in New York, where he is a successful artist. While he no longer channels Benjamin, he does channel some excellent artwork which can be seen at www.markVv.com. My best friend, Barry, now lives on an eight acre farm in Narrowsburg, NY. You can check out his fine home furnishings and accessories at www.rivergalleryny.com. Bellruth Naperstek remains in Cleveland and is the author of numerous books and tapes on visualization. Find out more at www.healthjourneys.com.

Anita Wexler died in 1989 while Wil and I were still traveling in the Winnebago. Niro Assistant went on to write a book entitled, *The Healing Yes*, and eventually returned to Europe and remarried. Charlie Swanson changed his name and went to work for the Disney Corporation. Greg Cassin still lives in the same apartment in San Francisco and continues to be an important contributor to AIDS, Medicine and Miracles. Eric Bailes died in 1995. Reggie, my beloved cat, lived to be twenty years old.

In 1999, Christine Hartman and I went our separate ways and are no longer friends. She lives off the grid near Yelm, Washington, where she continues to participate in the Ramtha School of Enlightenment.

Wil remained an active psychic presence in my life for most of the next decade. Most notable of our ongoing communications was a series of recurring dreams that began immediately after his death and continued for the next ten years. In these dreams, I would visit him in New York City, where he still lived in the apartment we had once shared together. Sometimes, he would instruct the doorman to turn me away. Other times, he would let me into the apartment but wouldn't allow me to stay.

I mentioned these dreams to Denise, who gave me an interesting take on their significance. According to her interpretation, the apartment in New York symbolized the bardo between life and death; a place where Wil could step his energy down, enough, and I could step mine up, enough, that we could connect and communicate. She was also convinced that these dreams afforded me a unique opportunity. "When you visit Wil at the apartment and he allows you to stay, you'll know that you're about to make your transition," she predicted.

In the decade following Wil's death, I dreamed only of him--never of my new partner, Syd, and our life together in San Francisco; it was as though they didn't actually exist. In the year 2000, I again visited Wil in the dream state in the apartment in New York, and this time something completely unexpected happened. He invited me in and told me I could stay. For the first time ever, I remembered my life in San Francisco. "Oh no," I told him, "I live in San Francisco with Syd." And with that, I turned and fled the apartment. I never had the dream again, and it was the last psychic communication Wil and I ever shared.

In the year 2002, Denise made her transition, and John stepped in to fill her formidable shoes. In 2006, with the help of a small grant from the Louise Hay Foundation, I produced a series of Reiki classes at the Center for Spiritual Living in Palm Springs, CA, where I currently reside. Today, I am as passionate and committed as ever to my spiritual growth and the process of planetary transformation, and am eagerly awaiting another ride on the Cosmic Slingshot.

To find out more about the author and to read his blog, visit his website at georgemelton.com. You may also contact him at georgemelton@ georgemelton.com.